The Scintillating Life of Iulia Hasdeu

Constantin Manolache

The Scintillating Life of Iulia Hasdeu

Introduction by A.K. Brackob
Translated by Diana Livesay

The Center for Romanian Studies
Las Vegas ◊ Chicago ◊ Palm Beach

Published in the United States of America by
Histria Books
7181 N. Hualapai Way, Ste. 130-86
Las Vegas, NV 89166 USA
HistriaBooks.com

The Center for Romanian Studies is an independent academic and cultural institute with the mission to promote knowledge of the history, literature, and culture of Romania in the world. The publishing program of the Center is affiliated with Histria Books. Contributions from scholars from around the world are welcome. To support the work of the Center for Romanian Studies, contact us at info@centerforromanianstudies.com

All rights reserved. No part of this book may be reprinted or reproduced or utilized in any form or by any electronic, mechanical or other means, now known or hereafter invented, including photocopying and recording, or in any information storage or retrieval system, without permission in writing from the Publisher.

Library of Congress Control Number: 2022941230

ISBN 978-1-59211-169-5 (hardcover)
ISBN 978-1-59211-490-0 (softbound)
ISBN 978-1-59211-232-6 (eBook)

Copyright © 2024 by Histria Books

For Lilica,

who departed this world too soon,

but whose memory lives on.

Introduction

Iulia Hasdeu is one of the most fascinating figures of nineteenth-century Romanian culture. Truly a child prodigy, she began reading at two and a half years old. By the time she was in grade school, she was fluent in French, English, and German, in addition to her native Romanian. Her interests included history, music, drawing and painting, literature, and poetry – the latter at which she excelled. Her intellectual prowess led her to become the first Romanian woman to attend the Sorbonne in Paris. Tragically, the life of this child genius was cut short by tuberculosis at the age of eighteen, but her legend and legacy live on more than 130 years after her death.

As the only child of renowned scholar Bogdan Petriceicu Hasdeu, Iulia was destined for an intellectual life. Her father was an esteemed scholar, historian, and philologist, as well as a writer and poet. B.P. Hasdeu (1838-1907) was born in northern Moldavia in a territory then occupied by the Russian Empire. He moved to Iași and then Bucharest, working as an editor and contributor on some of the most prominent publications of the time, including *Columna lui Traian*. Like most Romanian intellectuals of his day, Hasdeu was also deeply involved in political life, being an ally of the powerful Brătianu family. In 1876, he was appointed as Director of the National Archives. The following year he was appointed a member of the Romanian Academy and in 1878 also took a position as professor at the University of Bucharest. All of this placed B.P. Hasdeu at the center of cultural life in Romania.

His most important works include *Cuvente den bătrâni*, *Istoria critică a Românilor*, and his monumental project to create an etymological dictionary of the Romanian language, *Etymologicum magnum Romaniae*, which sadly was never finished.

Named for her mother, Iulia was born on 2/14 November 1869. Her father wanted his daughter and only child to follow in his footsteps and make a contribution to her country's intellectual life. Iulia started learning to read when she was only 2 years old. Driven by her father to excel, she began to learn French, English, and German. She proved an exemplary student, attending St. Sava Gymnasium and the Bucharest Conservatory of Music.

When she was 11, Iulia's mother decided that she needed to leave the country in order to further her education. They chose to send her to Paris. Romanian intellectuals had long had an affinity for French culture because of the Latin roots of both nations, and Paris was the vibrant cultural center of Europe at that time. So her mother moved with Iulia to Paris where she enrolled at Sévigné College. She studied hard and graduated at the tender age of 16, passing her baccalaureate exam that year.

Life was not easy for Iulia as the daughter of one of Romania's preeminent intellectuals. She was driven hard by her parents to study and had little time to enjoy a normal childhood. This led to periods of depression and anxiety. In addition, her fragile health revealed itself as she began to display early signs of the disease that would eventually claim her life. Still, she pressed on. Iulia took solace in writing poetry, something at which she was truly gifted. She also studied painting and music while in Paris, working under the acclaimed French painter Diogène Maillart, who would ultimately paint the portrait of her seen on the cover of this book.

Iulia enrolled in the Sorbonne in 1886, becoming the first Romanian woman to attend the prestigious French university. She distinguished herself, holding two lectures at the school, one on logic and the other on the second book of Herodotus, both of which were praised by her colleagues and professors. Barely 18, she prepared to begin work on her Ph.D., but her illness became progressively worse. Her parents took her to Switzerland for treatment and then back to Romania, but nothing could cure her. She died at the family home in Câmpina, Romania, on 17/29 September 1888, less than two months shy of her nineteenth birthday. She was buried at the Bellu Cemetery in Bucharest, where her grave can still be visited today.

Despite her death at such a young age, Iulia did not fade into obscurity. Her father was devastated by the loss of his only child and became obsessed with keeping her memory alive. He gathered all of her writings, prose, theater, and poems and published them posthumously to much acclaim. Iulia wrote mainly in French; thus, her work could be accessible to a wide audience. Her genius was recognized and continues to be today. A plaque is still attached to the building in Paris where she lived during her studies there, commemorating the tragic young poet.

B.P. Hasdeu was interested in spiritism, which was very popular in the nineteenth century, even before the death of his daughter, but with the loss of his only child, it became an obsession for him and his wife. He held numerous seances over the remainder of his life, seeking to communicate with his daughter and later his wife, who died in 1902. The transcripts of these spiritism sessions were recorded and preserved.

One day while working at his desk, Hasdeu fell into a trance during which he claimed to have received instructions from Iulia to build a castle on family land at Câmpina in her memory. Hasdeu wrote: "She ordered me to place the busts of Christ, Shakespeare, and Victor Hugo in the temple, forming the upper altar. It is this trinity whose unity demands a new trinity, totally new. It is what she ordered me, later, designating nine members of the family, whose portraits were to be placed in the frame of the window, on either side of the upper altar." The construction of this "temple," as Hasdeu called it, whose foundation has the shape of a cross, began in 1893 and was completed three years later. The Iulia Hasdeu Castle stands today as a monument to her memory as well as a museum visited by tourists from Romania and around the world.

Because of her remarkable story and exceptional talent, along with the efforts of her father, the memory of Iulia Hasdeu remained alive in the popular imagination. Numerous books and articles have been written about her life. One of the earliest such attempts at presenting her life is *The Scintillating Life of Iulia Hasdeu* by Constantin Manolache.

Constantin Manolache was born in Iași on 14 February 1883. He trained as a military officer and lawyer. He became a military prosecutor and eventually rose to the rank of General, becoming Inspector General, overseeing the military justice system and military prisons in Romania. Manolache also had a passion for literature and for French culture. He debuted by translating poems of Victor Hugo in the magazine *Floarea darurilor* in 1907. He contributed verses to many of the leading literary journals of the time, including *Viața Românească*, *Semănătorul*, and *Neamul Românesc literar*. He wrote plays and prose alongside technical works on military law. He also served as editor-in-chief of the magazine *Lumea Militară Ilustrată* (1935-1939).

Manolache was a strong advocate of traditional values and a keen observer of human nature, both of which are evidenced in his writings. His first novel, *Sfânta dreptate*, won a prize from the Romanian Academy in 1935. But the work he will most be remembered for is his romanced biography of Iulia Hasdeu.

As Constantin Teodorovici points out in his commentary on Manolache in *Din Atelierul unui Dicționar al Literaturii Române*: "Interesting is his attempt to reconstruct the scintillating life of Iulia Hasdeu (1939), using texts written by her, in which he makes a pertinent analysis on a psychological level, in a subtle attempt to reveal the transfiguration of external stimuli in spiritual impulses and works of art. He decodifies and sheds light on the artistic laboratory of the poet. The biographer-narrator resonates in unison with the heroine and her great frustrations and the ideas with which she came into contact, demonstrating a kind of consubstantiality, which helps him in his attempt to bring her to life...."

The Scintillating Life of Iulia Hasdeu was praised by such noted personalities as the renowned historian Nicolae Iorga. Ermina Walch, a childhood friend of Iulia's mentioned in the book, wrote to Manolache praising his portrait of the child prodigy, stating "long after reading your book, entire passages remained with me allowing me to relive those moments long passed."

For the first time, the story of Iulia Hasdeu is being made available in English in the hopes that the memory of this remarkable female writer of the nineteenth century will become even more appreciated on an international level.

A.K. Brackob

Chapter I

The Stem

St. Ilie Church in Gorgani, which today hides on Silfidelor Street, between the walls of modern blockhouses, was, at that time, an old royal establishment, raised on a "mound" in the nearby outskirts of Bucharest, small houses predominating the surroundings.

On the June 10th, 1865, when he stepped into this holy sanctuary for the first time, Bogdan Petriceicu Hasdeu was twenty-seven or twenty-nine years old. Two sources, both of them equally credible, state the Romanian intellectual was born either in 1838 or 1836. The first statement is based on the birth certificate found at the church in his native Cristinești, the other is based on Bogdan's own statement, found in his writings, as well as in a family letter. However, whether he was twenty-seven or twenty-nine years old, it's certain the Bessarabian native was a man in full youth and vigor, with a strong body, sharp eyes, aquiline nose, and red cheeks framed by a bushy dark chestnut mustache and beard. His figure, not having the classic beauty of his ancestors, had the expression of a lively spirituality and characteristic delicacy.

The bride, awaited in the church's nave by the groom, by the godparents, and by the usual people of the church, Iulia Faliciu (Falics — the original, official name), walked towards the table used for this joyful occasion with a straight and daring posture, wearing her finery with decency and sharing friendly looks with those who were assisting at the ceremony in which she would forever place her hand in the hand of the one who was becoming the pride of his nation, and especially her pride.

The girl was twenty-five years old and her face could be, as it was, envied by every woman in Bucharest at that time. Her eyes were not too big, but they had fighting sparkles in them, and she had the smile of a sensible woman. Her cheeks had a ripe peachy glow, above a mouth with thin lips, masterfully crafted by the god of the mountains. Her oval face framed the beauty that had stolen the attention of her husband from so many other willing faces, that were now waiting under the arches of the church, and especially outside.

Hasdeu walked her proudly to the altar and was now waiting for the holy service of the everlasting union under the gaze of his friends who were joyfully smiling at this match, breathing in the healthy air around them. And their joy was easily understood. This young man, so attentive to the beauties that had tempted him over the years, was now settling down with one that surpassed them all. Men and women who had never been his friends now came to see who this "hero" was who had managed to monopolize their preferences, and others — especially the ladies — came to make sure that the young poet was really getting married... The whispers were blending in with the waves of myrrh...

In a small group, the whispers mentioned a certain nobleman who would have known Iulia before Hasdeu; in another group, other whispers spewed opinions about that unkempt peasant figure, and nothing could be truer in this world, than the statements of women in such circumstances. Eyes that had seen her, who knows when, together with that man, ears that had heard the gossip in this case from trustworthy people...

The girl of the Apuseni Mountains, just like that white and silky flower of the cliffs among the peaks, vaguely sensed everyone's admiring whispers and the hum of widowed wasps in the nests, and that's why she kept her head up high towards the seraphim up top, who had stopped in flight, and towards the just God at the merciful temple of the altar.

The Church of St. Ilie resounded with excited voices. This establishment was even larger than the capital's cathedral, with countless rows of pews, some on the sides, others crossing the middle of the nave itself, on side and parallel lines, and it was chosen by the godparents, Ion and Felicia Gârleanu, whose parish it was.

The ritual took place peacefully in a sacred service. The priest, Ion Mihăilescu, Father Ioniță as the parishioners called him, was holding the service in a deep voice, contrasting the words at the right time during this Christian ritual, and with some pride that his humble church was chosen for such a wedding.

When the time came to announce: "God's servant Bogdan is marrying..." Father Ioniță looked at his birth certificate and looked back up slightly puzzled... He might have seen his baptism name Tadeu, which he even mentioned in this case, but at the sharp whisper of the one before him, he spoke... "God's servant Bogdan." From the mouths of those who were not really his friends, more or less schooled, the whispers start flowing again. The groom had changed his baptism name over the years and some now remembered that, not many years ago, he had signed something — even published business cards — with the name "Dieu-donne" and this was the time when the comments on the changing mind of this knight they knew were accurate... fully, not having the slightest idea that the philosopher and etymologist from Bessarabia, which was a part of Russia back then, had made a simple *boutade* like an elementary interpretation of the scholars, showing that Tadeu, Bogdan, or Dieu-donne were in fact, following the Latin-Polish, Slavic, and French language rules, the same name.

But the rumors and the tones increased especially when some, who had not received wedding invitations "at home," found out that a few others had followed the newlyweds after the wedding to the two rooms on Popa Rusu street, where Bogdan had chosen to live around the time of the wedding.

"Did you see, *mon cher*? Our friend S and his lady... we know... they were invited."

"Madame G. and her niece as well..."

"That scoundrel! Nobody has taken an olive from the hand of the great scientist."

"He doesn't have enough to share?! Poor ladies..."

But the ones who were unhappy about the situation were not aware that, on that day, all the groom had in his pocket for the wedding and the party were the "two poli" left from his hard work, from which he had also paid Father Ioniță for his trouble.

It was a summer day, warm and blessed by the first cherry blossoms that were now resting under the windows. There, Bogdan welcomed his godparents and two or three of his friends and celebrated for a few hours with Șaba wine sent as a gift by a few of his admirers in Moldavia. When everyone understood, after talks and snacks, that this was the poor wedding of a poor man, they hurriedly raised one or two glasses and then left the newlyweds in the confines of their modest home, but with great room for their happiness, for which Father Ioniță had given them his blessing earlier.

Iulia Faliciu was happy in this small room where she was together with someone whose early life she only knew a little, from the generosity of a few letters, but who's rich soul she had discovered by herself. More than that: the humble "mountain girl," as her chosen one would often call her, aside from all the honeymoon happiness she was feeling, was proud of being the wife of such a schooled young man who was so well-known, and also the wife of a noble boyar.

Her peasant self didn't feel any inferiority when it came to her origins. In the mountains of Abrud, in those years, noble Iancu's[1] tale of lighting the people's path and raising them to the conscience of their rights was still fresh. She herself was a fighter in body and spirit, guided by Father Balint's calling for awakening, feeling her blood and heartbeats, and they were one with the authentic nobility of her predecessors. In Roșia Abrudului, Roșia Montană as it's called today, the Faliciu family had long asserted its rights and titles. Iulia's brother had fallen, fighting under the Romanian flag for the awakening of the nation, and for him must be written the first words of the noble virtue of the family. Iulia's pride had a solid basis and explanation. Her serene face, her words and stories about her people, had stolen the heart, two years before, of the young scholar of Romanian rights, who was traveling through the lands where Trajan had given Decebal the honor of a true warrior's death.[2] That's why when Bogdan and Iulia met, their spirits had melded together from the beginning in an apotheosis dreamed of by the elders of both families.

But the one who had sought happiness and was now enjoying it fully in his home was Bogdan.

His life up to then had been a long series of victories and defeats. Obscure defeats resulting from glancing blows, victories obtained mainly through personal merits, that were unsupported except by the genius that emanated from his creative powers. The new life that this woman, who wasn't quite a scholar and lacked those sparks of intelligence shown through playful words, without diplomas, was giving him in the simple room where the most valuable furniture was a pile of books, magazines, and documents, felt to the poet, teacher, and fighter as a corner of divine wealth from the beginning.

He had dreamt about it, he had waited and longed for this life, and he had earned it. He was entitled to it, not because of what he had given to the culture of his beloved country, but for what he was going to give to it.

Bogdan had once considered himself a boyar, maybe he would brag in the future about the sparkle of his family crest that had been stolen by his enemies, but it is certain that neither his title nor his family crest were the inspiration and energy for his creations. He had many years of adventure, from the time he abandoned his

---

[1] A reference to Avram Iancu, heroic leader in the Romanian struggle for liberty during the 1848 uprising in Transylvania.

[2] A reference to Roman Emperor Trajan who conquered Dacia in A.D. 105-106, ruled then by Decebal.

officer post in Russia following a duel with a higher-ranked comrade that resulted in punishment, an officer commission that he had accepted as a consolation after the betrayal of a girl named Alina, from the tumultuous life he had lived in universities, with other evanescent loves on school benches, or in the homes of his friends and acquaintances, such as Agafia and Sonia. He led a life of hardship and misery during the first years after crossing the Prut River to Iași, or the town hall in Cahul that he had left after a short time for not bowing his head. This whole life in which his soul of great promise was alone and constrained, tormented by various hosts, in rented rooms, bars, and establishments. That life was over. The doors were wide open for contentment, quiet hours in which the emptiness from across the table, with its dust and cold cup of tea, was gone, replaced by his wife's hands and her heart vibrating around him with freshness, replaced by warm coffee.

Until this welcome change, Hasdeu had been a high school teacher, a librarian in Iași, a temporary archive director, and a member of the historical commission; he had written various articles, studies, lyrics, and prose, about which he wasn't pleased. They each held the symbol of his occupation or production, but besides the mark of competition and fighting spirit, they all reflected something of the restless life he was living. He launched a few ironic attacks, especially against V. Alexandru Urechilă whom he would always be mindful of because he had attacked him in the past, naming him "our esteemed fellow professor, phantasmagoric, and dramatic reviver of Dacians." Hasdeu in turn had exposed a few frivolities in his lyrics; or those epigrams addressed to Professor Ion Strat, who together with August Treboniu Laurian (who was later to become Hasdeu's friend), had signed a letter of condemnation on the occasion of the novel *Duduca Mămuca*,

That's why, gentlemen, that's why
I am upset and troubled:
This idea has been tormenting me for a long time
No matter what, I want to be like... Strat!

or some tirades against P.P. Carp, who got the police involved after the Răzvan-Vodă drama, etc.

However, a few public conferences had demonstrated to the public the knowledge, which in fact, the officials had found applied to him somewhat earlier.

But on this tumultuous youth, on this early knowledge and his affirmed talent, there was the fresh memory of that event that had brought him a great deal of unpleasantness. Hasdeu often didn't have a filter or control when he was writing. The diabolic irony would often sneak into his inspiration, often turning against him when he least expected it. Usually, people like Hasdeu, whose sharp spirits threaten to take over at any moment, are often overcome by this spark, clouding their wisdom. For a well-directed joke, irony risks untaught consequences, and jokes with double meanings are more incompatible as they start from higher up. The novel *Duduca Mămuca* in which "frivolity" was insufficiently masked, was a shadow over the serenity that normally rests on the face of a schooled man. Iulia was informed by some well-wishers about this novel, as evidence of the past of this "Don Juan," but the "mountain girl" pretended she didn't understand what they were talking about. The one that was affected later on by such a possibility for a titan of wisdom was his daughter, Iulia, Lilica who was as delicate as a white lilac, who always kept in her soul this deaf claim, not only for that frivolous and sour sketch, but also for the intentional cacophonies or obscenities included here and there in her father's writings. After her father was dismissed from the university as a result of publishing *Duduca Mămuca*, republished later on as *Micuța*, and after he was sent to trial, Hasdeu, however, emerged victorious, was acquitted and got his job back; but that didn't mean that, despite his combative personality, always on the offensive, he wasn't burdened by sorrow and guilt.

Nevertheless, in the short-lived *Aghiuță*, a magazine that contained sharp articles against political figures and especially against Mihail Kogălniceanu, and also doubtful venomous articles. Even if his wife wasn't schooled, her good advice rightfully told her husband what he should and should not write.

"My dear Hasdeu," she said in the first year of their marriage, "from such a schooled and fiery Romanian such as yourself I expect beautiful books about the past and the future life of our nation. Write, my dear, write, but write in the way that Bogdan Petriceicu Hasdeu must write. The struggle of this hard-tried nation must be told to those who do not know it yet. And nobody could reveal these facts the way you do."

"My dear Iulia, I understand, and I'll follow your advice. But I'm also a different type of fighter. Especially when it comes to stupidity."

"Well, Hasdeu dear, you can't banish stupidity from the world."

"I believe you; but I also cannot tolerate it around me, in the politics of my country, and especially in art. Neither stupidity nor ignorance."

"You'll make enemies; that's all, my dear."

"This keeps me going. The more enemies I have, the more stupid and ignorant men there are. And I can't allow them to flourish in this country."

"May the devil strike them, so you can beat them."

These discussions while enjoying hot coffee and a cigarette at the worktable had an immediate effect. Hasdeu saw the celestial finger blooming in the warm hand that his Transylvanian woman used to hug him, soothe him, and advise him.

Later he would write about this blessed guidance, with all the gratitude and love:

> My wife and her soul were a piece of gold from Abrud... Until my marriage in 1865, I had written a few newspaper articles, a few brochures, and a collection of documents.
>
> There was a night, close to sunrise, but not yet morning; I was just a small piece of myself, a tired and disgusting piece. From then to now, with my wife's help, I started feeling complete and bright... Thus, I could work, I really could, because my Iulia was not only soothing me during work but also was banishing all of my needs...

It wasn't only the conversations, caresses, and direct advice that contributed to this. Whatever was said about Hasdeu, this protean spirit, gigantic in possibilities and manifestations, often bad as he would call himself, could not be accused of not having one thing: gratitude. He had a sense of gratitude. This would even be visible towards his enemies, but especially towards his friends. Even in his categorical antisemitism, claimed in conferences and told in political prose, Hasdeu kept his devotion true for the good-standing Jews that had made his acquaintance. He was accused of not having any gratitude, he was even accused of being opportunistic, but whoever glimpsed at his private life saw the truth was only one.

Warmed by this fire that flared in his heart, Hasdeu, as it was later found, remained by his wife's side despite the clashes of married life. No accusation to her accusations. Only goodness, honesty, and righteousness.

This absolute love that his wife had for him was the first resort, as said by the words of Apostle Paul: "Love... finds excuses for everything, believes everything, hopes for everything, suffers for everything...." It is possible, but his vast soul was embodied in gratitude and through this, it can be said that Hasdeu was a good man.

Always on the run between classes and his job as an editor, between a conference and a political speech, his mind was slowly emptying at the sight of this woman and the peace she had brought to their modest home.

Strong and tireless, Iulia, his wife, was far from wanting a life of vanity as the spouse of a professor, deputy, minister that he was, and she didn't forget the manners she had learned in her parents' home in the mountains. She sometimes lacked servants, but even when she had one, Iulia woke up in the morning, dressed in her modest clothes and her silk kerchief, went shopping at the market for everything needed in the house, and came back with bags of everything she knew her Hasdeu enjoyed. Her kitchen was an example of tidiness and cleanliness, as every Transylvanian kitchen is, and always received her with freshness and richness. Between two stews, which she closely kept an eye on, the flavors and whiffs from the stove, blended with pieces of songs, visited her husband in his office. His pen then picked up speed, the paper becoming docile, and his smile showed from under his bushy mustache.

And then she came into his office, with her hands in her apron and smiling eyes:

"I cooked Transylvanian goulash for you, my dear Hasdeu."

"With pepper, Iulia, with pepper?"

"With Hungarian paprika."

"Oh no! Not this!"

"It's okay my dear. That's the only good thing Hungarians have: paprika in goulash! In a minute I'll make that Abrud pie that you love so much!"

"Bravo, bravo! My dear Iulia!"

"Now my dear, we both must go back to work!"

It's not surprising why Hasdeu, the poet, sang like no other husband about the virtue of this woman and about all the happiness she had brought into his life, which would become the prologue of the literary work *Răzvan și Vidra*.

In those poetic days of somber dark
Holding your hand in mine for inspiration,
I wrote this drama that became my life
As a most delicate "forget me not"

Oh, you, who shared your honest soul with me,
Making everything easier to conquer
You carried both our burdens on your shoulders
A gesture of pure love and poetry!...

But he wrote that much later from his memories after his wife had left to be with God, in a work for the Academy (1903) called "A Romanian Wife," which should have only been a fragment of his literary work called *Băbușca mea*, that he was intending to write as a romanticized story of their marriage, and especially of his wife who had been "as a lamp with soothing light" after the death of their daughter.

And this was not a simple statement of gratitude for the fruitfulness of his talent that his mountain girl had promoted.

In the two small rooms on Popa Rusu street, Bogdan Petriceicu Hasdeu worked thoroughly, produced impulsively, aside from some literary-political works, two of his most notable works of historical literature, works of mature creation that even today are taught in schools and found on the bookshelves of scholars: the drama *Răzvan Vodă* (later revised and renamed *Răzvan și Vidra*) and the wonderful monograph of *Ion Vodă cel Cumplit*. The latter one, however, would cast doubt on the home in which it was written: because in "A Romanian Wife," Hasdeu states that he wrote both works, and also a third one at the same house on Ioan Rusu street, *Domnița Ruxandra*; while in the second edition of *Ion Vodă cel Cumplit* he stated that he had written this history in 1864 (when he was not yet married) while living in the home of banker Mircuș (or Mircoush as he writes it) from the Theater Plaza where he had lived.

We attribute and honor the sign of his good faith, where forgetfulness might also lead to some errors, where they were written wasn't as important: (the prologue to the second edition of *Ion Vodă cel Cumplit* was written thirty years later). The fact is that day-to-day work on creating these literary pieces, which Hasdeu himself dedicated to his wife, was predominated by the solace of his home, from where the busy bee had managed to build a whole hive, with meals on time, with tiptoeing, with precision in the household, and — what Hasdeu missed — with small savings for the future. These savings were not a means of plugging the tap of honey in the hive. On the contrary! In her daily prudence, Iulia never allowed someone in need to leave with an empty hand. The poor were showing up every Saturday, which was a day dedicated to them, and the housewife would always find a coin or a slice of bread for these forsaken who were blessing her home and her soul. Later on, when his wife became even more generous, Hasdeu tried to talk to her about tempering it but without success.

"You're too giving, dear Iulia! I also help those in need, but not those who must not be helped..."

"Dear Hasdeu, do good and do lots of it! Because it won't harm you! There are a lot of people who don't have much. Don't worry! I know how to deal with it."

"Our life is hard, and you work too much to not save some money for your own needs."

"And I can deal with that, my dear..."

The balanced life, the aura of sainthood that was surrounding him, the contented soul of the intellectual worker, gathered now from so many foreign alcoves, in the quiet and healthy nest of his own home in which a clean body would satisfy his needs enough, the thought that sprouted long ago and was fed with the love of life and seeing his existence perpetuated in the future, all these brought the wish of procreation during the nights of caresses. The conscious introspection of the thinker with a gigantic mind was already giving him the impulse to break the barriers of time and break the limits. A child, maybe two, maybe three, would carry on, and maybe exhaust in years and centuries, the tumult he was feeling in his bones. It was a dream, a constant wish he had, ever since he had decided to get married. And it was not a coincidence that Hasdeu, the one lost among ladies and many admirers, or spoiled by a few generous windows, didn't fall in love with any of them. His ideal woman slowly took shape in his mind. When it comes to having children, Romanian peasant women have ancestral qualities and strengths. That's where all the pure essence is, the pure blood only touched by the coolness of the mountains and the heat of the sun. That must be the healing source of Hasdeu's line that he owed to his parents. The perpetuation of this family was not found in refinement, not in the subtlety of lives such as his mother's, the delicate Elisabeta Daucșa, who had given birth to him when she was around fourteen years old and had left him an orphan shortly after. No, this family had its strength in the thick and fruitful furrow of their land, where the seed for its perpetuation had sprouted, whose predecessors had counted lords, princes, but especially writers and intellectuals, such as his grandfather Tadeu and his father Alexandru, a man who resembled Bogdan's superior potency from many humane and cultural points of view.

But even in this natural and strong ambition, Hasdeu found an unexpected caution from his wife. She shared this holy wish to be a mother, just as it had been in the world where her mother and grandmother had originated from, hard-working women when it came to their homes and childbirth. This beautiful woman with a beautifully crafted body never understood anything else when it came to marriage. However, the homemaker had realized that because of the small space they were living in, only two small rooms where two people could barely live together without bumping into each other, bringing another person into it would be truly challenging.

But this couldn't really be considered an impediment since the mountain villagers in Abrud never put the crib of the newcomer in sparkling palaces, but together with the elders and with the many other noisy children in a single room. She was worried about her Hasdeu! Her husband was reading, writing, composing, going out, running, and he was always coming home tired, only to sit down and start working again. The last thing he needed was a baby. Every time the conversation turned to the child they both wanted, she always showed her worry with a smile.

"Don't worry about silence, dear Iulia. Everywhere I've lived before I had you to take care of me, I worked just as I do now."

"For your future works, dear Hasdeu, those that I and our people are waiting for, I consider protecting you from this is not unfounded."

"You're right, dear Iulia, but my poor mother brought me into this world and raised me with hardships as well."

"You think mine raised me any easier?"

"I know. We must think of our nation. If we didn't give it valued children…"

"We will, Hasdeu, we will… but slowly… *'langasam'*."

For Hasdeu, however, the child he wanted was not simple office work. That child would carry the eternal legacy of its parents who would gift it the treasure of knowledge and talent. Atavism preoccupied his mind, not only objectively, but subjectively as well. "The matter of the atavism," — as a physiological problem and especially as a psychological one he would later write in dedication to Paul Janet and Th. Ribot, on the occasion of editing the works of his daughter — "is all the more interesting as for several years now it has begun to be given more and more attention, and people rush to gather as much material on it as possible and choose the most conclusive data."

Between his poet and writer grandfather, his historian father, and his genius child, Hasdeu would later embark on bio-psychological research that allowed him to discover the most eloquent conclusions about the importance of atavism in transmitting the possibility of artistic creation. It's not sure if he had superior intuition, or just made a simple logical deduction when it came to the birth of a child that would be like him or like those from his family, that would be the golden link between the past and the future. Something mystical from the other side would spark this hope, which is the pride of any parent, a native impulse of love, and an impetus of life.

That's why, with pain in his heart and questions about why he watched his wife lose pregnancies, those first fruits of their love lost right from the start, made him ask himself many questions. The full and ardent senses would torment his soul and give him excruciating insights into life. He couldn't conclude anything disagreeable about the mountain girl from Roșia who had given herself to him so candidly and whose physical build was the definition of motherhood. Trivial occurrences that Hasdeu didn't react to were the revival of several anonymous letters when, in the first year of his marriage, he had those memorable antisemitic conferences about the Talmud, Three Jews, Shakespeare's Shylok, Balzac's Gobseck, Alecsandri's Moses, and those about national industry, foreign industry, and Jewish industry... Two or three anonymous letters ridiculed him as one that was a "Jew's grandson," cursing him for not being as intelligent as his Jewish grandmother and for God to not give him an antisemitic child. After wishing him infernal torture on earth, they finished with the supreme invocation of untimely death.

Hasdeu smiled, throwing them in the fire one by one, knowing in his conscience that his grandmother, Valeria-Cristina, the wife of Tadeu, had been more Christian than many other Christians, had helped build churches, and had worshiped Christ's cross.

A fatalist, with that mystical and unbroken belief in destiny, Hasdeu allowed himself to be carried by fate and by the decisions of the Parcae. "Not even God will change what has already been written," says the heroine of a drama he wrote in these first years. Later on, if that's how it was fated, for him to be the last of the Hasdeu family, who would be able to change it? His soul, however, was full of high refuges where he would hide this unrest in the "sarcasm" that saved him, in his smiling attitude, even more as an "ultra-optimist" such as himself couldn't drown his worry in hopelessness, but he told himself, as Corneille, that as long as life gives the man strength and hope, as long as love keeps his spirit alive, hope is the only horizon, because only death closes the borders with the earth.

Death alone extinguishes the hope of a man.

It will come. If not now, then it will come later! "Dum spiro, Spero." That bud of the vigorous and fruitful tree will come to dispel the storms of capricious destiny.

During that long wait, days and nights passed between 1865 and 1869. Hasdeu worked, day by day, with excitement, humor, and with powers enhanced by his quiet home. In those years he published the pamphlet *Satyrul*, throwing arrows of irony to the politicians of those times, taking a stand against Cuza Vodă[3] and supporting his removal, even though later on he would regret this and rise against the nation who turned on the Romanian leader; he rose against the foreign dynasty, even though later he would devote himself to it; he worked on turning *Domnița*

---

[3] Alexandru Ioan Cuza, the first prince of the United Romanian Principalities.

Ruxandra into a play, as well as the drama *Răzvan-Vodă*, which had a successful premiere. When it came to his career, he created a public course based on the "history of the Romanian constitutional right," and in the political sphere he campaigned for the House of Deputies, having liberal views but running as an independent, becoming a deputy from Bolgrad.

During the summer months, especially in 1867, he traveled to the Apuseni Mountains, together with his wife, where Iulia visited her relatives and the lands of her childhood, refreshing her being with the clean mountain air. Also, in the following year, he embarked -this time by himself— on a study trip abroad through Serbia, Austro-Hungary, Germany, and France, discovering and collecting important historical documents. He wanted to repeat the trip for scholarly purposes during the following year, in 1869, but that summer his soul was called back home with very emotional news. In the summer of that year, fatidical for the existence of the creator Hasdeu, maternity gave his wife strong emotions again. Hasdeu, after consulting his doctor friends Vlădescu and Măldărescu, gave his wife attention and daily care, making her follow the doctors' advice of moving slow and avoiding effort, while God listened to his prayers and was close to his thoughts.

Hasdeu had never been an actual atheist. He just had never conformed to the rituals and formalities of Christianity, believing that they obscured and reduced the proportions of infinite kindness and the beauty of divinity, but he had always believed in God's power, even before that adoring culmination that he would testify to three decades later:

I wish my heart to play one single melody,
One single spell for a late child
Who is so full of life, though not yet born
Hiding under its mother's heart, most helplessly.

I'm infinite, though I am made of flesh
My soaring mind not knowing limitations:
I'm an artist who knows no respite
Playing the songs of my imaginations.

The earth, sky, clouds, and solar systems,
And everything existing in this world,
Are specs revolving around their creation
Specs that started their journey from our God.

And my thoughts cry, yearning humility:
Until in the end — they say — I cannot surface;
Ecstasy by itself can only rise this high;
The ecstasy binding a man to divinity.

Such a display of adoration towards God was a revelation during those times in the fresh Romanian poetry. Not metaphysics, not mysticism, a simple cry of pain as it was said. It's a display of supreme faith.

For Iulia, however, Hasdeu's God was the other God, the one watching over simple mortals, and the church was the refuge of most intimate devotion. And not just once during this time of motherhood, the rituals and the prayers had taken her hopes to heaven during the communion with the body of God's son. Starting with the early signs during her first pregnancies, Hasdeu and his wife made plans for their awaited child. Those moments, somewhat rare because of his busy schedule, were dedicated to the name and the sex of the baby. If they had a boy, he wanted him to be named Alexandru after his treasured father, or Iuliu, after his beloved wife, and if they had a girl, no other name than hers… What would the child look like? A boy would look like Alexandru, the one with a serene face and soul, and a girl would only look like his beautiful wife from Abrud.

Amidst those plans of hope, caring for his wife, and closely supervising her, Hasdeu worked. He worked constructively and fiercely against politicians and political morals (....the bat, the horse traders, the porters) of the politics of those times. A convinced democrat, he launched his attacks in the *Traian* magazine, first published in 1869. Against all those who fought against freedom and individual dignity, Kogălniceanu was at the top of the sharp spear whose tip he used to stab all the "servants" of the ruler. He attacked Carol I, but he found him indispensable to the country and voted for him. He attacked cosmopolitanism, this "laziness to love," and declared his love for the country to unspeakable dogmas and didn't show mercy to anyone that encouraged foreigners in the country's seats of power.

All this brought him negative reactions — threats, and consequences were not far behind. In August 1869, while he was a candidate for the Academy, Hasdeu fell, fighting heroically and eventually throwing sarcastic remarks toward all those who had caused it because they were not comfortable with his presence.

Once he returned home, his consolation was always in the soft arms of his wife and the roundness of her belly that was growing healthy and protected.

Chapter II

The Sprout

The problem that would preoccupy Hasdeu later on, in the last chapter of his life, as a philosophical attitude on detangling and explaining his soul's enigmas, became a constant in his life. There's no sleep without dreams, he would empirically state at a later time. "The lack of dreams is just a prelude to sleep, or is the end of sleep, one of the two, but it is not sleeping…. All creatures when they sleep, they dream just like humans… Because the plant sleeps as well, for certain it has at least a crumb of a dream…" And on these postulates, the philosopher, tormented to the last fiber of his being by that boundless pain in his earthly body, would look for conclusions to help soothe his terrible loss.

A few days before that wonderful sprout would appear on the branch of Hasdeu's tree, a sprout that would be his daughter, Iulia Hasdeu, the mother had a dream that she didn't speak about to anyone, especially not to her husband, whose opinions she knew well. Her often introverted and focused personality had the patience to not divulge that dream, which she didn't consider a prophecy. But it would follow her for a time, and she secretly confessed it to a friend later on. She was in a palace, disguised as a poor woman, living her youth in solitude. Suddenly, a shadow detached itself from the arched ceiling of a hall, darker than any shadow she'd ever seen, turning lighter, somehow like a cloud of smoke, and surrounding the young woman, turned into a blinding light that danced around her. Terrified, the unfortunate woman was struggling to get away without saying a word. In its dazzling game, the shining smoke started changing shapes, changing its outline into smooth lines and precise shapes, and the girl felt her hands reaching for the cloud. But it was now a maiden, white as a lily, who surprisingly burst into laughter, spoke a few melodious words, and after that turned back into a white cloud, then into a fog, rose, and disappeared above the palace's spires. Iulia woke up moaning. Her husband asked her what was amiss, but she asked him to go back to sleep, as she was fine. Hasdeu had also had dreams like this one, or others, but he had never thought about their substantiality, but rather about the problem itself, that would torment him over the years, fueled by events and especially by loneliness. Heretical explanations never preoccupied him, and he never accepted them as signs of the future, because the problem did not impose necessity or a thirst for refuge, as it was imposed on him at the end of his life. His multiform activity, intense and vigorously mastered, was taking his time away from mystical preoccupations, as they passed through the human spirit. The realities of life would overlap daily, overwhelming him too much to allow him time to remember his or his wife's dreams.

Among these realities, the happiest one was the birth of the long-awaited child. In the evening preceding the event, the signs of the impending birth sent Hasdeu running to bring help, after which he came back to his wife's bedside, caressing her while she heroically suffered; he would go out again and come back, burning with the impatience of a sensible man. The following day, after sunrise had already blown the shadows away from the windows and had polished the room with the golden rays of the autumn sun, a little girl arrived in the clean sheets, round, with black wavy hair, brown eyes, almost black, and thin eyebrows, greeting her guests in the language of all frogs, like a sign of nature had lent its rich mosaic to this new being. The mother's good health and the ten pounds of the rosy newcomer gave the father a day of rare euphoria. There were sounds of strength in the small round body, in the restless hands, in the suckling greed, bringing strong hope in the home and happiness to their friends, whom Hasdeu had informed. In the editorial office of *Traian* newspaper, at the office of *Românismul*, whose president he was going to become, in the halls of the Academy, in the homes of his friends, and even in the home of Ion C. Brătianu, there was word of Hasdeu's child. Congratulations, well wishes, baptism plans, and his friend, Brătianu, agreeing to be her godfather all increased his fatherly joy. And the baptism soon came. When the recovered mother, Iulia Hasdeu, presented Miss Iulia Hasdeu to the guests, her big eyes gave soft looks to the smiling faces watching over her from above.

During the purifying ritual, after the newborn, stopping her loud protests, was passed into the hands of the great minister, following the customs of the place, a silver tray was brought with all the "amulets" full of symbolism such as a gold coin, a crucifix, a pen, a flower, a piece of candy, and many other objects considered prophetic. All these were presented to the new Christian, while the gazes of the attendees waited for the choice of the indecisive little hands that were gliding above the items, pushing and rolling them around curiously. Hasdeu hurriedly brought a book and set it among them. The child's eyes were set on each item on the tray and when her father expected her to choose the book, the little hand decisively grabbed the golden pen, which was a gift from her godfather, and her pinky finger hooked

The Sprout

around the thin stem of the flower. This prompted rich remarks, prophecies, and assurances of happiness to please the parents.

"She is going to be a schooled woman, just like her father, since she grabbed a pen," said the godfather.

"Why not a poet? She grabbed the flower as well," said Zamfir Arbore.

"Maybe a teacher, because she touched the book."

"Why not an honest priest's wife? I noticed she wanted to grab the crucifix first," concluded the priest officiating the baptism.

Hasdeu softened. His everyday focus towards this sprout that inspired hope for the future, the atmosphere lightened by her cooing, and the calmness of his home had wrapped his soul in the tenderness of patience. For a few months, he kept his arrows in his quiver, and Bogdan Petriceicu Hasdeu never had a richer Christmas in his modest home, than the one given by his wife that year.

During the first year, mother Iulia, a woman from Abrud, full of devotion like all mothers in the world for whom their child was their supreme jewel, was a caregiver, a governess, a diaper-washer, and a soother for the father who was often interrupted from writing by squeals that didn't always have a pleasant resonance in the home of a writer. After finishing the household chores, the mother always grabbed the stroller to take her daughter out for some fresh air, for a short time during winter, for a long stroll during the days of spring, and when summer came, she sat in the shade of the trees knitting happily.

Stopping his writing, Hasdeu sprung up from his desk when the stroller with the tiny queen returned, waited for her to wake up, and took the little body in his arms, a body abounding with charm and hopes. Not few were the times when his mustache and beard were tried by the fingers of this angel in a human body. Over those wide eyes, shadowed by eternal questions, with a comical seriousness in every gesture, the scholar's shiny eyes gave silent answers. Life transfusions, subconscious rivers of thoughts, of the future, hopes, and dreams, all these were sourced from this vigorous stem towards the sprout.

The writer's friends of those times were predicting the future victories of the baby that couldn't even sit up by herself yet. Feminine beauty had sketched outlines and accents that were already visible. Among those friends were her godfather, Ion Gârleanu, August Treboniu Laurian, the Transylvanian man known by the child's parents from the time when they were students in Iași, now the dean of the Faculty of Letters, whom Hasdeu had a beautiful friendship with, even though he had to sign the letter of condemnation not long before. They came to the modest home of

Hasdeu, with their white beards and serene faces; Grandea de Macedonian, the journalist who was still young but full of admiration for Hasdeu; the archbishop Ghenadie Petrescu, who would later become a metropolitan and who would send shockwaves with his brave attitude in an acute professional issue; the publicist Gh. Missail, the painter and professor F. Walch and his wife, Doctors Vlădescu and Grecescu, Nicu Dimitriu, poet Alex. Macedonski, Gh. Chițu, P. Aurelian, future ministers, and among the youngest of the former colleagues or students was Svârlescu, a history professor, Radu Novian, and some university staff members who celebrated the birth of this doll with a face as soft as a flower petal and eyes as dark as the night.

The undefeated active and combative spirit of Hasdeu, however, couldn't stand being too long in the calm given by his precious sprout. In the spring of 1870, *Traian* became *Columna lui Traian* and the first issue was published on the 1st of March, with a clear anti-dynastic tone. Hasdeu would explain later that nothing had attacked the ruling prince, whose personal merits he was well aware of, but his Romanian patriotic soul couldn't understand how the other newspapers were promoting an emphasized foreignism. "Romanian spirit in democracy and democracy in the Romanian spirit," the motto of the newspaper *Columna lui Traian*, couldn't bring him any inconveniences from the "good Romanians," especially not from the government of Manolache Costache Epureanu, the prime minister of those times, or from Alexandru Lahovary, the new Minister of Justice, who were both top political men.

At the same time, with *Columna* being published, a political insurrection movement that was foreign to Hasdeu began in Ploiești, where the well-known proclamation of a republic was made, as well as the demand for the ruler's abdication, a movement led by the famous former Captain Candiano-Popescu, who following his heroic acts during the War for Independence would become an adjutant-colonel for King Carol I, and, later on, even a general. However, the anti-dynastic articles in *Columna* were considered to be an instigation and a provocation towards the movement, which led to Hasdeu being arrested after he previously made the same hints under the pseudonym Puang-Hon-Ki in *Salyrul*.

Hasdeu's bitterness about his eight days spent in Văcărești prison was not necessarily because of the imprisonment itself: "...a prison for a political man worthy of carrying this title is just like a weapon for a good soldier, meaning honor and reassurance," he wrote after being released. More than that, Hasdeu couldn't have found better company, as he spent his imprisonment together with I.C. Brătianu, General Golescu, An. Stolojan, and Candiano-Popescu. His pain during the week spent far from his wife, and especially far from his dear Lilica, as he would call his little girl, was unbearable, especially when his wife and baby were strictly forbidden from visiting him. As a consolation during these days, Hasdeu wrote ballads, studied documents, and noted his findings.

It's obvious he sought revenge. His quill knew no respite. Between a metaphor and a fable, between historical memory and an epigram, his emphasis gravely fell on the government and the head of State. Beizadea Dimitrie Ghica, "the decorated blister" as he would call him, was especially the target of his invectives.

Sorrows for a fighter such as Hasdeu were easily suppressed by his constant stream of thoughts. One year passed and between speeches and studying documents, between lessons and newspaper articles. He found time for satire against those working for the *Convorbiri literare* magazine, the head of which was a mind of great proportions, Titu Maiorescu. Nobody could see an adversary like Hasdeu coming, as he was waiting and watching. The famous poem *Eu și Ea* (*Her and I*), signed with his pseudonym M. Elias, with an intentional cacophonic alliteration and childish content, was published by the magazine only because the original author was German and the direct one was Jewish, confirming what Hasdeu already suspected, the Philo-Semitism practiced by those in Iași.

While the nation's attention was focused on the prank, cumulating in sympathy and admiration, Hasdeu rushed home every day, impatient to feel the embrace of the child that kept his health and mood uplifted. He sat at his desk with Lilica in his arms, reading newspapers and magazines, showing her photos and faces, talking to her in his way in the language of the angels.

The girl started walking. She had already started babbling fragments of words before her first birthday, and she also started holding herself upright, with or without support, encouraged by Hasdeu's laughter and giggling that she could understand. The child had opened her eyes to letters and found them fascinating symbols calling to her, especially while in their company, she and her "papà" would find themselves caught in a mystical "présage." Pages were flying everywhere during her "philological" research, while Hasdeu tried to translate from time to time: father = *papà*... mother = *maman*, book = *livre*, milk = *lait*, and many more, all this delighting her, especially when *papà, lait, liv*... found original meanings in her mouth with cherry-colored lips.

Thus, the first two years of her childhood, which for most children means bottles, diapers, and crying with or without a reason, became years of precocity that was going to show itself very soon. Papà's French on one side, mother's German on the other side, during the time when articulated speech and basic vocabulary is barely showing in other children, came together in phrases, even though her pronunciation was typical of a two-year-old child. This would amaze all the friends and family during visits to their home.

Around Christmas in 1871 and New Year's in 1872, Hasdeu bought her various books with pictures and geometric shapes suitable for kindergarten, and in his few spare minutes observed that Lilica was looking at the letters, pronouncing them clearly but with a lisp. Shortly after, she could put the letters together, emphasizing the words, and on New Year's Eve 1872, Lilica could decipher a few dozen words before she was two and a half years old. On the same occasion, the mother prepared a surprise for Papà and the guests: a poem recited by the little mouth of the miracle child.

The poem sounded like this:

Izel, izelasul meu,
Loagăte lui Dumideu
Pentu sufeselul meu.
Eu su mic, tu fă-mă male
Eu su sab, tu fă-mă tale
In tot locu mă păzete
Si de lele mă felete.

Everyone present understood the solemn moment of the recital that preceded bedtime for the child and the party because it was a poem learned by every small child.

The explosion of applause and the kisses on the chubby cheeks were far from over when the mother picked up the little artist, snatching her away from her astonished admirers before laying her in her little canopied bed.

The surprise would be even bigger three to four months later when the girl would prove her reading competency while looking over spelling books with pictures and drawings that she received from everyone. They were in her native language as well as in French and German. Her father supervised the creation of her small library.

"Dear Iulia, I have hope that God has gifted us with a smart and exceptional child like no other…"

"I believe so too! That's why I've been preparing her."

"Yes, but we must be careful!"

"We are being careful..."

"We mustn't force her to do anything..."

"Not force her? Are you not seeing that she's the one forcing us?"

Her mother was also worried about this. Lilica's aptitudes were natural, however. She learned every answer she received to her questions about letters, she spoke in full sentences, and she understood everything. The child never cried about cookies or a hidden box of chocolates, only when her mother took her books out of her hands.

Her parents later learned to portion Lilica's reading capacity, but she also learned to get a stool while her mother was cleaning or cooking, to hide the book under her apron, and hide under a table or the bed to quench her thirst for knowledge.

Her old great-grandmother ended up living with them and she was tortured by repeated requests for her to tell stories, fulfilling them, even though not always as much as the child wanted.

"Tell me more, Grandma, tell me more!"

"I'd tell you more, dear, but I don't know any more right now." The venerable grandmother of Bogdan Petriceicu Hasdeu would find excuses after starting to live in his house.

Mother Iulia often told her Transylvanian ghost stories or real stories from Abrud, but the child had no limit.

"Tell me more, Mother! Tell me more!"

"I forgot."

"No, you didn't! Tell me more... a nice one..."

One evening the old grandmother was left in shock. Lilica had asked her to tell her some stories herself. And her little mouth had started pouring phrases and repeating, almost exactly, the stories she had heard, even the ones she had read in the picture books from her library.

"Once upon a time there was an emperor who had two children... Small ones... This small... And those children were beautiful... just like my mother... and like you. And those children were well behaved, just like Lilica..."

In her phrases and childish speech she could hear order and significance, the recital being more impressive as her memory, that she'd rely on her whole life, was passing the first tests. And this thirst for telling stories she also took to her father, making his workspace resound with her voice. When it came to Prince Charming being lured in by the song of a princess, or the emperor's daughter who found her prince with her voice, Lilica knew how to invent or quote the right lines. And the scholar found himself in the seventh heaven, where "ecstasy binds the man to God."

Lilica enjoyed telling stories to animals as well, who listened to her silently. She gathered the cats or the dogs that would become her loyal friends for the rest of her life, wrapped them in blankets in her bed, got their attention for what she wanted to tell them, and their expressionless faces listened to their tiny protector.

"There! Be good and Lilica will give you sweets. There! Once upon a time…"

And the green or blue eyes watched her lazily, pricking up their ears, blinking their furry eyelids and purring, wrapped in the magic of the terrible dragon that only ate people… And her father's bushy face would not just once fill with tenderness at such sights, watched from behind his manuscripts.

However, life was not always filled with tenderness; life means climbing up sharp cliffs to reach pointy peaks. It is also a treasure earned coin by coin by the healer knowing where it's hidden. Hasdeu was working hard, drafting great studies on the life of the Romanian nation, starting the monumental piece of literature that would become the peak of his scientific work: *Istoria Critică*, received with enthusiasm by scholars and commendation by Bucharest's mayor. The depth of the soul, similar to the layers of soil in which gold and lead are found, or the heights where thoughts find sunrays and storms, was not immobilized by tomes and parchment. Voluble and unpredictable, Hasdeu didn't forget the small incidents with his adversaries, and his serenity intertwined with philosophy, science, and sarcasm opened up to that intermezzo that the poet enjoyed so much. The second prank was even funnier considering the ones in Iași should have seen it coming, as the last one was not that far behind, and it caused a scandal around the joker. Pranks have their significance: *Istoria Critică* had received recognition, even though it wasn't quite unanimous. The ones in Iași, especially Iacob Negruzzi, V. Burlă, the proud philology professor who carried the philosophical debate around "the duck," as well as Cihac, had attacked his work, and Negruzzi had created a lyrical satire around it. A new bet with his most trusted friends, among which was Bishop Ghenadie, gave way to the acrostic *La noi* on the subject of a poet. "Here the apple is rotten" was signed by P.A. Călescu (Păcalescu — the Joker), an acrostic which resulted in the apple being rotten at the *Convorbiri* magazine. The prank was so successful, that Negruzzi admitted not being the center of attention that had resulted from the poem and invited its author to join the *Aghiuță* magazine.

In the house at No. 9 Dionisie Street (the Batiște suburb) where Hasdeu lived at the time, his friends gathered and filled his modest rooms with laughter at the ones who were "pranked." They only went quiet when Iulia Hasdeu appeared carrying the miracle child, summoned by the proud father to join in their joy and... admiration. Lilica was about two and a half years old and displayed a precociousness that everyone around her loved.

A while before that even, on the day of Saint John, Hasdeu, his wife, and their child had paid a visit to their godfather. Ion C. Brătianu, impressed by the visit, enchanted by his goddaughter, and especially amazed by her reading from the books on his desk and her poetry recitals, had predicted to her parents the miracle this little girl would represent in the future. Hasdeu had gladly received the confirmation of his predictions, as well as the advice to not force the sprout, even though she was eager to learn.

Under the trees in the Garden of Icons, where Iulia Hasdeu sat for hours with the girl, to sunbathe and breathe fresh air that was welcome after the stench of the city, many people's gazes stopped upon the little human who sat on a bench with a book in her lap, and with a comical focus on her face. The mother always smiled at the appreciation, managing from time to time to distract the soft eyes from the pages held by chubby hands with fingers that were tracing the pictures of children and colorful birds.

Around the girl's fourth birthday, she knew that bread was "blot" and "pain," that the bird was "vogel" and "oiseau," that "I love you, Mommy" was "ich liebe dich, Muttel" and "je t'aime, Maman," and the German words, as well as the French ones, came together in sentences in poems, with a precise meaning. So, her library kept growing with books in different languages that were suitable to her growing age. She signed her name on their pages as "Iulia Hasdeu," or simply "Lilica" next to small or more complex drawings that showed her artistic inclinations even then. Mrs. Charlotte Walch, the painter's wife, and her parents' friend offered to educate her in English, bringing her daughter Hemina, who was around the same age as Lilica, to make her acquaintance.

Among the first more complex German books Iulia received was a hardcover brochure: *Fivel fur die evangelischen Volkschulen*. The book was signed in pencil by a beginner in the art of writing: "Lilica Hasdeu," dated 1873, which might have been added later for documentation, as well as some doodles pretending to be drawings by a child that was not yet four. Underlined lyrics and markings proved the girl was learning the German poems from the book with the help of her mother, and later on with the help of a teacher.

1873 was a year of deep grief for Hasdeu. Alexandru Hasdeu, the writer, historian, great Romanian soul, Lilica's grandfather, and the loving father of Bogdan died in Hotinul Basarabiei, forgotten by his people, poor and miserable. His son only found out about it on the 20th of January, two or three months after the unfortunate event. Hasdeu's pain was even greater as he not only owed this scholar his life and various talents, but his great initiations in culture as well; that's why he only found solace in the diversion of two great events: the decoration given to him by King Carol I for historical merits and the prize awarded to him by the Academy for his book, *Istoria Critică a Românilor*. Evidently, he was no less consoled by the moments in which his dear daughter knew how to caress his beard.

Lilica progressed astoundingly. When she turned four years old, she could read fluently in three languages, could write with almost calligraphic accuracy, and could sketch faces of children and old people with remarkable facial expressions. She also started saying words and expressions in English. Every bird in the sky was thrilling in her voice. Minor melodies interlaced with some pretentious fragments predicted the major singer she was going to become. Hasdeu, who in his own words was a musical primitive, amplified these manifestations in his mind, and at the suggestion of Dimitriu the piano professor, and of Vasilescu who was knowledgeable in the piano trade, he considered buying her one, so Lilica would develop all her aptitudes equally. However, the lack of space forced him to give the idea up for the time being.

The questions were showing up constantly in the restless mind of the father; what would Lilica become when she grew up? A scholar? A musician? A painter? He could answer two of these questions. Would she be one to decipher the pages of history? Could she go on this path or the one of philology following the great path that he had paved for her, but which would be long and difficult? Why not? Her bright intelligence and her ease of understanding foreign words and speech, her attention, and especially her remarkable spirit of observation that her father was following closely, made him believe in the mirage of his work's continuation. A poet? No way. Poetry is an unrewarding and thorny career, even if rare, perfumed flowers grow amidst its thorns. What did poetry offer him? Only enemies! When it came to music, future predictions stooped to what his friend Dimitru the pianist told him about an artist failed by his musical ideas, or Z. Dimitrescu, the well-bred musician and composer, both embittered by a misunderstood and unproductive life and activity. How about painting? Ah! This is something stricter, more pretentious, but this career is also rough when it fails. The personal competencies of a skilled painter with real predispositions as Hasdeu had, made him believe that Lilica's lines were worthy of attention. She was young, however, and five years of age were not enough to make such discoveries.

Her progress with French and English, under the strict supervision of Mrs. Walch and especially of Hasdeu were obvious and more precise than with German, for which she needed a better teacher than her mother. The child was also showing a certain apprehension to this language.

But after every rain, there comes the sun. There were some arguments like in any other respectable home, that came to disturb the calm so lovingly cultivated by the mother. Her combative side was hard to bring to light, but sharp. For the life and work of her husband, the woman was also his inspiration, understanding that sometimes she had to abide by his rules. Women have keys, restraints, and silencers for many of their intimate resonances, aside from one: jealousy. And Iulia was jealous, legitimately jealous. "Mistakes" came easy to Hasdeu who cultivated them. He was carrying a fatherly seed that he knew about, but he couldn't contain it. He was a great lover…, as a certain writer from Bessarabia would say. Luckily his affairs didn't last. However, that didn't do any good to Iulia's eyes, ears, and soul, which carried a healthy and selfless love for her husband. The "friends" targeted by the sharp ends of the polemicist's spear, their wives, as well as the girls and the widows carefully informed the wife about the scholar's escapades, which showed imprudence unsuitable to the fighter that was his wife. Imprudence and a lack of… selection! A curvy milkmaid, a swarthy nanny, or a gallivant, all attracted him just the same. The satire man from *Satyrul* had significance. His suggestive eyes seduced these modern Eves without delay; his crafty words maintained closeness, and his masculine vigor finished it. That's why mother Iulia, no matter how calm she was, from time to time erupted in anger, ignoring her husband's clumsy protests and defenses. And the conflicts grew. Lilica once raised her serene head between the two and, to protect her from understanding, they started speaking German. They knew the little girl was not up to date with Goethe's language… and suddenly:

"*Warum zank' ihr euch?*"

The question fell like lighting between her parents. The almond eyes widened, her arms reached out, and the little mouth that had pronounced those words hid in her father's beard.

"You didn't say it quite right. But how did you know that *zaken* means to fight?"

"From the book you brought me from Mr. Stanilas from Vienna," she answered proudly, knowing her father had an uncle near the capital of Austria.

"Okay? Well, we're not fighting." He tried to smooth things out. "Your mother is a bit upset. I upset her."

Therefore, Hasdeu concluded that their future "debates" on the subject that couldn't be avoided had to be carried out in a fourth or a fifth language, Hungarian for example. Mother Iulia spoke it fluently, but Hasdeu understood it as much as Lilica understood German.

And the "problem" arose quite often, allowing the shadows and the murky waters of discord to invade their home, but Hasdeu felt more and more guilty.

Without a solid reason, Hasdeu was named as one of the most depraved scholars. One of the most depraved? Why? Who could have said that on the pyramid of libido the son of Alexandru Hasdeu would be at the top? Indeed, the physiologists, especially the ones in this specialty would dogmatize the law of neuro-physiological balance based on organic compliance. An organ that is too evolved, progresses to the detriment of another, or of others. The nervous energy especially decreases in the normal population but overflows in certain groups. Intellectuals, because of the high use of their brains, end up not being Don Juans. And if they abstain from that as well it results in a psycho-nervous imbalance and a state of mind that can be noticed. As proof, the great academic neuro-critics would say that Hasdeu was lacking so much, was so incoherent, and had so much of those inclinations described in *Duduca Mămuca,* that even the tragic end of his young daughter's life was attributed to this. But history would not be on their side. Hasdeu was just a man that was far from typical. We're supposed to only learn from the legendary wise Jewish Solomon, quoted in the Bible and school textbooks as an example of "wisdom," who was a poet of thought, nature, and love, with countless slaves and princesses as lovers, who compared the woman he loved in many ways, such as: "I see you as the mare harnessed to the pharaoh's cart!," or "I have sixty empresses, eighty mistresses, and countless girls, but my dove is only one…" Without losing ourselves in ideas about emperors or potentates of the Mosaic Bible, we are stopped by the memories of so many stars in the ethereal sky of human thought, who have such predilections.

Alexander the Great, who conquered the world, whose legend says he was conceived by a snake and a woman, was said to be in the graces of the irresistible Thais. Caesar, another man of the world who was schooled and talented, as well as King Melnac, were both known to have been unbridled seducers; Octavian

Augustus who is glorified by history for his wide knowledge and intelligence, Alcibiades, even Socrates, and Aristophanes, not to mention the wise but cynical Diogenes, who satisfied his carnal needs in the sight of people in the street; Horatius, Catullus, Martiallis, even Propertius are only some of the ancient ones worthy of being mentioned. The Prince of Conde who was a scholar of rare skill, Charles V who had a sharp and vigorous mind, Boileau, the angelic musician of poetic arts, Richelieu, the satanic bishop with a multitude of skills, the noble Molière, a restless lover, or the great and unparalleled Goethe who loved continuously until he was eighty years old, George Sand, Napoleon the Great; Stephen the Great, who in forty-seven years of dominion had just as many lovers and four wives; Alexandru Cuza, Mihail Kogălniceanu, Titu Maiorescu — to avoid mentioning contemporary figures these are just some of those who worshipped love and had gallant affairs, who never became less than they were before world history and human thought, neither were their offspring if they had any.

Why should Hasdeu be the only one to pay the consequences for extramarital affairs? While others didn't pay for it, he paid in his home and in his thoughts that tormented his mind with admission and maybe with guilt. All this even more so as he heard those cruel explanations — mentioned above — unfounded and unjust, about the early loss of the angel that was his dear Lilica.

Hasdeu's virility lasted until he was sixty-five, he called himself a "restless Faust," and in this statement, he denied the theories of physiological or psychological compensations. The principle that memory is complementary to intelligence was reinforced by the great person Bogdan Hasdeu, just like in other genius men with Napoleon I at their helm. His intelligence rivaled his memory and these two forces stayed in perfect balance. The words "rivaled his memory" could be misinterpreted by someone on purpose. The meaning they are supposed to have is that everything that formidable memory recorded was filtered by the infinitely clear lens of his intelligence, *inteligo* in the literal sense. A spontaneous perception, deeply straightforward, accompanied by an illumination given by his knowledge of so many subjects, this is the slightly described laboratory of this great brain.

And Lilica inherited it, as well as his spiritual devotion. Some have said the genius of the child surpassed her father's. It's possible. If we look at it from the angle of rapid evolution that was suddenly stopped and permanently suppressed by illness, especially during her time of creativity, this is easily observed. In time, compressing this genius, the intensity of the work that only kept increasing like a final alarm bell that was resounding somewhere in the zenith of her existence, always rushed and untamed, will explain the statement.

Lilica's memory would often surpass the understanding that age and precocity had given her. She would memorize with astonishing ease because she had an attention span of the same level. When she was reading something there could be bells and trumpets in her vicinity but the text had her attention. The child would not move her eyes away from its pages. Everyone knew about what she had read in her six years.

One afternoon, at the home of Pană Constantinescu, where a few friends and acquaintances had gathered for a visit, during a rare visit that Hasdeu made with his family, there was also the poet Macedonski, who, informed of the arrival of the magister and his daughter, as well as of the beauty with which Lilica could recite and easily memorize lines, he arrived among the first. After a few discussions and conversations, these rare aptitudes came up, and Macedonski, listening to the child's recital full of nuances and warmth, walked into a neighboring room and composed a poem on the spot, then came back and gave it to the little girl so she could recite it at first glance. Lilica took it, read it, disappeared for a few moments, and after she returned she recited the poem from memory, with a gesture of a winged poet, holding the paper folded in her small hands. The bard of Romanian symbolism was rightly left astonished.

After she turned six years old, Hasdeu started realizing his daughter was surpassing milestones that time and evolution had set in place for the other children. Beginner books had fulfilled their duty, geography and history books following the same path, and in her seventh year, she completed and aced the analytical programs for primary school. The girl could read quickly and could clearly analyze and synthesize, which were skills foreign to other children her age.

The miracle was even greater because Lilica had a chubby body and cheeks, and was very short, so she didn't betray her age.

Hasdeu's wife was called upon to volunteer for multiple charities, but she refused them all. Some say that Hasdeu stopped her because his wife wasn't able to face the arsenal of conveniences and especially the "precious" "savoir vivre" of the salons; others claimed that Iulia's jealous nature was avoiding the gazes and provocations that Hasdeu couldn't stop giving in such circumstances, as well as with certain mistresses of Bucharest. Others, who were probably closer to the truth, claimed the woman had her hands full with caring for her home and especially her flower that was growing in her eyes and didn't want to trade her modest home for the brilliant salons of the *haute-volée*, which were not always profitable to the modest souls that lacked artifices.

However, Iulia Hasdeu went to a few meetings organized by "Concordia," where two of her real friends were part of the committee, always on her husband's arm, with her pretty hair styled in thick curls, and wearing her most precious earrings which she'd received from old I.C. Brătianu, her godfather, at Lilica's baptism.

During one of these meetings, Iulia Hasdeu was asked by the committee to start the production program by bringing her amazing daughter, who already had a set reputation, to recite a few poems. She agreed and Lilica Hasdeu appeared on the stage in the room in a puffed dress, with curly hair and sparkles in her eyes. The applause at the sight of this small human, that was as big as a sprout and bright like a star, was so loud that the normally brave child, took two or three steps to the side, and she would have run away if her father, who was sitting in the first row, wouldn't have interfered and convinced her to stay and recite.

Her eyes widened and shot gold sparkles, her small chest heaved, but the words left her mouth easily, each wrapped in its nuance, forming warm and swaggering lines. It wasn't a recital anymore, but a declamation to which her father had a small prior contribution, because the spectators could see the inspiration coming from her spiritual warmth and her wonderful little head. Applause didn't stop when she finished reciting, the ladies' lips waited their turn to kiss the cheeks and the forehead of the small and charming artist.

Chapter III

The Corolla

The year 1876 was of a certain importance to Hasdeu and of great importance to Lilica. The philologist had wanted for a long time a place where he could ensure the stability of his home, which would stop the relocations from house to house and from room to room, that disturbed the order of his hard-earned books, especially the drafts and manuscripts, which were already quite disorganized. The opportunity came when the position of director of the State Archives became available after the departure of Constantin Aricescu. This position was given to Hasdeu, who was a long-time client of the shelves, trunks, and basements filled with documents.

And in the spring of 1876, when white lilacs, black locust trees, and lindens around the buildings of the State Archives were spreading their white, blooming branches toward the visitors, Bogdan Petriceicu Hasdeu, Iulia, and Lilica moved to that region surrounding the church built by Michael the Brave, so rich with history, vegetation, and humidity, and took over the residence where they would live for the next twenty years.

For future events and for the life that opened its gates to the genius of Iulia Hasdeu in the expanse alive with memories of this monastery surrounded by the poetry of calmness, flowers, and trees, with a church and surrounding graves, and a wide view over orchards and small houses, we must give a small description, because among them the child lived the most beautiful years of her childhood, or even her existence, and sketched the talent that proved to be generous.

Back then, the rectangular building of the State Archives didn't have the Romanian style and architecture that it has today, rather it looked more like an old ruin of a monastery with the church in the middle. The wide courtyard that surrounded the church built by Michael the Brave allowed for a graveyard to be set there.

Actually, the voivode had rebuilt this church in 1592 for the third time, because it was first raised by God and Vlad Dracul's will a century prior and was restored later almost from the foundation by Kaplea from Bolintin, whose grave, located near the church, was desecrated by her heirs. Her bones were scattered on the field, for reasons related to her fortune.

The fearless voivode Michael had his ruling seat in this building around 1600, and the church allowed him to pray there when, in 1593 as he tried to take the throne, he had been arrested by Alexandru cel Rău, who wanted to behead him. Later on, around 1793, this was the ruling seat of the greedy and restless Alexandru Moruzzi, and later of Alexandru Ipsilanti, the bright Greek, during his second rule in Muntenia (1796). He allowed the Greek monasteries on the land of the ruler to expand their gardens, raise bees, plant orchards with indigenous and exotic trees along the hills of Spira, and on a big part of Uranus and Izvor streets, which back then were on the outskirts of the city, where the Arsenal of today was founded in the vicinity of the State Archives.

That would explain why Iulia Hasdeu, the inspired poet, sang the songs of her memories among the cypress trees that were left in the monasteries' parks long ago when the Archives building was established.

Between the seventh and the nineth years of her life, when other children started learning the alphabet, Lilica had finished that part long ago, feeling the calling of more advanced knowledge. She started plucking the chords of her harp, and it's important to note that she noticed the poetry of those lonely crosses, resting among the bells, shadows, flowers, lights, and perfumes, and especially the view of the wide horizon that suited daydreaming and meditation. The home of the Hasdeu family was in the former xenodochium of the monastery, in the left corner of the rectangular building, which today serves as the entrance. It consisted of only two rooms, a smaller one and a bigger one separated by a wide hall. The basement contained a kitchen, a small living room, and a room for the servants. Hasdeu set up his work desk, library, and a small bed in the larger room on the right, which had belonged to the former abbot, leaving the left room for his wife and daughter. A wooden veranda that was quite unstable was used to hold a wooden table and a bench, on which the historian would work during warm weather, inspired by rose bushes and wildflowers. The stairs to the entrance rose to this platform and squeaked noisily at every step.

The girls' room had two windows with a beautiful view. One faced Izvor street with the trees swaying under it, thanks to the hill on which the whole building rested. The child's eyes gazed over them towards the trees and the bushes of Cișmigiu. The other window faced the monastery's orchards, where the administration had started building streets and houses a while before, demolishing the charming mills that rose there until Cuza promulgated the law of expropriation. The church was built in the name of Saint Nicholas, and the commemoration on the day of Saints Michael and Gabriel was done in honor of the brave ruler and son of Pătrășcu cel Bun.

The cellars were crammed with wooden boxes, crates, and piles of registers and folders, among which crawled obese rats and sneaky mice; the halls and the galleries surrounding the building with vegetation and swaggering pillars, the shady trees with benches underneath, and especially the graves with stones and old smoked or glittering candles set by the pious hands of children and friends of those sleeping for eternity, all these attracted the curious steps of the girl, either in the solitude in which poetry could thrive, or in preparation for the primary school exams that Lilica was going to pass shortly, for which Hasdeu had obtained a few books.

Professor Svârlescu and his wife became the most intimate friends of the family. The professor had bound his soul in admiration and boundless devotion to his magister, so Hasdeu chose him as his work confidant and organizer for the files that were misplaced in the mountain of books, documents, manuscripts, and registers on his work desk, which was always messy, even though it was organized often by his friend in fear. Hasdeu was a professor at the time as well. Shortly after that, when the mother asked him to discreetly check if Lilica had mastered the primary school subjects, he discovered the little girl wasn't just doing well, she had completely mastered the subjects, with knowledge and a rare analytical spirit. The poems of Alecsandri and Bolintineanu, the ones of Boliac and Gr. Alexandrescu had found a place next to La Fontaine's fables and Florian, and all the other lyrics from the French manuals, even the German ones. Hasdeu had followed her evolution from afar, but at the moment, when he was given a report on this unexpected progress she'd made while casually studying under a tree, or on a chair in the kitchen, as she had the tendency to hide while reading, he finally realized the extent of her training in grammar, and especially on the history of Romania. His Lilica, aside from reading about the deeds, eras, and years, made connections and deductions. His soul shivered with happiness, and he decided to send her to school to take her exams, choosing one because the director, Scurtescu, was also a poet.

This happened in 1877, during the War of Independence, when Bucharest was filled with Romanian troops, cannons, Russians, and noise, and when Lilica turned eight years old.

The school curriculum didn't mention any such exam aggregations. But Hasdeu, who despite his combative attitude stood his ground against his adversaries, as well as against the officialities, bringing forward his title of philology professor at the university and a member of the Academy, as well as a representative of the Ministry of Instruction who had been assigned a scientific mission in Kraków. The scandal caused by his quill was successful. Therefore, Iulia Hasdeu was given a waiver to take all the exams of primary school.

And that's how the brown-haired little girl, with round cheeks and big eyes, took her seat and passed all four exams in turn before the professors and especially before the poet Scurtescu, who had been informed previously of who the important child that answered all the questions so seriously and gravely in her shyness was. Her mother sat in a chair in the back of the classroom, listening, full of pride, her eyelids fluttering with the emotion of that moment. The teachers felt that a phenomenal child was sitting before them at the desk, and they had the same feeling when she stood up and filled the blackboard with numbers. Scurtescu understood a diversion would be appropriate to distract this student that had managed to confuse the teachers.

During the history examination, after answering all the questions, she was casually asked something about Ion Vodă cel Cumplit and his rule. The answers she gave surpassed all the information found in the history textbooks.

"Are you sure of what you're saying? Who told you all these things?" asked Scurtescu.

"No one," said the candidate, a bit surprised. "I read it in my father's book. Please read it and you will see I'm right."

"I read it," said Scurtescu jokingly, "but I didn't find the information you're talking about."

"You read it? Allow me…"

"What?"

And Lilica focused her gaze in a corner of the classroom, then moved her eyes to the teacher, somehow scolding him…

"You didn't notice that my father portrays Ion Vodă as 'a great administrator, a great political man, and a great general'?"

"Yes, but that doesn't tell me why! For example, why was he a great general?"

"Because he amazed everyone during the Jiliște battle; first, Ion Vodă subjugated Wallachia, then he decimated the enemy's army which was a lot bigger, while Moldova's losses were few. Doesn't this mean he was a great general, professor?"

"Well, good job little girl, you are right," said Scurtescu in admiration. "I wanted to see how well you mastered what you read."

All the members of the commission were smiling, and Scurtescu was barely restraining himself from picking her up and kissing her.

Naturally, she passed the exam with flying colors and the director shared the news among his colleagues and acquaintances, after which he visited Hasdeu, took him aside, and confessed the amazement of his friends and his own admiration.

From that moment, or maybe even before that, Scurtescu became one of the most devoted and intimate friends of the family and of the titan from the Archives, for whom Lilica would hold venerable respect. Meanwhile, her progress with English was equal to her progress with French and greatly surpassed her skills with German. Mother Iulia wished that she would master them all, and her father, even though he wasn't a fan of political Germanization, understood his child was spoiled by destiny and was a sprout whose rosy corolla announced the bloom of her glory. Lilica had to become a schooled woman and the pride of her nation; this was his strong belief. He knew that especially when it came to history, the subject dearest to his soul, and philology, strong German was indispensable. Coincidentally, aside from Mrs. Walch, her English teacher, her mother had an acquaintance, young Ernestina Feichtinger, a German tutor who was also quite good at piano.

During important days such as her parents' birthdays, while her parents were not home, she found refuge in the living room and wrote cards on special paper with floral patterns, that was either bought like that or drawn on by her own hand. They were written in French and English but shortly, thanks to her new tutor, in German as well. The content of these cards was not simple phrases like "Dear Father, for your birthday I wish you... etc.," but true literary compositions with very few grammatical errors. Whoever has studied French and especially English knows how hard it is to avoid grammatical mistakes, that even French or English high schoolers make in their native language. The base of these epistles predicted true literary possibilities, with colorful expressions and pure honesty given by the poetry that was sourced from her mind and reabsorbed by it.

The events of that time, the news of the war taking place across the Danube by Russians greedy for vodka and wine, the defeats and escapes, but also of the brave Romanians who were fighting for a noble cause, gave the girl an opportunity to be embraced by the arms of the muses and transpose the news into lyrics written in her notebooks or on scrap paper found on her papa's desk.

Her teary eyes were also showing fear at the sight of stretchers and ambulances carrying the injured, the horses rushing through the neighborhoods of Bucharest. Mother Iulia, with her natural generosity, helped the injured with clothes, sheets, cigarettes, and milk often giving more than she could afford. Lilica watched and because she understood everything that was happening, she felt strongly and wrote her feelings down in lyrics. Her parents suspected she did it, but she destroyed them later on when she came across her creations of those years.

But her soul was not best revealed by these inspirations.

The dark-winged demon watching from beyond what is known, that covers the eyes of those trying to banish him, touched in these cruel early years the soul of the child with prophetic aptitudes, if a prophecy is what is in the souls of authentic poets. The ambiance in which she lived also contributed to it, and the ambiance in which her childhood was sometimes paused, and the pain of the world weaved webs around her.

She never went out by herself, not even to visit her friend Matilda, the daughter of Pană Constantinescu, or Florica Zaharescu, or Hermina who was her most intimate friend, not even Maria Mavrodin, who was a bit older but very dear to her. She received them in the Archives, their play being reduced to climbing trees, or running among the graves. The girls would always talk and make confessions, but Lilica didn't feel any quality resonance with these girls; so, the moments of childish joy were very few and especially relative. Florica, more than Hermina, tried to get to know her struggles but being a normal child, she was unable to see the demon that was building walls around her mind. However, Lilica kept her close to her heart. She walked with her, gravely talking about the philosophy of death, about the dead they rushed past, who were lying there forgotten, even though they had forged ideals and had wanted happiness at one point, just like them.

From time to time, Lilica stopped her friend before gravestones eroded by rain, and both tried to decipher the stone words of the one lying in silence in the ground. She read the stone of a man who during life had been known as Ioanis Rossetti, a name under which a granite rose symbolized the remembrance flower of those who had dug the grave; then a name with a resonance: Zinca Dissescu who was actually the grandmother of a great juror and minister, or Elena Vizula, or Teodosie Contopol, one of the last abbots and builder of churches, as well as many other names.

But two of these gravestones kept surfacing in the mind of the child, one with a shorter but more visible inscription, the other with a longer poem which was more faded.

The first contained one of those epitaphs that was often read in graveyards that was either prose or poetry. Instead of piety and condolences, they were almost always sarcastic through a solemnity that trivialized pretentious sentiments:

"Passer-by, —
Contemplate — *Don't pass by*
My life here — *The cold remnant.*
And what it is — *I was once,*
And what I am — *You soon will be."*
(C. Mărculescu)

For Lilica's soul that was inclined towards melancholy, such warnings, that she took as they were, produced impressive echoes.

The other stone sounded more human, sourced from a mind full of honest gratitude, and — according to the church's bishop — was only a fragment of a eulogy by I.H. Rădulescu, written after the death of a close friend's wife. The stone was cold but true:

"The stone talks: it doesn't have much to say.
Here underneath me, a rare woman lies,
Who lived by God and brought joy to her parents,
With honor and with love,
And in her husband's home, there was pride and peace,
The stone says much after the wife is silenced."
(Maria Arindinschi, born Geanoglu)

This inscription also made an impact on the poet child, through the naive but honest confession of the husband who had set it there, that was certain. This would probably become the funerary stone she was going to remember a few years later when the gentle poet would write the poem *Le Cimetière* (*The Cemetery*), that was dedicated to her friend, Florica:

I still can see the forgotten slab of marble
Forgotten here while we try to read it
A faded name, old tears, a long-lost sparkle;
The name of a lass who had once suffered;
A lily plucked by the ruthless hand of Death.

Who laughed as she was meeting her old lover…
I still can see that forgotten slab of marble…

When her friend's steps stopped, Lilica asked Florica: "Do you think people can come back to life?"

"I do! That's what we're taught in religion class, in the chapter about the symbols of faith…"

"And how do you think they are when they are resurrected? As they are now?"

"How would I know, dear Lilica? I think so."

"Well, no! First, what dies is only the body, the flesh, the bones. In the ground, they turn to what they once were. But the soul is immortal, is always conscious. Up there, somewhere, I don't know where."

"With God?"

"With God, or even higher!..." claimed the genius child.

"Even higher?" asked Florica, with her eyes widened in surprise.

"Yes! What I mean is that our soul doesn't die. You have no idea how glad I am that it doesn't die, and that's why I don't fear death! You should be glad about it as well… That way we'll live for eternity."

"Yes, but we'll be terribly old…"

"Not so! Since our soul merges with God, we won't age after death… The spirit will always be young… That's what my father says… And if it wasn't like that…. Everything would be so sad…"

On the nights with a full moon that Iulia Hasdeu would write about so many times in her lyrics, her melancholy and sorrow increased, starting with those years of her childhood. The outlines of that heavily anchored cross on the church tower surrounded by moon beams had fatidical and threatening lines, enhanced by the tragic calling of the owls. The occasional cry of the sentinels guarding the Archives at night, accompanied the dire cry of the nocturnal birds, making the child shudder in the solitude of her soul, seeming to predict her death.

So it is not without grounding, the early inspiration for the poem *Moartea* (*Death*) which the child wrote when she was eight years old. It was never published by Hasdeu in his posthumous collections, but it was the seed of obsession of the other poem about death that was written around the time she passed, in which she showed the proportion of her illuminated and deep spirit before being released from her bodily form.

Hasdeu confessed in one of the annotations in the play script *Alcee et Sapho* that Lilica had written when she was fifteen years old, in which one of the main characters, Erinna, mirrors the author by sacrificing her youth. He said that ever since Lilica was eight, nine, and ten years old she had written three poems in Romanian; the first said she had to die young, the second described her death and consoled her mother, and the third said she was an angel before she was born and had asked God to give her a mission in the world, a world she was going to leave disgusted. Was the lab that was her mind capable of making true prophecies from beyond this realm?...

Her mind didn't know any respite. Between toys and short joyful songs, she read every book she got her hands on. Verses filled her notebooks; her gaze was always watching the thin horizon for the boundless lines that were contouring her soul. Among these she also received her high school textbooks, math which she felt no inclination towards, but her sharp soul managed to dominate, Latin was just as hard, in the beginning, but was tackled in the end, and then geography which was limited to memorizing details and didn't engage her, lastly world history and Romanian history, which her mind had mastered and turned into her toy. And her classes began. At first, under the supervision of Professor Svârlescu, who was helping her and her father daily. Then there was the young tutor Frățilă, another of Hasdeu's devoted friends, who made the classes pass easily with dexterity, blending in with the English, French, and German lessons given by Charlotte Walch and Ernestina Feichlinger. But Lilica's requests and aptitudes had to be satisfied with other subjects as well. She finally received her piano, which amazed the child's playful eyes, and Professor Dimitriu set in place a schedule that Lilica had to follow with Ernestina for piano, and with him for canto. The warm but raw voice of Lilica Hasdeu needed technical modulations and art in phrasing the melodies. Her voice, but also the ambition of her prolific aspirations! The pen and pencil drawings she made everywhere, on book covers, on cards, on sketch pads, demanded time as well. Professor Walch discovered these aptitudes and talents, and from time to time she even received drawing lessons, so this child forgot completely about playing, about trees, about the owls' screeches and the wind blowing through the branches with blossoms, and devoted herself to her studies, under the supervision of her father who had great trust in his phenomenal daughter's abilities.

Often, while relaxing on the verandah at the front of their home, Hasdeu took his daughter on his knees to tell her jokes, improvised stories, or more complicated stories meant to test the evolution of her mind. The child always listened, laughed about the first ones, and widened her eyes at the last ones. The eternal "why" was something often heard from her mouth. She never accepted arguments without grounds. Causes and explanations didn't give her a superficial understanding. The more clear and complete, the deeper it sunk in! Hasdeu was compliant, replying and throwing in a joke here and there, a charade or an anecdote to relax the charged laboratory of her mind. But the trick never worked, because the serious questions always came back with a vengeance. Great-grandmother Maria, who had visited them in the past, was now a permanent resident of her grandson's home, and she started taking Lilica, willingly or unwillingly, to liturgies or evening services. The child listened to the religious services, caught bits and pieces, made connections and deductions.

And based on this, that balcony became the place for debates between the forty-year-old father and the eight-year-old daughter:

"What is the Holy Spirit, Papa?" asked Lilica.

"What? It's the thought, the spirit of God that was sent to people to show them the path they must follow in life."

"So it was sent by God, right?"

"Of course!" said the father, between a hug and a kiss on the forehead.

"Only by God?"

"Of course, dear Lilica!"

"Not by Jesus Christ as well?"

"No! That's what you learned in your religion class."

"Yes, but Ernestina says the Holy Spirit comes from Christ."

"That's what Catholics say, not we of the Orthodox faith."

"Okay, Papa, but how can people admit or reject what God created in a certain way? Could we deny what God says?"

"God doesn't talk to people how we, father and child talk, in a conversation," said Hasdeu after a moment of thinking. "To talk to him you must have powers that you don't have yet."

"Does Ernestina have them?"

"Her neither."

"How about *grand-maman*?"

"Her neither."

"Then who has them? You, Papa? You do have them! You're the smartest father in the world."

"No!"

"Yes! You hide things from me because I'm young. But I'm not young, Papa! I'm grown and I want to know. Tell me the truth."

And that's how the subject of God, the origin of life, the mystery of death, in relation with her growing age tormented the mind of the child, while her friends of the same age only though about playing, about the dresses in their wardrobes, or about the riddles told by August from the Circus.

On one of the pages in her Algebra textbook that is reproduced here, and from the first year Lilica came into contact with this annoying subject, that she would defeat, however, with will and obligation, after doodling "ah, ah, ah, ah!" on the cover she sketched in perfect French a dialogue story, titled *Le Père des Enfants* (*The Children's Father*), in which a little girl of Iulia's age keeps asking her father similar questions:

"Who is God?"

"He is the Father of us all," says her father.

"Then, you're my brother," says the spiritual little girl.

But seeing that her father keeps avoiding the straightforward answer she was waiting for, as Hasdeu did to her, she asks her older brother who tells her that "God is the Father that created the world."

"But who is Jesus?" asks Sophie, the little girl.

"He is His celestial Son because we are His earthly sons," says Louis, her brother. "He opened the gates to Heaven!"

"Heaven? What is this?"

"It is a garden in the sky where people's souls go after death!"

"So, the soul doesn't die?"

"No, because the soul is the breath of God!"

And the dialogue continues until a serious lady gets upset hearing the characters talking about such things at their age and tells the children if they want to understand God to learn: "*Pater*," "*Ave*," and "*Credo*." The ending itself shows a spiritual balance and precocious maturity.

On the same book, written around the same time is another draft: *Dieu et Jesus* (*God and Jesus*) that starts on the right page after she had tried a few algebra formulas, a draft in which the mystery of God and human salvation preoccupied her. Further on there's another draft, *Jean le Bossu* (*Jean the Hunchback*), and a crossword with Corneille, who had attracted and captivated her ever since then through her work. And all this was happening when Iulia Hasdeu was between six and nine years old…

The little girl was always asked intelligent questions that excited her and which she answered correctly, which could also be seen from the multitude of arabesques, flowers, or faces, and from the repeated notes on book covers or random pages, lines the child used to express her reveries, meditations, and hard answers.

In an English book titled *The Bracelets* written by Marie Edgeworth, Iulia signed her name calligraphically as "Iulie Hasdeu or "Iulie B.P. Hasdeu," and in the first years, the writing had those curly tails that every child liked, giving it a bit of importance, superiority, and sign of uniqueness. She signed the same way on another book, *My Darling Album*, a storybook for children with beautiful and colorful illustrations or fonts chosen in such a way to make the child learn the language willingly. The purpose was reached because next to the text, the drawings in the book are copied by her hand.

The stern lessons with her teachers and under her father's supervision followed their course. In the summer of 1878 when other children her age were preparing for the first or second-grade exams, Lilica was getting ready to take her first high school exam.

Meanwhile, Hasdeu, who was a chosen member of the Academy in the philology section, was working on his serious piece called *Cuvente den bătrâni*. At first, he wanted it to have great proportions, but he then limited it to three volumes because he wanted to write *Magnum Etimologicum* without suppressing his work as a publicist and a polemicist.

A common view of their big worktable was Hasdeu sitting at one end, with his beard over old books and thick tomes in dozens of foreign languages, working tirelessly with his small handwriting, with his head bowed like a woman, and at the other end his Lilica, with her straight handwriting, working on her lessons, especially on Latin with which she needed daily help from her father.

These unforgettable moments had a certain friendship and somehow a collaboration, because they brought Hasdeu true inspiration for his work, and they would come back to his mind, especially after his small friend at the table had passed away…

Sfântul Sava High School for boys, which was recently established and only had middle school classes, had well-known teachers that Hasdeu appreciated, which was the reason he chose it as a place for the exams. Among these teachers were Bonifaciu Florescu and Tănăsescu (French), Z. Herescu (math), M.G. Iacomi (Latin), N. Codrescu (geography), Priest Ovidiu Musceleanu for religion (Priests Musceleanu and Vasilescu were the priests at Mihai-Vodă Church at the Archives), N. Bărcănescu (history), Mândreanu (Romanian), and Podoleanu (music), etc.

Chapter IV

The Flower...

In the summer of 1878 when Iulia was not yet nine, she passed her middle school exams. She was small and shy and was intimidated especially by the great presence of her scholar father who accompanied her everywhere. She also passed her first high school exams with an overall grade of almost nine. After that, the father took his daughter by the hand and started walking, but her stops to look at various objects made him think, for the first time, that even though she had so many good grades in many of the classes, Lilica was too crude for her age and the pressure she was under. Even more so, aside from studying for the exams, she also had music, art, and foreign language lessons at home, and other struggles that were still unknown to him, related to plays, poetry, and reflections... very deep reflections! The child wrote them on sheets of paper or old notebooks that she made sure to hide well.

A new sensible and devoted friend entered the Hasdeu family. He was a young professor named G.I. Ionescu-Gion, freshly returned from Paris after getting a position at Matei Basarab High School. He was also a journalist, writer, and former disciple of Magister Hasdeu. Ionescu-Gion had a great mind of deep reflection and knowledge. His cold and severe look was also fair, his attitude was reserved, even proud, and he tutored Lilica at geography, Latin, and natural sciences, subjects the young student had not gotten a ten in before. His personality balanced Lilica's and even though there was a twelve-year difference between them, they developed a friendship, with her seeing him almost like an equal, and him being protective over her.

The child's psychology was highly analytical. Her spirit was constantly evolving, jumping from one subject to another, and it was always craving knowledge, which caused her to ask questions repeatedly and didn't give her mind a moment for respite. The child was always trying to uncover the unknown, taking elements apart, and rarely putting them back together. Her restless curiosity, which people that didn't understand thought to be harmful, was a characteristic of her personality. She took apart toy cars, took down bird nests with eggs, and ravaged them, not out of malice, but from a demonic impulse to discover the mystery of life. The child wasn't creating anything durable. She started many things, left them, came back to them, and moved on, always prefacing her creation but never coming to a conclusion.

Without evading this state of mind, Lilica Hasdeu was prematurely acquainted with the other spirit of older age, of synthesis. Hasdeu had observed God's gift from this point of view as well. Ionescu-Gion had confirmed it. During discussions about history especially, which was a comfortable topic for the young professor, he found the mind of the girl found relationships between cause and effect, between premise and conclusion, made observations, and gave explanations, accused and agreed. Gion's soul, which was often closed to the outside world, opened up fully, so the discussions between them were similar to ones between two teachers. Using small convenient tricks, he found out that Lilica was writing poetry, commentaries, and that she was drawing. The student denied, laughed, and continued to draw, portraying the professors who had examined her, each with their unique element, with their expression, with humor, sometimes exaggerated, that proved the student had examined them more than they had examined her.

And Lilica was barely nine years old.

In the following years, the home-schooled girl passed her second, then her third-year exams. That time she had perfect grades and received first place in her year and a crown of flowers as a reward. For eleven subjects she received a ten in nine of them, getting an 8 in geography and natural sciences. That was the time when the professors finally realized that Iulia Hasdeu was a phenomenal child. Her memory wasn't the only one that was durable and true, nor the only intuition for school psychotechnics, but her rationality and the connections she made between ideas and knowledge, and that *pourquoi de la chose* (*why it is like that*), which was so familiar to her mind were the evidence of an extraordinary brain that highly excelled the ones of the rest of the students. On this note — said one of the teachers to her father — the ten she received in a normal class would be the equivalent of a twenty for Iulia Hasdeu. And the history scholar smiled sarcastically under his bushy mustache when learning of this *à la Palisse*.

Bogdan Petriceicu Hasdeu lived fully the most beautiful years of his life. Glory favored him; his hopes magically came to be. His daughter, a very healthy child, full of aptitudes and especially of love, with eyes that smiled at internal discoveries more than outside ones, adorned his existence with the flowers of divine gifts.

His plays were on stage, and a new one received the amusement and applause of the spectators (*Ortonerozia* or *Tre crai de la răsărit*) and Lilica's joy. She started going to the theater after receiving multiple invitations. Hasdeu received a seven-year term as the general secretary of the Romanian Academy and the secretary for the Literary Section; the high forum awarded him with 5000 lei in gold (worth more than 200,000 lei at the time this book was first published) for his two volumes of *Cuvente den bătrâni*. Even so, the arrows of his polemic didn't blunt but became sharper; finally, he traveled to London for research, where he studied the *Gospel of St. John* from 1574 for three weeks straight in the British Museum. From there, he extracted especially "lexical, phonetic, syntactic, and phraseological archaisms." He became one of the initiators of raising a statue of his forerunner, Heliade Rădulescu, for whom he had always carried great respect.

In his household near the church of *Mihai Vodă*, his wife Iulia surrounded him with her boundless love while closely watching the meal preparation for her gourmand husband and making sure he had a quiet work environment. The health of her daughter was always on her mind, as she fed her the best meals multiple times a day. Their doctor friends, especially Măldărescu examined the girl every time small indispositions kept her in bed, aware of her hard work that wasn't proportionate to her physical activity. She was prescribed to take long strolls in the park, much more milk, and rare steak which were imperative for her anemia, and of course, rest. Her mother followed the recommendations thoroughly, but Lilica preferred halvah to milk and black olives to bread and butter. This caused small arguments from which the young "philosopher" always emerged victorious, the nickname given to her by her mother because of her infinite reasoning.

For the girl's health, her parents decided to take summer trips to Câmpulung or Valea Prahovei.

Hasdeu's escapades disturbed the quiet home life of his wife. Her friends were always eager to tell her all the gossip they heard from letters, whispers, or in confidence. One brought her the business card of a lady who often came to her home, another whispered in her ear while she was knitting, the mysterious name of a Polish blonde woman, Olga, for whom the Romanian scholar was having a dispute with an infantry captain. The Polish woman didn't live far away.

The bitterness was always felt stronger than happiness, and when the first came from jealousy, the taste of happiness suddenly disappeared.

In her suppressed pain and resignation, one single worry persisted in pulling a shroud of forgiveness over everything: the child. Lilica shouldn't have to find out about the gossip, especially since her sharp hearing gave her much to dwell on and no diplomacy at all.

That's why, while her confidantes enjoyed the fruits of their actions, the wife of the seductive master, between biting her lip and her twitching eyelid smiled falsely but kindly. And when one of them spilled the last drop of poison among the "honest" pity, about a possible divorce, Iulia looked for the best reply, which was unconvincing, but insolent, saying her husband was too much of a patriot for her to break up with him. The reply was, however, sharp just like an ax meant to cut down the thirst for gossip from her "friends…"

That didn't mean his actions had a long life because whatever gets too full spills out. When Iulia, the patient wife, opened her mouth to speak, she was unstoppable. The fighter under the Balint's flag from the Abrud Mountains had those "weapons" that any woman would have under such circumstances, which were sharp on both sides. And if the saying about the two things that make the Romanian leave his house, smoke and a woman's tongue weren't true, Hasdeu started believing the contrary and realized that sayings never lie. In the beginning, he protested about the "deceptions," but after a while, his protests weakened, then stopped, and the husband took off down the stairs under the bell tower, to where nobody knew, glad at least that Lilica was away with her grandmother for the evening service. He had to heal his scolded soul.…

"You cheated on me again!" This is how his jealous wife received him on his return.

"Are we at it again, dear Iulia? I was just walking around… taking a breath of air!" Hasdeu tried to justify himself.

"Don't give me excuses, because I know. I know well! I found out everything. At first, I thought my friends were lying to me, but it's true, and you'll be sorry for it… you'll see!"

Meanwhile, Professors Svârlescu and Frăţilă, who were normally at the house, were inquiring about the twelfth grade for which Lilica was studying thoroughly. The student didn't take any time to finish reading the textbooks and wanted to learn the subject from the "source." Her father's rich library was used daily, with a chair on top of another chair to climb the shelves like they were cliffs. Between reading world history, G. Zotu's Greek literature that was covered in Iulia's arabesques, Latin and Greek dictionaries, Gorjan's geography atlases, algebra textbooks, V. Cătulescu's sacred history textbooks in which the girl was writing literary drafts, or the practical French course written by Than. Tănăsescu on which she marked down various notes, Lilica often read Shakespeare, Corneille, Alecsandri, Eliade Rădulescu, the poems of Victor Hugo, and especially the many volumes about Napoleon I. All these had her full attention and interest, causing her to cast aside all the other works that she considered bland. On a stylistics textbook written by M. Strajanu, which her father had received signed by the author, Lilica, after repeatedly scribbling Xida, Xida, the name of an acquaintance of the same age who wasn't her friend, she noted the following:

"Mr. Al. N. Gussi is one of those people, who after signing his name on the book cover, signs it on the first page, and on every page thereafter. *Le nom d'un fou se trouve partout. Nomina stultorum omnes cognoscant...* (The name of a fool is found everywhere. Everyone knows these names)."

We couldn't uncover who Mr. Gussi was; if he was a teacher, a scholar, a friend, or a colleague, but he certainly was one of those unbearable people that had poisoned the young poet's innocent soul with sadness.

Stilescu was placed in the same category by Iulia Hasdeu around the same time, but we don't know anything about his personal or professional life. All we know is that he was a textbook author.

So, in the book by Cornelius Nepos, the famous Latin historian and poet whose chronicles of the great men of his time the student was translating, after scribbling her usual signature, she wrote "Third-year middle school student, ten years old, studying at St. Sabba High School in Bucharest," and in the back of the book, she wrote a few ironies addressed to Stilescu. (It is possible Stilescu was a professor teaching at St. Sava that we couldn't find in the very few registers that were left for this school). On a page from a notebook the student was using for her third-year middle school studies, she wrote exercises on Latin comparative from which we could see Lilica was working alone on these lessons as well as on the translations, the last with a bit of help from Hasdeu who was assisting her with the vocabulary. We also found that Stilescu's method annoyed her. That page contains around twelve exercises on forming the comparative, which the child resolved in part, choosing to draw a doodle of this man with a spear instead of a pointer finger, signing it with her usual swirly handwriting, and a note, this time in Romanian: "Iulia Hasdeu,..., who is horn-mad; her work, written by herself, following Mr. Stilescu, the mad professor at St. Sabba."

A note on another book she had received as a prize during this time, a book on *Elemente de Fizică* (*Elements of Physics*) by Bacaloglu, says:

"First prize with honors; 1880, June 29
Given to
Ms. Iulia Hasdeu"

And on the back of the first page, the first-prize winner started a small love story (the author was ten) in French, which was written in perfect syntax but had small grammatical mistakes, with two drawings of the two main characters that showed the girl was a beginner at drawing. The author wrote on random blank pages of the book; pages 1, 72, 121, and so on. The naive plot predicted Iulia's dreams of a chivalrous love that the daughter of Mrs. Rouges, Othele, feels for a brave young man with a sword, each receiving the gift of romantic commitment accompanied by their respective sketches drawn in her hand.

By writing all of these in books, the child was somehow trying to be discreet, and she managed to do so as Hasdeu would state later on. Even though he had known about the poetic dispositions of his daughter, he only discovered her work during the last two years of her life.

Was it a good or a bad thing this literary and philosophical work of the precocious thinker? It would be a paradox to assume. It might have been bad if by revealing her creations at that time, her father had pushed her and guided her. It might have been good because chained talents and susceptible personalities such as Lilica's, either deviate from their native talent or are disappointed by seeing their creations mutilated by corrections. The proportion of Iulia Hasdeu's native talent was sufficient to show her strength, especially when she was the age of an April bud with petals barely starting to unfold.

But her multiple preoccupations by the time she was barely ten didn't even give her the time to revisit her drafts on hidden pages. The writer didn't have time to revise and finish them, not even when she got older.

Her studies for the last year of middle school didn't allow for respite, and rest would only allow her to get fixated on intimate thoughts.

Ionescu-Gion started visiting Hasdeu's home more often. His interest and work in history were compatible with the great magister's occupation which often brought him to his work desk. But her mystical link and curiosity might have sometimes been confusing to other people and impossible to understand during that era, a feeling for the precocious and joyful girl, who even though she was chubby and small, like any other child her age, had started to show advanced intelligence that was more similar to a university student. The father was very pleased with the maturity of the young professor, the more so as he saw that his teaching was showing great results, reflected by Lilica's mind. Her progress with French, English, and German with her chosen tutors was added daily to her mind in which the subtle fluid of her soul was flowing.

We shouldn't forget that at the same time Lilica was a student in the Conservatory whose director was Wachman. She was studying canto, theory, solfeggios, and piano even if, normally, at ten-eleven years old no "music master" can focus on vocal studies because their vocal cords are undeveloped and unstable. Her voice, between second mezzo-soprano and contralto, showed precocity in this field as well, her teachers being very hopeful in her abilities. The girl sang with ease, her warm and curved tone being able to reach high and grave notes. Her studies, as we will show later, would often lure her back to the staff and clefs, as well as compositional keys.

Lilica studied Than. Thănăsescu's *French Theoretical and Practical Course*, the professor before whom she took her last French middle school exam, and a course in which the student and writer drafted another literary fragment, somehow as a refuge from the difficult textbook, one that was not suitable to her culture.

When the exam started, Iulia Hasdeu came as always with her parents, without whom she didn't even leave the house, and sat at the front of the classroom. There were a few other home-schooled students in the class.

She stood up, barely reaching the height of the other students, ready to answer the questions. The professors asked their questions and she answered in turn to each of them with very high accuracy.

During the math examination, the student was asked to use the blackboard. And even if the professors who knew Iulia's value wanted to freely interrogate her, Hasdeu asked them to treat her like any other student and allow her to pull a random subject from the urn. Iulia stuck her fine hand in the narrow opening of the urn and pulled one of the most difficult math problems: "the value of π" with the origin, calculations, and the process of obtaining the sixteenth letter of the Greek alphabet. Iulia tried to write on the blackboard by standing on her toes, but she couldn't reach it. Two of her fellow students, one of which was still alive at the time this book was published, a venerable man and a distinguished poet who would later collaborate with Hasdeu, stood up from his seat and moved the blackboard to its lowest point, Lilica's hand finally reaching the middle of this panel representing death for all those scared to death of math. She started writing and displaying the theory by giving details and showing, to the amazement of her father and the other professors, that π was the abbreviation of the Greek peripheral, meaning the circumference, and why its value is equal to 3.141592… etc. The blackboard was covered in numbers, symbols, and algebraic operations.

The beard of Haş-Deus, as he would later be called by poet Duliu Zamfirescu, a nickname the satirical poet would use in a telegram, raised in a soft smile, and his lively eyes stung with unshed tears. Professor Herescu stopped the student that was still going, thanked her, and — because the highest grade was ten — gave it to her…

During her history exam, after she was assigned the "French Revolution," Professor Băcănescu, smiling jokingly, tried, just like Scurtescu, to confuse Iulia Hasdeu on Napoleon I, who he deprecated and accused, asking the student to mention the reasons. After glorifying the genius general's rise in the French political state, Iulia Hasdeu frowned at hearing the professor's words and protested. She couldn't bring any accusations to the one that was going to become her life's model.

"What? You don't know about any damnatory deed of his?" asked the professor smiling.

"No, because there are none," answered the proud candidate.

"But what about Duke d'Enghien, whose assassination…"

"He was not assassinated, Professor. The Duke was sent to trial and sentenced because that was the right way of doing things. France was required to do so, as it was being threatened by political plots…"

"Yes, but all the historians reprehend the way the trial was held. Do you know how it happened?"

"I know, that's why I don't blame him. Napoleon never blamed himself…"

"It's actually said that he blamed himself," insisted the professor.

"I don't believe that Professor, because I read in the *Memorialul de la Sf. Elena* that Napoleon said if he had to do it all over again, he'd do it all the same!"

Her reply had the echo of a historian raised among rolls of parchment and she disarmed the professor. Băcănescu gave her a ten with the same resignation as Herescu, his smile an homage to her.

Lilica had to take exams for twelve subjects and obtained two 10s, two 9s, one 8, and… one 7 in the oral French examination. That 7 was given by Than. Thănăsescu who, during a lengthy conversation with the student was left confused, and attracted numerous ironies and satires, not just from Iulia, but also from the historian who used the professor's signature "Than." (from Tanase), which coincided with the first letters of Thanatos = death, and after the exam, he attacked him in every way he could with his sharp spear.

Her grade in French didn't diminish the unanimous praise of the other professors, including Than. Lilica obtained first prize with honors, given by Vasile Boerescu, the Minister of Public Instruction, who wanted to congratulate the exceptional student.

On top of that, she was successful with her exams at the Conservatory, for canto, solfeggio, and theory, as well as piano, for which she had worked every day during the very few hours she had left after studying. She received a prize from the Conservatory as well for her display of talent, but especially for her serious studies.

A few acquaintances used that event as an opportunity to gossip in hiding, envious of the family's success. "Of course, she's Hasdeu's daughter… that's why! Hasdeu can get everything he wants!" But he found out about this and knew how to respond to the "well-wishers" for their gossip.

The beginning of the following vacation allowed Lilica to relax. She played, laughed, and told everyone stories about the exams, including the questions and the answers. The cats and dogs that accompanied her and were the recipients of her affections in her arms and her bed, were now curled up and yawning, tired of playing so much. But these companions that knew their owner so well, were patient even when she was rough with them and took part in her happiness with licks or meows, whenever she would allow them to get out of her arms.

Florica and Hermina were the first ones to join her and learn about the success of their friend under the fruitful cherry trees all around her home. However, Lilica didn't brag about anything. Her modesty didn't allow her to put distance between her and her friends. Their laughter was childish and naive, somehow interesting for her.

Iulia's mind was similar to one of the beings whose souls struggled inside, in the obsession with the great calling. She was reserved before strangers, even though she could answer any question thanks to her sharp mind. Before her friends, however, she was relaxed, cheerful, sweet, even humorous. Who could have ever believed Iulia Hasdeu had a happy and playful side at first glance? Ionescu-Gion could.

"Wouldn't you like to be a medieval knight?" asked Lilica.

"Why do you ask?" riposted the historian gravely.

"Because looking at you I think all you're missing are spurs and a horse?"

"?"

"Yes, yes! You're imposing and have something that reminds me of Bayard."

"Me?"

"Yes, Professor. Your mustache!" said Lilica, bursting into laughter looking at his frowning mustache.

And suddenly, isolated and lonely, she went back to her thoughts, guarded by that demonic shadow. There, behind a bush, hidden on a bench under a tree, or hidden in the attic, the callings wrapped around her with claws of steel. That's where the child disappeared; those were the places where contact with herself, with the connection with so many past generations, and the thirst of answering to herself kept her stuck. She spent hours in this way; her mother looked for her with food or milk; she could hear it, but stayed quiet, dedicated to her books and her pencil. She wrote, worked on projects, composed poems, drew the characters of the books she was reading that were mentioned before, made up legends, scripts with well-defined characters, and well-structured acts. She made up her characters on the spot; Mrs. M, Ms. N, Professor S. But reading the "blue tales" was what had most of her attention with their magic. Fairies, princes, castle towers with barred windows and pale faces of princesses watching from behind them, shy like moon rays at the sight of their princes, the lakes with swans and delicate lotus flowers; lyrical girls that sang unknown songs about their dreams and ideals, these were what kept the child's days full in her hiding spot, while the outside world felt distant, foreign, strange, and cold. Her imaginary world had universal proportions, a world that nobody could know. In her craving for everything beautiful, for everything that impressed her from the words of poets and writers, Lilica started seeing the possibilities. It was not mistrust, but the sharp consciousness towards what she was going to write at one point, those works for which she as a child exercised with discretion, all for the great exam that was awaiting her and the victory she was hoping for.

Nobody found out about this, not even Professor Frățilă, Hasdeu's close friend, or Professor Svârlescu, who visited the home often, or Ionescu-Gion. Lilica had a great deal of respect for Svârlescu, even though he was a simple and mediocre man. When it came to Gion, however, the girl started feeling somehow reserved because, despite his seriousness and ability, she glimpsed that demureness that often casts a shadow on real merits. Modest as she was, she realized this modesty was even more valuable as it rose higher on the scale of human "values."

Ernestina and Charlotte were held in very high regard by Lilica. She had more work to do with English, and especially with German, and Charlotte Walch, who had a delicate nature and was unhappy in her marriage with her proud and violent husband, made Lilica feel a great deal of compassion for her.

She was kind and loving to her great-grandmother, Maria, and to Mrs. Svârlescu, who loved her dearly. She was especially close to Mrs. Svârlescu because at that time she was shattered by the loss of her husband from a severe illness and almost lost her mind. That's why, at his generous wife's insistence, Hasdeu decided to take the woman in and help her overcome her grief, especially since she had great affection for his daughter and his wife. He might have calculated something in this charitable deed. Iulia had started with reproaches, threats, and angry outbursts towards his affairs, and she needed someone to talk to while he was away, even more so as his affairs produced loud echoes. His wife was struggling with the idea of getting a divorce, an idea suggested by her friends, and the only impediment was her love for her dear Lilica. A woman close in age to her was welcomed with open arms.

Among all these events, there was one that seemed fated. Following the girl's intense work, doctors observed her face was pale, and that was not only a result of exhaustion but also of a blood deficiency. Lilica was anemic, and the only things helping with the anemia were the rich meals served by her mother, which were also greatly enjoyed by Hasdeu, and the repeated requests for her to eat more. As in previous summers, doctors advised them to take a trip to the mountains.

But Hasdeu was too busy with his projects. He was working on the third volume of *Cuvente den bătrâni* with its demanding and tiring linguistic research. He had the time to work on it after his newspaper, *Columna lui Traian* was shut down. Therefore, he couldn't find the time to leave, but he didn't try to stop his wife and daughter, even though he knew he would miss his Lilica. His wife was set on taking this trip, not just for the girl's health, but she also thought her month-long absence would bring back that pale spark in her husband's heart. Either way, her absence, and his longing finally proved to him what she meant in his life and his home. The trip was preceded by a new argument. His wife was already corresponding with her acquaintances in Brașov, so they could help her find a room for her and Lilica in the city, or in Lunga, or especially in Noua where there were lush evergreen forests and fresh air. She was cold and hostile when they said their goodbyes to Hasdeu, but Iulia felt great sadness for the girl.

Even though they tried to keep her away from their fights, Lilica felt, heard, understood, and suffered quietly because of it. Her delicate and gentle mind didn't understand the bitter reasons for the arguments, but she didn't change her behavior, even though the arguments abruptly ended at the sight of her. The atmosphere in the room was no match for her sharp spirit of observation. The love for her father was far from being overshadowed, Lilica loved her parents equally. His comforting arms that often moved to the rhythm of her songs, his warm and colorful words, her daily presence in his work environment which she looked at curiously and with great interest, the lingering smell of cigarettes in his mustache and beard, all these had an undying place in her heart. If for her mother this trip was an awaited vacation, for Lilica it was hard to handle.

"Do you think we're going to have a good time, Mother?"

"I'm sure of it. But this is not about me enjoying my time. It's all about your health."

"You have to enjoy it also; both of us... We should celebrate..."

"You don't believe it?"

"I don't know, Mother... if Father was with us..."

"!!!"

Iulia had prepared the suitcases, excluding books completely, just as the doctor had told her. Lilica had to rest, sit in the sun, and breathe in fresh air! However, the girl managed to sneak in some books written by Hugo, Lamartine, and Molière between her clothes.

But another seed of discord was sprouting between her parents. Following the advice of Charlotte Walch, Laurian, and other friends and colleagues, Lilica Hasdeu had to go to Paris to complete her studies. The advice was resounding like an echo in her soul. Paris! Paris! She had discovered it in books and panoramic illustrations that seemed to her like a fairytale. She was longing for it every night like it was an impossibility, a fantasy. So many dreams had taken her to Victor Hugo's Paris, especially over the chaotic and sharp towers of Notre Dame de Paris, or on the web of streets with their statues, antique shops, boutiques, on the Seine flowing under bridges with the hiding places from *Les Misérables*, with the secrets from Sue's *Les Mystères de Paris*. She was seeing Old Paris in her dreams and illustrations, and singing about:

During the winter evenings, I always stroll around
To visit the old Paris, from centuries before

And I love this mirage, I'd like to remain about
To feel I'm truly living in those times that I adore.

Lilica found support in her mother's ambition of sending her to the "city of lights," however, she was hit with her father's strong opposition. The arguments happened when the child was not present, but the doors were too thin not to attract attention. That's why the trip to Brașov didn't take place under pleasant circumstances. Despite her father being far away, she enjoyed the new views, the new color of the horizon, the mountain peaks, and the forests, which inspired her and made the days go by calmly, effectively, with fresh air and flavors for those lungs clogged by smoke and mold. She learned a lot of new things, but made no friends, even though her mother tried to help her. In the hours her mother spent talking to some Transylvanian women, her eyes were gliding from Tâmpa or Postăvaru towards the spiritual depictions of Paris, where Jean Valjean's bravery and Cosette's sensibility refreshed her. She secretly wrote in books, sketched with her pencil, and fed herself with hope. A few days into her trip she sent her father a few illustrated greeting cards and a letter about her vacation. The letter was warm, confiding, and communicative. Hasdeu replied to her in the same manner, making his dear Lilica the ambassador of his thoughts, but mentioned her hostile mother as well. It was a difficult and delicate task, which made the girl enter their arena against her will. Her spirit, inclined only towards beauty and harmony, was foreign to these feelings and thoughts. However, she took on the mission. She thought long about what she must say, and her endearment was one that only a bright little girl could come up with:

"Mother, why don't you write a few lines to Father?"

"You already did. Why would I write to him as well?"

"Because, dear Mother, he must want to see your handwriting that he cares for so…"

"Cares for…" Her mother sighed.

And her eyes suddenly turned towards a patch of grass somewhere, anywhere, trying to end the conversation, or avoiding answering.

"Please Mommy!"

"Maybe later… I have many things to do…"

"Poor Father, how he suffers in our absence!"

"That's what he wanted, Lilica! And regarding his suffering…"

"Mommy, maybe... maybe…"

"What?"

"Maybe you also... You know, those arguments..."

"He's the only one at fault... Did you eat your ham sandwich?"

"Yes, I did! Mother, we women are often the cause of misunderstanding in a marriage..."

"That's ridiculous! What makes you say such a thing? 'We women'!?"

"Why can't you get over it? Why can't you get over these small disturbances when Father treats us so good and is so famous?"

"Everything is as you say. However, he causes me a different kind of sorrow... one that we shouldn't talk about..."

"Write to him, Mother!"

"Maybe later!"

Lilica understood that no matter how much she insisted it wouldn't work because her mother must have a broken heart.

An opportunity allowed the mother and daughter to take a few days' trip to and around Tușnad. There were heights with waterfalls and cliffs, and many evergreens; but it was cold and cloudy almost daily. A few days later the mother caught a cold and they had to return to Brașov under the care of her worried daughter. It was the first time she was responsible for anything, and that was her mother's health! For that, she did everything she knew: lime tea, quinine, and a massage with her small child's hands.

Hasdeu found out about this incident from his friend, Frățilă, who was passing through Brașov, and he wrote to his daughter affectionately. He was sick as well for a while, maybe from working too much or from catching a cold, because his headache wouldn't leave him. He was scared. He had the impression he had the same symptoms as Svârlescu. The silence from Brașov also contributed to it; it was not quite a silence, but more of the post being slow, taking three days to deliver a letter from there to Bucharest.

Solitude was too difficult to handle for Hasdeu when he was at home with only the two old women: Mrs. Svârlescu, who wasn't completely sane, and his grandmother. The thought of being left by his wife became unbearable, especially when he thought about both her and their daughter moving to Paris for months, even years away from him... With that obsession in mind, he wrote a letter to Lilica:

"You should take Paris out of your mind, especially if your mother doesn't want her husband in the mental ward at Mărcuța, because all these hardships combined with working so much would send any man in there, even one stronger than me.

What would happen to you then? And why does your mother hate Bucharest so much, when everyone respects her and where our family was seen as an example to follow until some created intrigue? If your parents truly love you they must live together and not believe every ill-wisher, so their child doesn't end up like Alexandrina! It would be terrible for a boy, but even more so for a girl!"

He concluded, "I send you thousands of kisses for both you and your mother. Yours forever, Bogdan."

His words, weaved in fears and unspoken wishes, rattled the hearts of his family in Brașov. She could see the break between her parents and the role her father suggested for her, precisely her, to convince her mother to abandon the plans of going to Paris. The letter displayed obvious remorse for the break between them, as well as the wish for reconciliation: "I send you thousands of kisses for both you and your mother!" and especially that "yours forever," that was aimed directly at his wife's heart.

But she kept her silence, so Lilica became the sole one responsible for replying to his letter. The child thought long and hard, gathered the most subtle, deep, and honest words from her soul for her beloved father, and with diplomacy, and maybe some naivety, with the logic of a laborious mind, she wrote a consoling letter to the man that was most tortured by their absence. She added a few doodles and took the letter sprinkled with tears to the post herself.

During the second half of August (1881) the travelers returned to their home. Hasdeu greeted them in the train station, kissed his wife's hand, and hugged and kissed Lilica after examining her posture and the color of her face. He was glad his little girl looked healthy, and he wanted to believe his advice had been acknowledged.

A few days passed during which the family tried to get readjusted to their home routine, and the issue with Paris came up again. At first, the girl tried sweet tricks, then the wife started imposing it.

"Daddy, I missed you so when I was in Brașov!"

"I believe you, Lilica! Do you think I didn't?"

"I know you missed me as well. You have a lot of work to do and that was another burden to carry."

"Oh no! If I didn't have my work I would have lost my mind..."

"Work, dear Daddy, work. I'm glad that work distracts you from being upset."

"What do you mean, Lilica?"

"It comforts me to know that when I'll be studying in Paris you will..."

"Paris? Didn't you understand that..."

"But I must! Everyone says that... I will carry your name with honor over there, dear Daddy; people will talk of you, you'll see... I'll be worthy of you..."

A few supporters of this process brought their "friendly" contribution with insistent arguments and perspectives. While trying to read, Hasdeu dropped the philology book, rubbed his beard, stood up at his table, sat back down again, and delayed the decision. It wasn't just about their financial situation, which was fairly new and strictly budgeted, but the most painful thought was Lilica's absence. Superior studies? Hasdeu didn't even know why the Paris curriculum was so special, and why he should send his daughter away when Bucharest had a great curriculum and talented professors. Professor Frățilă, who was held in high regard by the master, was one of his few hopes. He could be the one helping Lilica prepare for university. And after that... Maybe a future chance would allow him to accompany Lilica during her studies at Hautes Études or the Sorbonne.

Mother Iulia, however, was getting ready to leave with the help of her friends, trying to find good accommodations in Paris. She was looking for prospects, information, and housing offers. A week or so later, she had most of the details in place. There was still one problem, the most important one: travel and rent money. Her modest savings were put to good use, passports were obtained, and the date was set. Hasdeu assisted passively in everything, not knowing how to react. However, he used this time to get used to the idea, knowing there was no point in fighting it and borrowed some money for them as a sign of defeat. Finally, his wife, who was only talking to him when she had to in front of Lilica, decided to explain the situation to him and show him everything was settled, the leave was necessary, not just for her but especially for Lilica and for her future.

And so, Hasdeu put aside his stacks of folders with documents and manuscripts and went searching for travel necessities with a knot in his throat and tears in his eyes.

Meanwhile, Lilica's heart was feeling excitement and happiness for finally being able to travel to the country of her dreams but also sorrow for abandoning a person who adored her. She tried to calm her feelings with books, poems, and songs. But the books closed themselves, lyrics avoided her, and songs couldn't come out of her restless chest. Her only solace was the piano. Not Mozart! But Beethoven and especially Chopin. In the nocturnes of this musical poet, her head could slowly turn from one shoulder to another, her fingers run gently on the keys, her soul merging with the one of the unhappy Polish genius.

Hasdeu listened to her from the couch, on which he was resting and trying to banish the thought of separation, listening to the tumult of arpeggios and musical phrases for which he had no affinity, but finally understanding their meaning of depersonalization, resignation, and wishes that were foreign to him. The keys went on with their game, as the whole world was singing the lament of its life, the prose of hardships that took the shape of an elegiac poem. Lilica was leaving. Lilica was playing... Was she happy to leave? The rhythm of the allegro would say she was. The andante melody would say the contrary...

Iancu, the servant, picked up the suitcases and took them out on the verandah. Lilica was wearing her hat and carrying a small travel bag with magazines and books. The carriage arrived. The impending departure was real and difficult. After pacing in the train station, Hasdeu chose a compartment, looked for friends or acquaintances as travel companions for his family, kissed Iulia's hand, covered Lilica in kisses, and watched the train start, whistling and creaking like a scaly dragon. Iancu had given Lilica her favorite dog to accompany her to Paris, with Hasdeu's blessing. Finally, the train was almost out of his sight, and his daughter's fluttering handkerchief made a final imprint in his mind before disappearing...

He had friends by his side that were also watching the train departing; Theodor Speranță, Frățilă, Doctor Vlădescu, the musician Dimitrescu, historian Ionescu-Gion, some with their wives, others without them. Hermina Walch and her mother were also present. After Maria, Florica, and Mrs. Svârlescu dabbed their teary eyes, Ionescu-Gion grabbed the magister's arm as a comfort for those difficult moments, and they each left for their homes, where maybe a warm heart was waiting for them...

Chapter V

The Uprooting

The train ride lasted days and nights. The passengers got glimpses of faraway places, shadows, light reflections, riverbanks, and hurried people getting on and off the train on crowded platforms, giving some diversion for the souls of the tired travelers. Towards Paris… Towards Paris? "Am I dreaming?" Lilica asked herself. "Is this just another one of those dreams that kept repeating?" But the path she was traveling on had Paris at one end, and the image of her father at the other end, her father on the platform waving his handkerchief so she wouldn't see his eyes, her father alone, alone, alone. Her good traveling companion, Madame de Staël, a woman with masculine features, distracted her from her melancholia and thoughts. *Corinne* kept her busy with images of sunny Italy, but the book was too short.

"Mommy, I wonder if the home on Rue de Tournon is suitable."

"I don't know, Lilica. It was recommended to me as suitable."

"I wonder if it gives an open view…"

And her mind repeated the history she knew of France and Paris: "Rue de Tournon! Rue de Tournon!" It seemed to her that once those words were spoken aloud, even the train's wheels were going in a rhythm with "Rue de Tournon." Who was Tournon and why was there a street in his name in Paris? Was it the old Cardinal de Tournon, the wise statesman who had brought the Jesuits to France? Or maybe the Count of Tournon, a statesman who during the revolution had switched sides from Napoleon I to Louis XVIII?

Her mother only had one answer to her questions: "Stop thinking about such things, Lilica, and eat a piece of apple and vanilla cake!"

"I'll have two," said Lilica, naturally hungry after such a journey.

The border control officer confirmed they were about to enter France. France!

"Your passports, ladies!"

"Here you go," said Lilica with excitement.

The Uprooting

The girl looked wide-eyed at the man in a uniform, who was the first French person she met in authentic France.

Paris, finally! She wanted to see it from afar, but they arrived at night. Early fall brought the same frost to Paris that she was used to. The coachman wearing a top hat pointed the whip at various landmarks, dark monuments, institutions, and parks. The girl's initial impressions were disappointing. There was nothing magical about it. A huge city, with a lot of people, and that was it!

She watched the tall building they were going to live in, with all its windows, lights, and curtains. After climbing many dark and cold steps the concierge (the building administrator) showed them to their apartment. They had two rooms and a kitchen on the third floor; it was quite welcoming.

"Is your little dog clean?"

"Yes madam, very clean!" said Lilica.

They fell asleep fast. The rooms were welcoming, and the windows facing the street made her feel like she was so high up that the people underneath seemed like children running to school…

The next morning they woke up early. The loud voices from the street and the horns sounding from the barracks had disrupted their sleep.

Even though Tournon Street was in a Latin neighborhood, it wasn't one of the friendliest ones in Paris. It was only around three hundred steps long, meeting Saint-Sulpice St. on one end with the great historical palace and Luxembourg Palace on the other. Her mother had probably chosen the location for its proximity to the school and the wonderful park with a Renaissance style, which was the work of the great architect Debrosse, parceled with alleys, decorative trees, basins, and bronze busts depicting Chopin, Fabre, Sainte Beuve, Watteau, Alfred de Vigny, and others, as well as artworks by Dubois and Husson. Lilica and her mother would visit this park many times in their free time when she was not in school.

This historical park was surrounded by the most important schools: Sévigné High School, the Sorbonne, St. Louis High School, the Polytechnic, the French College, etc.

During her first day there, Lilica sent a short telegram to her father to tell him she'd arrived safely, forgetting to say that they had decided to live in the building on Tournon Street from among the two to three recommended options they had. She then followed the plan that she'd set in place ahead of time, which was to visit her chosen high school. Sévigné High School was named in honor of the famous female scholar, Madame de Sévigné, and even though it was new, it was considered one of the most serious schools for girls in Paris. More so, as it was directed by the great philologist, Michel Bréal, whom Hasdeu knew from his reputable works and from the scientific correspondence he'd had with him.

Sévigné High School was not too far from their home, on Condé Street, neighboring Tournon. Even though it was new, its fame came from the exquisite classes taught by valuable professors, among which were Maurice Albert, the son of the other great scholar, Roy, Giry, Gazier, Passy, Picot, Grig, etc.

Lilica and her mother were helped with everything by the Romanian ambassador, Calimach Catargiu, a friend of Hasdeu who he'd warmly asked to help his family around.

After all the preparations, and after the Romanian student presented her documents and diploma, she was enrolled in the fourth year and started attending classes regularly.

When the student went into the principal's office with the wish to be enrolled in the fifth year she argued with Principal Bréal. He saw before him a small but exceptional student, who spoke to him in excellent French, and even though she was modest, she was confident in herself and her knowledge; but the curriculum was the curriculum. The subjects taught in Romania did not correspond to the ones in Paris. Lilica had not learned the subjects required for the fourth year.

"I will pass the fourth-year exams in summer."

"At the same time as the fifth-year exams? It would be too difficult because you're too young," said the principal, "and it will be tiring."

"I don't believe that. I read a lot and I learn fast, sir."

"I believe you, miss," said the principal, "but I don't believe you'll manage it. For example, did you learn the Latin prosody required here?"

"No. But I will. I'll request private tutoring for Latin."

"Excellent, but for that, you also need permission from your father."

"He'll allow it," said the small, excited student.

"I don't think so. He has written to me already, saying he wants you enrolled in the fourth year. I agree with him, especially since there are many other subjects..."

That argument defeated her. Lilica gritted her teeth. One year lost... But she was resigned. She'd make up for it.

Her priority was informing her father by sending him long letters about the classes, about the way she was welcomed, impressions about her classmates, spending reports, and her intention of helping her mother perfect her French.

Lilica had an authentic Romanian soul that she had inherited from her parents. She wasn't quite anti-Semitic. Hasdeu's occasional fights against the Jews had left imprints and had possibly determined a certain attitude, but her poetic, artistic, and humanitarian soul lifted her over any resentment she might have had. For this reason, Hasdeu was careful to hide the fact that his grandmother was Jewish, emphasizing that she was an eminent Christian. The girl found out about it from gossip but was reserved and kept quiet about it. She also discovered that Principal Bréal was Jewish, as well as some of her professors and classmates.

Hasdeu made sure to ask her to be careful around Bréal and his wife and advised her to get acquainted with them by paying regular visits to their home. This recommendation marked Hasdeu's anti-Semitic nature, which could have also been a phobia towards a race or the undesirable individuals belonging to it. He felt respect, even friendship towards Bréal, Ascoli, the great Italian philosopher, and for Lazăr Șaineanu the philologist. There was no opportunism involved, because Michael Bréal, as well as the others, had the same respect for him, and a student such as Iulia Hasdeu didn't need favors or protection, as people liked to gossip in Bucharest. Hasdeu wrote that this gossip had started like a swarm of wasps buzzing around his daughter's success at St. Sava.

One of the first letters he'd sent to his daughter said the following:

"I don't want the people in Bucharest to assume you ran away from easier or more difficult studies. I'm glad you have the opportunity to make new friends among better-educated classmates, to whom you must prove that Romanian girls are superior to the French through their intelligence and hard work. I'm convinced you're the only Romanian student in the school, so your duty of making our nation proud is even more sacred…

Dear Lilica, I hope you won't betray your father's trust. You must know that talent doesn't mean anything in the world if you don't have a good character, so you must have both. A girl of the high class must have her talent chiseled by studies, a strong and noble character, as well as manners in which gentleness must equal dignity, but in which modesty must not turn into shyness."

After telling her about their budget and about the 6-700 lei they were going to receive monthly from him, as well as about the State scholarship he would try to obtain for her, and the money her mother spent that he was going to replace immediately, Hasdeu added in the same letter:

"Your mother will convince herself — I hope — that she has been unfair towards me, basing her feelings on slander and ridiculous intrigues. Oh, how I'm waiting for Christmas so I can embrace you both…"

Through this letter, he also asked them for the school curriculum, so he could see if and how Lilica would be able to pass her final exams. He asked them to write to him every weekend and ended the letter with thousands of kisses from the "loving husband and father."

The lines of that letter written on September 11th, 1881 contain three important things: Hasdeu had a persistent and mystical regret over the departure of his daughter to study in a foreign country, a regret fueled by the longing he was feeling for her, then his Romanian soul was jealous of the prestige of the Romanians living abroad, and finally, the heartache caused by his wife's attitude after she believed gossip, even though his burning wish was to see both of them, so he could embrace them.

This letter, as well as the ones that followed, showed the warm and forgiving nature of the good soul Hasdeu had, even though at times he spewed poison.

Lilica started classes. She showed up looking like an exotic rarity among her French classmates. She was a small child, the smallest and youngest among them. Her natural modesty and shyness, which her father knew well, caused her to be reserved at first, watching this foreign environment with wide eyes, an environment she would dominate shortly. A few questions from her professors that she answered correctly in French, maybe with a slight accent, would prove the genius Romanian girl had knowledge that surpassed that of her classmates. That made them gather around her and show their honest appreciation for her knowledge.

The letter mentioned above showed a fourth fact, which in this case was not directly related to its content but showed a more generic picture of his way of thinking, of psychological and moral problems he had as a scholar. We're talking about the advice given from the perspective of philosophers and educators on the qualities a girl must show: "gentleness must equal dignity" and the "strong and noble character" must reflect manners.

Why did Hasdeu give this advice? He had suspected Lilica didn't know how to prove herself. That was not admissible! He was seeing things from the perspective of a husband and a father… The letter the husband had received from Paris was unexpectedly a kind of money order, "an accounting report that didn't mention

The Uprooting 75

more important information." The girl's pen had been guided by someone else, indicating a certain doubt as to the "manners" of the letter's author... Hasdeu knew why he had to give that advice, especially since she was far from him and he couldn't watch over the child, even though he was trying from where he was to make sure she showed a beautiful character in addition to her gifted intellect in school.

The thought of these manners that had to match the society her classmates with higher social standing came from, made her parent send her another letter on the 15th of September 1881, in which he insisted Lilica must eat breakfast at school, so she'd have the opportunity to learn high-class manners and socialize with her classmates. Hasdeu knew about the manners of the women in his life, even if they were living in Paris...

The letter was not sent with malice or hints to her nature. Hasdeu honestly and respectfully loved his wife just the way she was, even more so as she was the mother of his dear child. He was worried about them being all alone among strangers, with no servants or housekeepers.

"You must get a housekeeper; I don't want your mother, who suffers from migraines, to handle all the household chores by herself and burn herself in the kitchen."

Hasdeu did everything possible to ease their life.

During free days, especially in the beginning when studies and duties didn't take up Lilica's time, she and her mother toured Paris. They first visited Les Invalides, the dome containing the "Austerlitz sun," Napoleon I. Lilica's steps were full of emotion when she approached the funerary hall where statues with flags depicting victories were guarding the massive porphyry slab on the grave. It was the place where the genius Corsican was resting, the hero of heroes who had captured her whole admiration and her sympathy. Emotion uplifted her and made her feel fluid; not feeling the cold stone under her feet, she was a spirit, a memory, in ecstasy. Two tears flowing from her lashes brought her back to earth, earth ennobled by this priceless treasure. Her mind resounded with the last wish: "It is my wish that my ashes may repose on the banks of the Seine, amidst the French people, whom I have loved so well," read the testament of the sleeping immortal before her.

They didn't visit anything else that day. It was a cold autumn day as most autumns are in Paris, with the sun shining over the metropolis, and the wind blowing through the sparse leaves. They stopped on a bench near the dome in silence and recollection that her mother couldn't understand. It was afternoon and signs of the evening started appearing over domes and parks. People were passing by in a hurry; the leaves were falling slowly…

"Don't you want to visit anything else today?"

"No, Mother. It's beyond my power!"

"Are you tired?"

"Maybe!"

"Let's head back then. The sun is starting to set."

"No! Let's sit here a bit more… This is the Mecca of my soul."

"I don't understand you."

"He was not understood either, Mother!"

They started walking home slowly, with heavy steps.

Once there, Lilica took a sheet of paper, drew something, wrote a few lines, and threw it away. The twelve-year-old muse didn't have any place in her heart for that at the time.

"I wish I had the piano! I miss it. How about we write to Father and ask him to send it?"

"What? How could he even do that? Your father has other things on his mind…"

"Of course, Mother. But his first concern is his family…"

"Yes, he proved that all right!"

"Yes, Mother, he did!"

"His concern is to always scold me. Scold ME!"

"But he loves you, Mommy." The little girl stood up, wrapping her arms around the neck of the person that was caring for her.

"If only… How about you drink your coffee with milk, butter, and honey?"

"Okay Mother, but after that, we must write to him and tell him about the piano. And you will be kind as always and add a few lines of your own…"

The giant bumblebee with iron and silver wings was buzzing outside over the roofs, on the streets, and under the hooves. Paris was tired of the weak September sunlight and was smothering the night in favor of the lights from the theatres, cafes, and boîtes.

Lilica sat at her desk and turned the light on, her mother pulled the curtains, and suddenly the room on Tournon Street had the atmosphere of their room in the

Archives... The table was covered in schoolbooks, folders, blocks, candies; the nightstand had books by Hugo, Molière, etc. The mother was watching her closely... And slowly a sturdy silhouette appeared, not too tall, belonging to someone with a graying beard, a serene face, and the eyes of a wizard! He was next to her... holding her hand, whispering to her... "Yes, yes... the piano... yes, yes... nothing is impossible when Lilica asks for it... Why would that be difficult? Only one thing is difficult... separation... I can't handle loneliness, your absence, Lilica!..."

Mignon the dog disturbed her dream by jumping in her lap. She could feel her owner was missing something from home...

Lilica wrote, her lines flowing automatically, even though the light was poor, and her eyes were worn.

The child was suffering from myopia that had started bothering her a year before. She had to lean over the sheet of paper to see. She was leaning closer every day. Sometimes her nose would touch the hand she was writing with. Whenever her mother saw her, she would ask her to straighten up when writing, like the defect was somehow related to her spine... Her father knew the cause. He always gave her good advice, to work in good light, with her back straight, and focused. Every time she wrote a line she would repeat his words in her head: "Save your little eyes; if you force yourself not to read too close, your myopia will heal..." He thought reading up close was the cause of myopia, not an effect, as he was a great scholar, but not a great oculist.

Her father's advice had another effect. Lilica's conscientiousness kept her for hours at her desk for schoolwork, but especially for the matters of the soul. Studying so much wasn't the best for her eyes. Schoolwork took most of her time: authors, logarithms, commentaries, dictionaries, and sometimes... morality. She was especially preoccupied with Latin. Professor Gazier was an excellent Latin teacher, and he was very demanding. She didn't waste any time. Every time she looked out the window towards the French horizon she remembered the text, Latin constructions, recited Cicero and Ovidius, and went over the vocabulary. She did great in French, never reading the text fragments, but going straight for the entire works of the authors. It was the same with history.

Her young age and the years spent in the mountains helped her with her work, just like the piano responded to her consciousness after hard studying.

However, her father's letters were like whip lashes for that hard work. He asked her for eminence during exams so that he could ask for a scholarship in the Deputy Chamber in Bucharest. She needed that scholarship to ease her life in Paris.

And that whipping would continue insistently for the rest of her life because Hasdeu didn't realize her eyesight was the result of effort.

Finally, her father replied to her on the matter of the piano, informing her that the transport would be too difficult, too costly, and with a high risk of damaging the instrument. However, he would try to sell the one at home and send her the money so she could buy herself a good one in Paris, as that city was renowned for their quality and brands of pianos. That was the best choice.

In the same letter, he had another request for her mother; he wished she'd write him at least two lines.

To satisfy the need for comfort in their home, Lilica asked her father to send them two big trunks with items they needed, especially books, sheet music, her palette and paintbrushes, a few items of clothing, and other light items… Petrică Chiță, the son of one of Hasdeu's friends, helped them procure items they needed, even found them a new apartment that was close to the one on Tournon Street, on Saint-Sulpice Street.

Other sons of his friends that came to study in Paris brought other necessary objects, especially books, even a few presents from her father.

Among other things, Lilica informed her father that she didn't always meet friendly individuals among the small group of Romanians in Paris and at school. After finding out about the girl's success and observing her attitude, some smiled, some mocked her. The child could feel all of this, and her sensitive heart caused her indignation and a few tears wiped away by her mother's hand. This was her first taste of loneliness among strangers…

In turn, Hasdeu let her know that Xida, her and her mother's "friend" in Bucharest spread rumors about Lilica being forced to start with the first year of high school in Paris; other people made up stories about her mother choosing to leave after cheating on her husband.

However, Hasdeu wrote to them with a manly attitude, like a high-bred fighter that was aware of the suffering people sometimes have to go through: "I find it odd that you, a small and innocent being, already have enemies. It gives me strong hope that you'll get far in life because the only ones lacking enemies are the ones that mean nothing."

After informing them of everything happening at home, Hasdeu tried to cheer them up with a comical situation he had gone through. Mrs. Svârlescu, the inconsolable widow, who was taking care of the house in their absence, had a commemoration for her late husband and asked Hasdeu to send them a slice of funerary cake to Paris…

This letter softened the heart of his wife but reminded her of what she had left behind, in the home in Mihai-Vodă they had worked so hard for. The longing for all of this determined her to grab a pen and write a letter to her husband after Lilica finished writing to their friends in Bucharest. She wrote it but the lines, even though they informed him about everything, and especially about Lilica and her hard work, started with "Mister…" Another reason she might have had to write the letter was the need for money. Their new apartment in Saint-Sulpice Street, even though it was more elegant than the other one, was not furnished, and Iulia had to spend her last savings to buy a few pieces of furniture that looked good and were quite expensive, and she still had a small debt to pay.

Hasdeu sent them the money as soon as possible, money that included their monthly allowance as well as a sum meant to cover the mother's expenses. Even though her letter was cold it managed to light up a feeling of affection towards her.

"…However, I am grateful for you breaking your silence, because you and Lilica are mine, just like I am yours, so both of you should keep me in your mind while we are separated against my will."

The phrase "against my will" that emphasized the father's letter was received with tears of gratitude because from far away his family could feel him watching over them and struggling to offer them a comfortable life with tuition for Lilica. He used the words of an experienced professor in matters of the heart, and a loving parent.

Aside from the advice related to school and to the way the child had to learn, for example, Greek language, which was hard and demanding, required weekly private tutoring, Hasdeu had received the curriculum for the fourth year and realized how difficult it was. So even though he wanted his daughter to be the top of her class he slipped a bit of different advice between the lines.

"Dear Iulia, don't force her to study; allow her the time to relax and play like any other child. Power can enhance the force of a human, but at the same time, it diminishes the genius which thrives from freedom. I only write these words to you, and please do not show them to Lilica…"

Furthermore, knowing how Paris, the cluster of foreign lights, was full of adventurers, assassins, corrupt individuals, and scammers, Hasdeu taught her how to pay attention at her new home:

"Inquire about who lives above your apartment and below it, to make sure you don't have scoundrels as neighbors.

Lilica has to be protected because Paris is a nest of all sorts of crimes despite all the icons and crosses on Saint-Sulpice Street. You remember how we both watched over her at home, so she was never alone, not even with the tutors. In Paris, even women are dangerous; servants, caretakers, washerwomen, who come in the home or are inside the home with despicable plans in mind. But I'm sure you've already thought about this…"

In truth, Iulia and her daughter had already thought about this issue and the lines in Hasdeu's letter prove the great spiritual connection between them.

"I'm so happy you did it, Mother. You wrote the letter so well. And because you listened to your daughter, your daughter will listen to you more."

"You're a good child, Lilica, and I like listening to you when you are right. Yes! You must follow your father's advice and try to resemble him as much as you can, but only when it comes to knowledge…"

"Yes, Mother, I'll try to also match his kind and loving soul… and not his knowledge because not many people can match my father in that!"

The girl's words were just natural conclusions about the treasured mind towards which Lilica had honest appreciation every time someone compared her parents' intellect, personality, or way of thinking. She couldn't precisely weigh the levels of sorrow in her mother's soul, but she knew something else; her father's love for both of them and his genius had been proven so many times. Her appreciation showed nonetheless for the everyday devotion of her mother, which was simple and often overwhelming, going so far as to follow her and control her. However, Lilica's explanation for that was done with logic and understanding. She never blamed. Few parents, more or less schooled are so preoccupied and understanding of the needs of a child. Hasdeu made sure to sneak in a mention of her exam at St. Sava in the *Românul* newspaper, which also mentioned her reception in the fourth year at Sévigné. The girl received a copy of the newspaper from Uncle Stanislas Hasdeu in Vienna, whom she would have to write more often, as her mother was advised by her husband in the same letter:

> "...Whatever you said, as you are a misanthrope, her uncle will leave her a beautiful fortune, even though we have to care for her schooling first, which is the only real treasure of our century..."

He then talked about Lilica, who had to have everything she lacked or wanted:

> "You didn't tell me. Where do you dine and what do you eat? Are you still a vegetarian? If you are, please allow Lilica to eat meat...
>
> I send you loving kisses and respect.
>
> Bogdan."

"...Loving kisses and respect!," said Hasdeu to the woman who had addressed him as "mister," the wife who once had felt so much for him at a time when he had not betrayed her love and respect. But that's why Hasdeu's generosity was more obvious and, of course, more remorseful...

Lilica's letters to her friends in Bucharest, written either in Romanian or French, depending on the recipient, produced indescribable joy to them, and no less to her father. Pană Constantinescu, his close friend, and his daughter Matilda, Lilica's friend, carried these letters with them to show everyone who loved or was inspired by this exceptional child how her spirit was thriving in Paris. It was understandable why her parent was so glad to get her letters as well. They were the legitimacy and the authenticity of her developing talent for the eyes of all those who were doubting it.

Lilica's progress in school, which became more and more distant from her classmates was constantly the reason for pride and happiness from Hasdeu, who shared how he felt with his daughter:

> "Your mother told me you do well in school and focus on studying, which makes me so happy. You've probably already heard the old French saying 'nobility obliges.' I don't refer to the nobility of blood, which is something that doesn't matter so much; but you were gifted by nature with the superior nobility of intelligence, and this nobility obliges you to grow your reputation every day, the reputation you were given from the time you were a baby."

So, Hasdeu was constantly modulating between these "whip lashes" and his care towards her health, without being able to balance the two or show a preference towards either of them. Because after advising her to accelerate the rhythm of her work, he immediately mentioned she must take care of her eyes, those beautiful eyes that "for a woman, they are her best adornments that ennoble her whole figure and expression." This recommendation even became similar to a threat:

"If you won't force yourself to read from afar, if you won't listen to your mother when she reminds you of this, when I come to Paris, I'll have to bring a doctor to give you surgery...."

Hasdeu didn't know that, while reading his letter, Lilica smiled with superiority, maybe even with pity, because she knew she didn't deserve that threat. She did everything in her power not to hunch over the notebook, to keep books far from her eyes, but her will was not enough to heal her disability, which could only be corrected with glasses. Her parents avoided getting her glasses for a long time believing they would "spoil her vision," even though it was the opposite. Hasdeu didn't understand this problem of cause and effect until his wife wrote to him to explain what was happening.

Her myopia was hereditary from her mother's or her father's side, and another possible explanation for it was her anemia, as well as her habit of reading by candlelight or under lamps with a weak light until late at night, which over time weakened the sight of the girl that had to sit in the front row to be able to see, even when she was going to the theater with her parents.

While trying to advance in class, a struggle that wasn't just hers, reading during the night to keep up weakened her sight even more. The girl was studying diligently every day and every hour, and her teachers were seeing results.

Her past struggles with Latin, the exceptions, the irregular verbs, and their place in sentences were fully mastered; even though it had been difficult for her before, they became completely familiar. During one of her classes, while reading the students' tests, Professor Grazier saw the participle "pulsum" in a translation of Caesar. One of the students was asked what the infinitive was, but she confused it with the one of the verb "pulso."

"Are you sure?" asked Professor Grazier.

"Yes, I think so," answered the student.

"Who knows?" he asked her classmates.

"I do," said another one, standing up.

But the answer was not exact, and the rest of the class became confused.

A small head with curls and dark but sharp eyes raised from the second row: "I know," she said.

"Please, tell us!"

"*Pulsum* is the participle of the verb *pello, pepuli, pulsum, pellere,* and is easily confused with the verb *pulso*, because that is the frequentative of the first one, but the participle of *pulso* is *pulsatum*."

"Thank you, Ms. Hasdeu! That's correct! And how is it written," he asked the first student questioned, "with one *l* or with two *ls*?"

"With two when one is between two vowels," she answered.

"Whenever one is between two vowels?"

Silence.

"What does Ms. Hasdeu think?" asked the professor.

"*Pello* and *pellere* are written with two *ls* because the syllables containing *l* are emphasized, and *pepuli* is written with one *l* because it's contained in a syllable that is not emphasized."

The precision of her answer convinced the Latin master of the serious training of the exotic high schooler, that he had noticed a while before...

During another class, the French professor asked the students to write an essay to explain what conscience and remorse were, following a case in which the conscience of a student in the class was absent. From among all papers, the professor stopped at one of the two which had been graded a 10; the first was filled with twelve lines from the poem *La Conscience* (*The Conscience*) by Victor Hugo, in which the genius poet showed how "the eye" following Cain everywhere didn't even abandon him in the coffin.

Then, with his children, clothed in skins of beasts,
Disheveled, livid, rushing through the storm,
Cain fled before Jehovah,
Cain fled before Jehovah. As night fell
The dark man reached a mount in a great plain,
And his tired wife and his sons, out of breath,
Said: "Let us lie down on the earth and sleep."
Cain, sleeping not, dreamed at the mountain foot.
Raising his head, in that funereal heaven
He saw an eye, a great eye, in the night
Open, and staring at him in the gloom...

This paper belonged to Iulia Hasdeu, and we know Victor Hugo's book was her favorite.

"Ms. Hasdeu, you must know that *ténèbres* (darkness) is written with a sharp first accent and a grave second accent," added the professor casually.

From the girl's letters, and maybe from Bréal's who liked to keep her father informed from time to time, Hasdeu learned about her success.

"You cannot even imagine," her parent wrote to her immediately, "how glad and proud I am since I found out you're the top of your class. This is the only way to prove that your accomplishments in Bucharest were not due to my protection, as some like to claim. No matter how knowledgeable you become, don't ever forget to be happy, funny, and full of laughter; because only the ones with mediocre or malicious personalities are bland…"

Such eulogies followed by fatherly advice were repeated in numerous letters. She was advised to steer clear of the water in Paris which was not the best and to mix it with wine; to wear a flannel during autumn (which was written in a letter from the second half of October 1881).

Hasdeu found out from Iulia that because of her generosity towards people in need, who were really needy or just pretending to be, she found herself in need of money, and advised her to reduce that "angelic generosity" because:

"If all people were angels it would be acceptable; but unfortunately, an angel among people always becomes a victim. I ask my dear wife to not repeat what she did in Brașov where she took care of everyone coming from Bucharest, because if she found herself in need none of these loafers would help her. I, myself, generously repay others' services, but only real services as they are given, unexaggerated, repaid according to my budget, without forgetting that I still need to care for you and myself. Let the world say I'm cold-hearted, but I am warm-hearted for my family…."

Whoever knew about Hasdeu giving money as a reward to his most valuable students, as well as to his few but honest friends, would believe these lines and wouldn't question his morality. He was not stingy but measured and calculated.

Lilica received great news; her father had sold the piano at home and had sent her 600 francs obtained from its sale that she could use to buy another piano in Paris; he'd also sent a few items of furniture from their living room, so they could use them in their apartment.

Lilica hugged her mother around her neck, and Hasdeu would later admit to having received the rivers of happiness from the little pianist as well as from her mother, the one gifted with "angelic generosity."

His family's joy was even greeted by their new apartment that was now furnished, happy with their new life full of new impressions of Paris with its museums and works of art they visited during every free day. One day they visited two to three rooms of the Louvre, another day they visited three to four other rooms, a week later they visited the marble Palace of Versailles, the historic frescos, and the giant lush park that was as large as old Paris; another day they visited the Opera and listened to Manon or Faust from the gallery, which for them were unforgettable moments.

But the dusty trips in the dangerous crowds of Paris were not entirely joyful, as the city was full of disease and epidemics.

One evening while working on her studies, because she was unusually tired, Lilica felt her face was hot, and her head heavy, as well as a light burning in her throat; her eyes were watery, and she couldn't stand the light anymore. Repeated sneezing and a dry cough stopped her from working.

Her mother approached her with fear in her eyes, saw her cheeks were red and that she seemed to be getting chills. She tucked her in bed without delay, brewed her a tea and gave her some quinine, but the child was burning up... After a sleepless night for both of them, the mother called the doctor early in the morning. He took her temperature and found it to be 101.3, examined Lilica's throat, and saw it was inflamed with white specs. Her eyes were bloodshot, and her nose was stuffed and bloody. Iulia's fear was increasing, even though the doctor told her there was no reason to worry and gave her some recommendations.

Finally, he gave a diagnosis: measles. Lilica explained to her mother what it was. The doctor advised them both that she needed a long break from studies.

For the first time, her mother felt lonely not having Hasdeu next to her to help her in this new struggle. She was panicking. What should she do? Write him a letter? What for? What could he do if he was there? But how could she not write to him?

"God, have pity; protect us!" But the suffering didn't end. On the contrary, it got worse, especially during the night. The dream Iulia had around Lilica's birth, that dream she always remembered every time the child was sick or when she had indigestion, the one she never told anyone about, came back to haunt her while watching over her. "What could that dark cloud be? Just the worries that every person feels? But the cloud resembled a maid for a short while, then turned back into a cloud. No, no! Begone! It was only a dream! God protect us!" She followed the doctor's advice closely and waited for a divine miracle. On the third day,

Lilica's fever broke but she got a red itchy rash on her cheeks, then on her neck, then on her chest, and finally on her whole body.

A student from their group of friends sent a short telegram to Hasdeu: "Lilica has the measles." When Iulia learned of the telegram, she decided to write to him.

Meanwhile, Hasdeu received the telegram and was shocked. Measles? What could this be? In Moldova they used another term for it, so he'd never heard this word before. How could Lilica get sick? His Lilica! With those words in mind, Hasdeu went beyond his power and over the rituals in which he didn't believe, fell on his knees in front of the icons, and prayed like any other Christian with pain in his heart; these instincts were always stronger than reason. The instinct of praying is dormant in every atheist, and Hasdeu was not even an atheist. He was struggling like a lion in the cage keeping him away from Lilica. A part of him wanted to take the first train to Paris, another part of him blamed himself for allowing the girl to leave, one was urging him to run and talk to a doctor, and another was asking for God's mercy. And with those thoughts in mind, he was walking around his table, sitting on the bed, jumping back up, all the while hallucinating about his daughter. He was losing his mind.

He was seen running at dawn to Dr. Vlădescu's house, and from there to Dr. Măldărescu. Both tried to calm him down. They told him the disease was not serious. Most children went through it because it was an epidemic. What was very dangerous were complications. That's where they had to be careful. Lilica couldn't leave the house for six weeks because her lungs could be gravely affected and she could get tuberculosis.

This information was just as threatening in the mind of the father, and he rushed to send a letter to Paris because he thought the French doctors might not be aware of these things. The consequences of the disease worried him tremendously, especially the risk of tuberculosis.

In the second part of the same day, he received his wife's letter, saying the disease had a normal evolution, the doctors had given her recommendations and she was following them accordingly. Lilica was not in danger anymore. (Forever, perhaps??).

Even so, Hasdeu could not calm down. He sent her the advice of the Romanian doctors, as well as his advice for his wife: "I worry about you now because you need rest," said the loving soul. Regarding Lilica's studies, he was convinced this wasn't going to affect them much "because Lilica is already more advanced than the rest of her class."

Finally, the disease ran its course. It was terrible for her parents, especially for her father who was not able to work, starting and abandoning manuscripts, sitting with his head in his hands not able to focus. He was worried especially because his family was not writing to him often enough.

"Dear Lilica,

Why do you punish me so, sending me letters once every two weeks? Do I have to remind you to write to me by telegram every time?"

The news from Ermina and Charlotte Walch calmed his nerves a bit. They had just returned from abroad and had visited Paris and their sick friend for a few days, bringing her flowers, warm words, and details about life in Bucharest.

Lilica was well again, but she didn't follow the doctors' advice of staying inside for six weeks. She was busy studying again. Florica, Marie, and Matilda all wrote to her asking her to slow down, sending her good wishes, and telling her about things that would cheer her up. The girl's wish, as well as her father's, was for her to pass the fourth-year exam in December, so she could be transferred to the fifth year with the certificate necessary for the scholarship. Hasdeu's greatest wish was to take a few days off and visit Paris at Christmas, especially since C.A. Rosetti, the prime minister in Brătianu's government wanted Hasdeu to take Urechia's place as a minister.

A few days before, Hasdeu was scheduled to take part in the unveiling of I. Heliade Rădulescu's statue in front of the University of Bucharest, the event where he gave that wonderful and pious speech about the essence of Romanian culture, a speech made even more brilliant by the lackluster official speech of Minister V.A. Urechia, which was not even published in the *Românul* newspaper. Hasdeu's speech was published extensively. For this, Hasdeu received high honors from Lilica.

The girl was working as hard as she could, but the long absence from classes made everything harder. The exceptional grades the professors were giving her also caused envy among her classmates. However, Lilica was disappointed in some of her professors who were unfair and didn't take her disability into account.

Her letters to her father were full of sorrow and her parents felt it equally.

"What you're telling me about school upsets me. No matter how things are you must try and be the best in your class, and when I come to visit you at Christmas, we'll see what we can do to fix it, even though I suspect you exaggerate the matter a bit!... What's most important is for you to not know any less than what the second-best learns during class; it would be ideal if you knew more because you are Romanian, and you're Hasdeu's daughter…"

"Hasdeu's daughter!" Lilica knew well what place she deserved for her hard work. That was the reason for her sorrow because she was working hard and was not appreciated enough. Her wish to pass the exams in December didn't seem feasible at that moment. The disease had weakened her, and her progress was slow. She was suffering greatly.

Her only consolation was the beautiful piano she'd managed to purchase with the help of some friends. It was a true masterpiece of resonance and construction. Its exterior was sculpted in mahogany with masterly-made pearl inlays, and it had a special key device that made it a rare piece of instrument, contrasting with the rest of the charming furniture.

After the hours in which she struggled to read but her eyes wouldn't cooperate, Lilica got up and walked to the piano, relaxing with the rapid scales and arpeggios, with Chopin's ballads gliding over the keys. Her contralto voice rose slowly like in a dream, while her mother who was working nearby stopped in her tracks to watch her child blooming in a different reality, in the silence floating around her.

Her wish of seeing Lilica healthy kept her working hard for it. She cooked in the kitchen after purchasing everything herself, and she made sure there were extra portions that the student needed. But Paris didn't have the same food as Bucharest, and the two found it difficult to adapt. Lilica received an authentic Sibiu salami from Bucharest, as she loved spicy food, but she was craving black olives, and especially halva which people in Paris didn't even know about. However, someone far away was kind enough to send her a few round boxes of vanilla halva, and a box of caviar that Lilica adored but for which her mother's budget was not enough to purchase in Paris.

The mother had asked the giver of these delicacies for something else, and that time the present came walking. It was a servant sent from Bucharest who was to help her constantly, not just for a few hours like the ones for Paris did, coming to work in Louis XV heels, dusting superficially, or only there to take a letter to a mailbox two miles away…

Hasdeu considered such an expense was beneficial to his Lilica and he didn't think twice about doing it.

Lilica's friends wrote her regularly with news from Bucharest, and she never forgot about them, replying to their letters with news from Paris, details about her classes, gossip about her teachers, and enigmatic lyrics. The letter exchange was constant, relaxing, and the girls took the letters and shared them among themselves.

However, she sacrificed most of her time of respite for her studies, taking time off only to read French, English, and German literature. During her time of convalescence, on the fourteenth of November, she turned eleven years old, and her mother gifted her a storybook by Clementine Helm: *Das Vierblatige Kleeblatt*, a book better suited for her mother's cultural level than Lilica's. However, Lilica wrote on the cover in French: "Gifted by my mother for my birthday on the fourteenth of November 1880, for turning eleven years old. Julie Hasdeu."

So, aside from reading *De Bello Gallico* by Caesar, *Les Mots Grecs* by Bréal where she wrote grammar observations, and the mandatory bibliography for school, Lilica Hasdeu fed her soul by reading French prose and poetry by her favorite authors, especially Hugo, Lamartine, Vigny, and Musset, memorizing and reciting to her mother her favorite lines from Hugo's words.

But Christmas was approaching. Lilica was burning with longing for her father and couldn't wait to spend the holidays with her family despite not having the familiar ambiance from home that had captivated her from the time she was a child and which she loved so. That's why she wrote to him and asked him to drop his speeches and his dusty manuscripts and get to Paris faster.

Her father complied, especially because of the longing for his child that was burning him worse and worse.

He gave Mrs. Svârlescu instructions for the home and the animals, packed his suitcases with food (halva, caviar, olives), a fur coat for Lilica, and especially a straw basket in which he stuffed his wife's favorite cat, after struggling to make it stay still and endure the trip to Paris; it left behind heartbroken tomcats at the Archives… And he left.

The train was slow as a snail. Faster! He had to make a stop in Munich to see a friend from whom he hoped to get a German servant, maybe even a housekeeper. The stop lasted a day, an endless day that felt like a month. He found what he needed, and the next day he added a short and talkative redheaded housemaid to his luggage. She was perfect for Lilica.

He had arranged his trip in such a way so that he would reach Paris in the morning. He got off the train on the eastern platform, in the market full of cursing carriers, holding a bouquet of roses for Lilica that he gave her between tight hugs; his wife's gift was the jewel in the straw basket. It was a scene worthy of a Romanian scholar that amused the passersby. Excited to see her cat, Lilica opened the basket and tried to grab her fluffy friend, but scared and crazed by the noise around it, it jumped out of the basket. Hasdeu grabbed it by the tail, and her meows of protest blended with the laughter while the animal went back into its enclosure. To all this turmoil we must mention the cries of the scared Bavarian servant.

Their apartment which was often quiet was now full of joy, jokes, stories, and all sorts of stories about friends, events, cats, and Hector from home. Lilica was lying in her father's arms telling him about everything. Her mother couldn't stop talking about the girl's illness, about the sleepless nights, trying to avoid asking her husband about his love affairs in Bucharest.

"Those are only the opinions and malice of others, dear wife. Woman's worst defect is believing that love turns men into saints," Hasdeu said in Lilica's absence.

"Just so you know, I'm not as stupid as you think, dear Hasdeu. You a saint...:"

"I'm not talking about myself. I'm not worse than other men, dear Iulia!"

"I never said that; however, I suffered a lot..."

"I know because you allowed yourself to be influenced by envious women... I know you suffered. But know this, I suffered as well; yes, yes, a lot..."

"So what can I say?"

"You punished me... You cannot imagine how much I suffer for this distance you've put between us."

"Me? Lilica as well..."

"Her? She's an ambitious child... Yes, yes, Iulia; ambitious like me... and like you... But we must let fate take the reins... We both must watch over Lilica because I can see how weak she is."

The week Hasdeu spent with them in Paris was a blessing, especially for Lilica. They dined a few times at restaurants frequented by foreigners, even at the Grand Restaurant de l'Odeon, a place with servers in dress coats and silver cutlery because their housemaid only knew how to cook Bavarian dishes. They visited museums, monuments, and friends every day, and Hasdeu took a few hours to visit people from his field of study. He paid a visit to Bréal, Berger, and Bergoigne, who in turn took him to the Linguistics Society to introduce him to their friends, with whom Hasdeu was already acquainted.

A short glance at Lilica told him it would be sacrilege for her to take her exams at that time. She was visibly thinner than she was when she left, and her efforts were consuming her. His eyes showed worry and a thirst for knowing her thoughts, and love for that beautiful and intelligent head. He found enormous progress. She knew Latin, history, and literature very well. She was just starting to learn Greek; it was okay, but she had work to do. Hasdeu had already spoken to Bréal about everything and he had honestly praised the child's aptitudes but recommended a tutor to help her with Greek. Hasdeu talked to Lilica and insisted on that.

"You must not neglect Greek, my girl. Nobody can do great with Latin, especially if they are a philologist, without this classic base."

"I will do my best, Papa, I will do my best."

"Yes, my girl, do your best, but take it slow. Your health should be a priority, especially your eyes. They worry me just as much."

"I'm worried about them too."

"Me too," said her mother. "I always tell her to straighten up."

"But I can't! How can I keep my eyes away from the notebook if I can't see? Other than that, I feel good. I still cough from time to time. The doctor said this is normal after measles and it will pass."

"I hope to God! You must take care of yourself. Take the prescribed tonic, so you get your strength back. You have a lot of studying to do for the exam, and you must pass it with flying colors!"

"Yes, yes! That's also my ambition, Daddy, believe me!"

The day of parting ways approached, with dew on their lashes and in his beard. He gave them recommendations on Lilica's myopia, as well as hiring a doctor for their home on a monthly salary. The discussion about glasses came up and the doctor was going to do it if he thought it necessary.

The mother wanted to increase her quality of life by housing one or two girls, but Hasdeu didn't agree with it unless the girls were family of his friends; he decided to inquire about it.

On the second day of the new year, Hasdeu left. The departure was painful for the two souls that adored each other. He was no less upset about being away from his wife and a tear unwillingly dropped on Iulia's hand.

The cruel life regained its overbearing rule over the two ends of the steel road separating them.

Lilica took the advice. While trying to strictly conform to the recommendations the girl found her everyday consolation in the whispers of her father that made her days pass by easier, and her tears dry faster.

The Bavarian girl was more hassle than help. She didn't cook well, talked a lot, and was careless. Iulia wrote to Hasdeu and told him he gave her a burden. The girl was fired politely and given money. Hasdeu replied to her letter agreeing with his wife's decision and sending them some good news. *Columna lui Traian* had been reinstated and he had been given membership in the Linguistics Society in Paris with the majority of the votes.

Iulia had also told him in the letter that Lilica was doing well in school, but she refused to eat more, sometimes even answering back to her with harsh words...

In the reply letter he added a noble response to her past accusations and a bit of direct advice regarding Lilica:

"...I don't doubt she does well in school, and I need her to stop upsetting you, give you a break, and listen to you because there are few children in this world with a better mother...

...Write to me often, otherwise I can't focus on my work because I get migraines..." (1st of February 1882).

The next letter was addressed to Lilica. Following a matter related to money, about a theft in their home that had also caused losses to Mrs. Svârlescu, a theft Iancu, the servant was suspected of, Hasdeu returned to his eternal recurring theme.

"...I'll do everything I can but you must do well in school, behave appropriately and never upset your mother. You must never forget that your name is Hasdeu and our family's division is country, honor, respect.

In the February issue of *Columna* that will be printed tomorrow or the day after you'll find something that will amuse you, a letter to you about the portrait of Stephen the Great..."

Shortly after, Hasdeu informed them that Urechia had dissolved the permanent council of the Academy, a council he was part of, and with that position, he had lost 280 francs a month, but another door had opened, and he had been chosen as dean of the Faculty of Letters. The fatherly whip lashes were also a part of that letter:

"...I have to ask Lilica, again, to study and not upset you anymore..."

His words had a constant echo. The girl picked up pace when studying, working day and night while also getting ready to take the exam.

Chapter VI

The Foreign Furrow

The partial exam was scheduled for around Easter. Lilica was ready more than any other candidate. Her answers were complete, researched, and amazed the teachers.

Besides French, Latin, Greek, history, etc. the student stood out in another subject.

People say the French know everything, except geography. From that point of view, Lilica was a true French girl ever since she was in elementary school. She was a great student but was not great at geography.

This time, however, the Romanian student was above her classmates yet again.

The professor asked her a few questions about Africa and the new media of communication implemented there.

The candidates gave answers about the railway system from Algeria, Tunisia, and the other French colonies.

"But how about new ones? Tell me about a new one," said the teacher.

"The Suez Canal," said Talois, one of the students.

"Very good," said the teacher, "but is this French?"

All the students were silent. They couldn't imagine the contrary, but none of them were sure about the answer.

"Obviously," said Iulia Hasdeu.

"Are you sure?" asked the professor, knowing it was someone else who had opened the way to New India.

"I said obviously," answered Lilica, "because even though the Suez Canal was established by the English with the help of Said Paşa, the Khedive of Egypt, at the request of the English minister Disraeli, the plans and the leadership were attributed to the great French engineer Vicomte Ferdinand Lesseps, a genius whose statue you can still see today in Port Said; this canal is a French work of art."

"Well done, Ms. Hasdeu! I like your answer especially since you are a foreigner with a French spirit."

Her mother proudly wrote to her husband and bragged about watching over the child and about her success, and Hasdeu wrote back enthusiastically, congratulating her for her accomplishments, and showing his respect for his wife:

"...You have a mother that you must be proud of and love as you love God because there are few mothers like her in the world...

Don't neglect your health while studying. Have mercy on your eyes, keep your back straight, and exercise, because being sedentary at your age is very dangerous."

The collection of letters between them shows something from the subconscious of the "mystic from Câmpina," as old Hasdeu was going to be called after withdrawing in his castle, a time when spiritual conversations would become his last conscience. It was the loud resonating pedal he always cranked when preoccupied with the girl's over-activity and the deaf fear of her health and the inevitable consequences her diligence might cause to that precocious child...

But at that moment the joy for Lilica's achievement was exhilarating.

Hasdeu bragged loudly about it to his friends and published it in the magazine for everyone to see. His friends, among which were also Caragiale and Barițiu, were honestly happy for him.

"Such a parent must have such a child," said Caragiale during one of their meetings.

"Such a parent must have such friends," said Hasdeu.

"May God protect her," said Barițiu, patting him on the shoulder.

"Let's raise another glass for both of them," added the author of *Scrisori pierdute*.

"I heard the great Bréal congratulated her!" remembered Barițiu.

"Exactly. And the famous Talois, the top of her class is not the second-best. Did you know that?" said Hasdeu, rubbing his beard.

That letter of congratulations was concluded like this:

"Everyone is inquiring about your studies and your success and they are right to do so because you are the essence of the whole Romanian nation."

Lilica's friends were also very happy about it, Hermina, Maria, Florica, Mița, and Alexandrina sharing the letters. Mrs. Svârlescu sighed and shed a few tears, missing the child she loved so.

Old I. Brezoianu, the highly learned magistrate went to Paris, brought word from Hasdeu, and presented the girl and her mother with his homage of admiration. In turn, Frățilă, who was loyally helping with the editing and publishing of *Columna lui Traian*, also sent a letter of congratulations and health wishes for the girl.

Meanwhile, Lilica seemed healthy, sturdy, and happy, playing with her classmates during recess, telling jokes, and playing harmless pranks. She was especially combative. Her last success had given her great volubility and growing prestige despite the small intrigue and envy in her class. The girls thought Iulia Hasdeu was the top of her class, not entirely because of her own merits but maybe because France was giving more importance to its guests…

Being away from her country had made her see that dreams were beautiful, but the reality was oppressing. France was beautiful, Paris was charming, but her country was above all the other charms of the world. She wrote about it shortly after:

You're often looking for the flaws
Of your poor country;
Despite its madmen and its fools
She's always loved dearly!

……………………………………

If you're abroad for a long time
So far away from it
You learn your country is sublime
For the unfaithful heart…

It was not just once that during conversations with her classmates the words of the twelve-year-old child uplifted Romania in the eyes of the listeners.

"Why did you leave then?" asked one of them.

"Because I had to learn to love it more by coming here."

"Admit that your love is quite distant…"

"Romania has never been more beautiful and dearer to me as it is from here. There are simple and bad people there, just like everywhere else, just like in France, but my people are good and brave. No other nation has fought to save Europe from the hoards as much as Romania. If only you knew how much we've suffered! If only…!"

"We know, but France was no less brave."

"Of course, but the resistance dam is hit by the waves differently than the distant beach," replied Iulia Hasdeu.

Hasdeu found out later about these dialogues and she had only told him a little bit. But if he had been present when they were happening, his pride would have reached the sky.

Even though Lilica had just finished her exams, she had to work for the general ones, under the pointless advice of her mother. She hired a Greek and a Latin tutor, but she didn't forget about the predilections of her soul. Her free time was not dedicated to lying in bed. She drew, painted, and especially took piano lessons at school and at home.

Hasdeu found out about that and wrote to her mother, asking her to put her foot down.

"I'm asking you this not because I'm worried about money, because I don't think about money when it comes to Lilica's future, but I don't want her to overdo it, as she's still frail. When does she have a moment for respite? Think, dear Iulia, and then think again…" (5th of May 1882)

And it's known Hasdeu made compromises to afford it all; he reduced his smoking, made two cigarettes from one, worked for prizes, and often took credits from Mircuș the banker so his family had a comfortable life. He was happy he could do that for them, and he was content with his wife who showed kinder feelings towards him, and their marriage was going strong despite the distance, all that for Lilica's happiness. He was glad for it especially since the marriages of his friends were swaying. The Walch family for example. The arrogant and violent painter tormented his wife, even beat her. The wife and Hermina ran away from home in fear.

"That wretch!" exclaimed Iulia, reading his letter.

"Poor Hermina!" added Lilica.

"I never believed it would get this far. Charlotte is my friend and she's such a good woman!"

"Just like you, Mother."

"Is that so?"

"Yes! But Walch is not Hasdeu... Nobody in this world is like my father. Am I right, Mother?"

"You're a smart girl, Lilica, a very smart girl!"

"I'm so excited to see him again soon."

Hasdeu was getting ready for a new trip to Paris, ready to spend his whole summer vacation there, especially because he was worried about his wife being bored. The administrator of the apartment in which they were living was an evil, annoying, and rude woman, who even turned the servants against Iulia. His wife complained constantly about her, even though Iulia could do a lot more from there, by calling the police, than Hasdeu could from Bucharest. However, he wrote to Odobescu who had ties to law enforcement in Paris and asked him to help his wife.

His wife calmed down a bit when she found out he was going to arrive on the 14th of July. He also thanked her for the dresses she had bought and sent to her friends in Bucharest.

"...I congratulate your mother for the nobility of her soul that she's always shown, and that you must also inherit, dear Lilica. But, for the love of God, stop bowing your heads before the administrator..."

Hasdeu started his trip to Paris under moral and material conditions that were extremely favorable to him. He was sent by Brătianu's government to Paris to represent Romania at the inauguration of the monument dedicated to the great political French man and historian, Jules Michelet, a beloved honorary Romanian citizen.

He was greeted by Lilica and her mother a few days before July 14th, 1882, on the day of the inauguration. During the train ride, he read everything he could about the scholar and wrote his speech. He brought news from home, greetings from their friends, especially the good wishes of Ionescu-Gion. He also brought news of his own about his eternal adversary, Urechia, who had asked him back to the permanent council, even more, had proposed his name for the Romanian Crown Award in the grade of commander, a proposal that Hasdeu had refused, claiming he deserved the rank of high officer.

And then it was time to talk about the administrator.

"But dear Iulia," he said seeing the administrator, "how is it possible for a fighter like you with warrior blood in your veins to be afraid of a creature like her?"

"I'm not afraid of her hands; I'm afraid of her mouth... because she talks a lot and I can't understand what she says..."

"It's a good thing she backed off, otherwise I would have turned into the devil," said Hasdeu.

"That's what I was telling Lilica, because we were already getting ready to leave."

"Ever since she was visited by the police she calmed down some, but one time I got really scared…"

"That devil!"

"May she get stomped by a black cow," concluded the mother.

All three went to the inauguration of the monument where the two Iulias were in the front row. Hasdeu had poured all his talent, research, and especially his learned and patriotic soul into the speech, so that he could praise the great historian and protector of the Romanian cause. The speech was a eulogy for the one depicted in bronze, as well as for the speaker. Many congratulated him and the press reproduced it with an emotional appreciation for the Romanian historian. *Le Temps*, *Le Rappel*, *L'intransigeant*, all the newspapers rushed to praise Hasdeu, his friends cheered for him, and the Romanian event ended with a joyful feast.

That was not all. At the same time, the event was honored by the daughter of the speaker, who came to complete his glory. The general exam at the end of the school year brought her words of praise from Bréal's mouth, as well as from Picor, her history teacher, and Gazier for being the top student in the fourth year. Small and flattered in her modesty, the girl couldn't sit still on the chair, smiling happily to her father.

So summer started in prosperous circumstances. The increased financial means allowed Hasdeu to take his family to the seaside. A few days in Marseille and a few weeks in Geneva. He had chosen these resorts a long time before, so they could take advantage of their libraries and archives. While Lilica and her mother were baking in the scorching sun on the wide beaches, Hasdeu was cooling off between the walls stacked with shelves and documents, later publishing a rare discovery in *Columna lui Traian*:

"It's curious that the first document I found in the Geneva Archives was issued by one of my ancestors…"

After close to two months of rest and fresh air for Lilica and her mother, and work for the father, in the second half of August, Hasdeu went back to his country, and his family went back to Paris. The lack of servants or housekeepers upset him and despite his inquiries, he couldn't find a trustworthy one that could be a real help for his wife. When he got back to Bucharest he met Ernestina Feichtinger and convinced her to go to Paris as a housekeeper. Because the young woman loved his family so much, she accepted and decided to leave for Paris as soon as possible with a salary of sixty francs a month.

The mother was stuck on getting two to three students as tenants, not just to supplement her income, but so Lilica would have some friends to distract her from her many occupations.

Lilica was hoping to have Florica Zaharescu by her side. She had graduated middle school as well, and even though her parents were pushing her to study in Paris, she couldn't bear the thought of leaving them.

Hasdeu did everything he could to convince his friends' daughter to change her mind, just so Lilica would have a beloved soul next to her, especially since he had realized she was spending too much time studying and the overwork was making its presence known through those terrible migraines. Her father was overwhelmed by the work that had started during what was supposed to be his summer vacation, as well as by the loneliness that was made even greater by the two months spent next to his dear family. He was asking all sorts of questions regarding Lilica's routine.

But just like an addiction, every time culture and talent stimulated each other fiercely, in addition to the sparkling potion of superior refinement, it deposited the destructive ashes of intense burning into her body. She was caught in the vicious circle of her mind while trying to cultivate French, a language that was closer to her thoughts than her native language. Lilica was daily absorbing a big part of her reading, and her literary preoccupations were calling her insistently like a warm and private refuge. The mind of the 13-year-old girl knew no respite. She could compartmentalize school studies, her dreams, inspirations, and plans for great works of art. The views, poetic readings, memories, all under the deep refractions of her mind made her sketch impressions, reflections, play scripts, novels, poems, or hymns. Every time her mother saw her daughter's tired shadow, she didn't realize the girl's spirit was going through a random compartment, not knowing which one to settle upon. The poems that would later get a final shape (even though not finished) were being laid in notebooks, books, on blank sheets accompanied by drawings, the same way she'd always done it. However, she didn't miss any of her classes and her professors didn't notice any lack of quality in her work.

Ernestina was doing less housework than Lilica's father wanted, but she continued tutoring her in German, and helped her with piano lessons, even though there was not much she could help her with. That was a new problem for her mother. She couldn't fully rely on her new helper as her husband wanted, so she complained about it in letters to him. However, she didn't follow her maternal instinct of asking Lilica to step away from the ocean of books, notebooks, and exercises to send her with Ernestina to visit the parks and squares of Paris during her free time. She was happy her daughter seemed strong and happy, which would prove to be a deceptive appearance of the genius being.

The new school year started with diligence and rewards on Lilica's part. She suffered because of her father's absence but felt closer to him than ever. Their written conversations had reached the next level and they were closely analyzed by the schooled poet. In the last letter sent to her, he gave her a few useful pieces of advice and aesthetic guidance.

Hasdeu saw Lilica almost as a colleague and noticed her progress of one year was the equivalent of the progress of a decade for others. He was so proud of it the proportions of his inner philosopher were diminished... He was always preoccupied with money, and he was following the stock of destiny that Satan was tempting him with...

On the 14th of November 1882, Lilica turned thirteen years old. On the same day, her grandmother, who was spending her time visiting relatives, showed up in Bucharest and took up residence in her grandson's home despite his reservations. Mrs. Svârlescu was not happy about it either, as she was having a hard time running the day-to-day chores in the Archives. The woman was almost ninety years old, proud, and mouthy. She had seen a lack of respect in Lilica's attitude. There was nothing more upsetting for an old person than a lack of respect, so not knowing how to obtain it, she pretended to deserve it.

Old age itself is ill-natured, and the rotting log was not taking kindly to the strong green-growing sprout. There was something of the imminence of the matter's transmutation in those facts. Nature wraps its vigor and sap around the sprout, to make sure it continues to grow. After using all its tools to ensure its continuations, nature discards what it doesn't need. The beautiful flower becomes a ripe fruit, enough for the seed to thrive, sprout, grow, and continue its mission. But when it comes to people, old age is supposed to be like a high rank gifted by the heavens on a silver platter, like a reassurance given at the right time.

Maria Daucșa was a simple woman who had bloomed late in life. She was far from the generous grandmothers who charmed everyone with their wisdom; she was selfish and arrogant. Lilica loved her because of her late blooming and for the comforts she had given her from time to time.

"Bogdan, do you truly believe Lilica will be noticed in Paris?" she asked a few days after arriving at his house.

"I do, Grandmother, I'm sure of it."

"Oh please, I've seen so many children going there as calves and coming back as…"

"I'm sorry, Grandmother, But I won't allow such ideas relating to my Lilica…"

"Okay, okay! You'll see later I'm right… You'll see… You're spending a lot of money supporting the lifestyle of Madam Iulia and your daughter, and you lack a lot here at home… You can't even have a tenant."

"We live decently!" replied Hasdeu.

"But they pretend they're princesses over there… Your love for Lilica has blinded you! They're vain, my boy!"

It seemed the old woman had found something out from the "well-wishers" and was sharing their bitterness. And there were so many of those that aligned themselves one next to the other that they could reach Paris. There, Hasdeu's vanity and his authentic princely origin had caused smiles and ironies among his Romanian and foreign friends. But grandma's "boy" found out about it and got upset. He sent his family a few issues of *Columna* that contained his works and a printed supplement in which he had proven his origin and his forerunners that he was very proud of. He advised them to distribute them when needed, at the right time and place. His wife rushed to fulfill his wish, but Lilica preferred to throw in her arguments.

To prove his fatherly sacrifice, from time to time, Hasdeu sent news about their friends to his family in Paris, friends that didn't equal his ways as the head of the family, even proved themselves heartless. For example, he said that Hermina, "the poor girl," was being cared for by her old governess because her mother had moved back in with the painter. As a consolation, he added that she and Lilica might be able to correspond more often, and that his headaches were getting worse because they were not writing to him often enough… (November 1882).

Hermina also sent Lilica a long letter in which she lamented about her fate, a letter that was sprinkled with tears from both her and Lilica while she read it. The girl remembered her father had brought her a book from Hermina's mother,

Charlotte Walch at his last visit: *Carl Krinken: The Christmas Stocking* with the following dedication:

"A lily, from her affectionate friend and teacher," Charlotte Walch... Bucharest 1882.

Lilica took the book and put Hermina's letter in the middle so it could hug the epistle tightly... How could Charlotte Walch not do that and leave her daughter in the care of a stranger? How was that possible? How could some parents be like that? As a reply, Lilica went behind her mother who was knitting on the couch, hugged her, and kissed her cheek.

Lilica and her mother received wonderful news that meant they would have a more comfortable life. The government had awarded Iulia Hasdeu a scholarship worth 3,000 francs a year, thanks to their political and personal friend, Gheorghe Chițu, a valued philologist and instruction minister of those times. Hasdeu communicated that news to them and asked for discretion to avoid "inciting envy." He was happy about the painting Lilica had sent him to appease him while they were apart until Christmas or Epiphany when he was going to try to visit them. He also informed that Bishop Ghenadie was helping him to relocate Grandmother Maria to the monastery where Brătianu's sister was living, glad to be rid of her fastidiousness.

So, around Christmas Hasdeu traveled to Paris again, impatient to see his dear daughter, who had recently passed her partial exams with flying colors. Winter was hard, the road was long, and the train was slow, but there was a treasure at the end of the way. Christmas was holy even for a nonpracticing Christian such as Hasdeu, offering him warm days of privacy with his wife and daughter, and especially relaxing visits to museums or his friends. It was a time during which the father and the daughter conversed like two colleagues.

"So you prefer philology and history?"

"Yes, Father. I like classic and modern philology, but I also adore history and philosophy. Don't be upset, dear Papa, but philology compared to philosophy and history seems like chemistry to me, trapped in retorts and vials in a laboratory compared to the daring answers of the philosopher that go through centuries and limits of the mind. Am I right?"

"Well, dear Lilica, you are right and you are not."

"How come? I'm either right or wrong."

"This is why you are right: the work of a philosopher is tedious, time-consuming, linked to books and old documents, much knowledge, analogies, and conclusions, with a dose of linguistics and analysis. However, you are wrong because philology doesn't constrain the bounds of the mind, as once the origins, evolutions, morphologies, semantics are set in place, the truth becomes wider unexpectedly, and history feeds itself from those ideas that give it unexpected conclusions that come to crown philology with gratitude."

"I admit that what you're saying is true, dear Father. I treasure philology because it is close to my soul, and I hope the subject you've thought about for my doctorate corresponds to my aspirations, but…"

"I'm sure of it," said the father.

"But I'm barely in my fifth year of high school. I still have time to decide. Until then I can think and meditate…And especially learn."

"Obviously! What matters is that you are healthy, and you must be free. But especially healthy."

"Free?" asked Lilica, somehow suspicious…

"What I mean is that you must keep the freedom of your soul. You must be the way you are now, a child, a true candid child, influenced by nothing and nobody. Your whole love must be for your mother and me, and especially for our nation."

"Why are you telling me this, Papa?"

"Because you are thirteen and you're an exceptional child. You have the psychological development of a girl over twenty years old. Do you understand?"

"I can only assume."

"I want to talk to you like a good friend. In this world, there are bad people… especially men. You've noticed that yourself when you have young men such as Ornealu visiting you."

"They're insufferable and stupid."

"Did Ionescu-Gion write to you?" asked Hasdeu.

"Yes, Papa, he wrote a few lines to my mother with good wishes after my illness…"

"This man is serious and a good friend… You should write back to him as often as you can…"

"I'll do as you say!"

"But," Hasdeu stopped for a moment, "but… how is your poetry going?"

"My poetry?" said Lilica, pretending not to know about her hobby. "What poetry?"

"Do you still write poems?" insisted Hasdeu.

"Oh, no! Sometimes I have inspiration, but I don't write them down. Or even if I do, I throw them away. I don't have time for poetry when prose and school keep me busy all day… I'll have time for that later."

Hasdeu nodded knowingly, changed the subject, and they both continued their stroll through Luxembourg Park covered in winter sparkles. Lilica held her father's arm and enjoyed those moments to the fullest.

Hasdeu had found out that even though his daughter was keeping the truth from him, during the last exams she had suffered from migraines; but he had calmed down knowing that during his time in Paris his daughter had not complained of such things. Rest might have been the cure she needed.

In fact, the girl wrote down everything that popped in her head, drew faces, and read Shakespeare's *Macbeth*.

She had the opportunity to see Sarah Bernhardt's representation at the peak of her career (1882), when she was still young and playing Lady Macbeth, the sad queen of Scotland, with Marais as her partner in the main role. She critically examined everything with a precocious competency, even though she was barely in her thirteenth year of life. She dissected every character, compared the acting to the original text, and everyone's roles were analyzed comparatively with the classic Greek roles of Cleopatra, Agrippina, Electra, etc., just as Paul Albert, her forerunner, had done it. Here and there, Iulia Hasdeu's writings were completed by fine pen drawings; the faces she saw in her mind, and the ones she saw on the stage in the original English script, with critical observations, especially the ones of Taine (who was probably consulted at a later date, because the study was retouched in 1884 and 1886), with the conclusions of Victor Hugo on the masterpiece *Willy*. She compared Lady Macbeth with Frédégonde and explained why, studying the second one in the same year by invoking the studies of Jules Michelet, Cousin, and reproducing the original text of Euripides as a comparison. Iulia addressed the work of great Shakespeare in her study called *Mon Shakespeare* written from the way she understood him. Even though that work was finalized in the following years, it was still the brilliant study of a thirteen-year-old girl.[4]

---

[4] Theatre p. 193.

But school started again, her father was mostly away, and her mother realized that Lilica was suffering from migraines again and let her husband know about it. Even though he was mostly content with his life, he found himself shaken again and worried.

"I'm crushed by Lilica's migraines. What could they mean? As soon as winter is over she must take cold baths in the Seine…"

1883 was the prelude to literary inspiration for Iulia Hasdeu, that she constantly wrote down, but it was also a year of suffering that started quietly, then showed visibly in the few years she had left on earth, years full of diabolical diligence that filled the rich mind of that girl who loved everything beautiful, a year of creativity and everything else that diminished gradually until the time physical strength left her.

Following Al. Odobescu's example in the Romanian legation in Paris, Hasdeu wanted a position in the capital of France, an office, a teaching position, that could allow him to stay beside his daughter permanently, supervise her daily, take care of her, help her with classes and homework, as well as generally. That "what could that be?" had an immediate answer in his mind that originated from his advice for her to take cold baths, which was the usual treatment for neurasthenia. The girl was exhausting herself studying, taking so many other classes outside of school. Her father didn't know exactly if, during the night, when the mother was asleep, his daughter was sacrificing sleep to the calling of creation. There was only one truth.

"Dear Lilica, your head hurts because you keep reading at night," said her mother, "and you keep your book too close to your eyes."

"But I can't see otherwise."

"And what do you keep writing at night? Are you composing poems?"

"Oh, no!"

"Leave them, dear! I did nonsense in my youth as well. It wasn't to my advantage…"

"But Mother, there's nothing more beautiful in this world than poetry!"

"Okay, okay! Let others do that, not scholars!"

"Yes, Mother," said Lilica to her mother who was getting ready for bed.

But it wasn't the scholar working in the pale light of the lamp, writing thoughts, answers, or poetry, it was work inspired by the muse of the night or by the "alter ego" of a true poet, struggling in her soul like a butterfly about to emerge from its cocoon… And jailed thoughts escaped on the paper anonymously. Why? She didn't know. What demon was asking her questions about freedom? "You must be healthy and free." What angel gave her the answers? What "Pierre Dupont" came to free her from the terrible thought of having her life tied to a sick old man... while the young one was on his knees:

"Oh! My dear Louise (he said kneeling) you are so good! Dear child, I love you so much, and (he kisses her hand) I will always love you..."[5] (says young Pierre).

Thirteen-year-old Lilica saw love as a problem, just as it had gone through centuries incomprehensible at any age. Theoretically, her soul was trying naive solutions that were suggested to her by romantic novels and embellished even more by her imagination. What was love? What bitter filter separated only tears and poison from it? That's what was written by Hugo, Lamartine, Musset, George Sand, Shakespeare... Especially Shakespeare, whom she was reading in original, the complete edition,[6] printed in tiny letters among which Lilica drew women's faces, maybe the faces of the main characters as in other books in her library that are now collected in the State Archives.

That question tormented her day by day, year by year, until she passed... It was tormenting as she only knew the imperative meaning of love, the one that couldn't be denied or solved, the cruel meaning.

One of her thoughts on this problem was noted down as one of her scribbles: "Not loving is the worst crime." And as it would be seen later nobody would take more steps or fly higher through the obscure lands of it than her.

By that age, she had already read the romantic "contes bleus" or their adaptations such as *The Four Sons of Aymon*, Huon of Bordeaux, Amadis, Genevive of Brabant, Jean of Paris, the poems of Villion and Charles d'Orleans, Joung, Ossian, Schiller, Goethe, Bernardin of St. Pierre, Lamartine, Musset, and especially Hugo, who was her favorite. Her opinions about the world and the deep feelings in her heart were easily understood for that matter. Breezy, ideal, sacrificial, noble love was the only sentimental icon Iulia revered.

During the private visits mother Iulia and her daughter paid to the Bréal couple when Hasdeu visited Paris, the professor and the scholar realized the student was overwhelmed by the "evil of that century" as romanticism was called during the

---

[5] "Buvez de l'Eau" — proverbs. Terminé le 25 Aout 1883 — Volume Theatre p. 34

[6] The Globe edition, 1881.

eighteenth and nineteenth centuries because her thoughts were scattered, and her mind was aiming too high for her age.

"When do you have time to read that much, Ms. Hasdeu?" asked Michael Bréal during one of the visits.

"During my free time, Professor."

"So at noon and during the night, right?"

"Exactly! And during holidays."

"Do you think that is okay?"

"I don't know, but I know it's good for me…"

"I like your wordplay, but not your answer; because after mandatory studying you must rest."

"I rest when reading my favorite authors."

"Your romantics!"

"Yes, Professor, which are also your romantics."

"What do you mean?"

"They are my favorites, but they are your countrymen."

"Ms. Hasdeu, just so you know 'let's say' our romantics are not romantic at all in their private lives. Villon was a thief, Bernardin of St. Pierre was a traveler with no character or honor who never kept his promises, Musset was always in love and cheated on his lovers every day; even Hugo, your favorite, has many regrets related to his personal life. So, if you have the talent, you can write as they write, but you must not live as they live, and you mustn't have imaginary heroes, or idols. Other things mean more in life, such as science and philosophy which your father honors remarkably. Yes, yes, believe me!"

"I believe you, Professor, and I probably already proved it. I bow my head to science and philosophy, but I adore literature. I thank you for the information you provided about some authors, however…"

"True information!" Bréal rushed to add.

"Of course, but I think when it comes to literature what is important is the beauty of the creation, not the beauty of the author! Forgive me, I mean to say the beauty of the book, its value. Whatever was the private life of Villon, St. Pierre, or Hugo, their books are their work of art, their genius works…"

"I like this answer coming from a thirteen-year-old girl, but when this girl is twenty or older she will see that romanticism, no matter what genius wrote it, caused too much harm in the world..."

"It also caused plenty of good, Professor, because it made us dream of a better world..."

Bréal coughed, stood up, stroked the peachy cheeks of his student, and realized his casual conversation was not with a student, but with a small colleague...

Lilica finished her piano lessons because Ernestina had hardly paid much attention to them and had left their home after an argument, so the girl was playing it only for herself and not as often. She knew enough scales, arpeggios, and German *fingergeläufigkeit* (fluent fingers). The child had seen Pugnot, the great French pianist in a concert in Colonne. His touch was of another quality; it was soft, shaded, not like the rough one of Ernestina Feuchtinger. And there were so many other good artists.

Since she had studied piano and German with the same tutor, the girl had more free time to write drafts that were quite naive, as well as thoughts and interesting metaphors that she made sure to hide carefully. Even more, the letters to her father became true literary and satirical works, which Hasdeu was proudly reading to everyone after congratulating the small artist through his warm letters.

Around February 1883, Dr. Vlădescu died in Bucharest, even though he was still young. Hasdeu was heartbroken by the loss of his dear friend and wrote to his family in Paris, especially since Vlădescu had assisted in Lilica's birth, had taken care of her as a shield, and had loved her dearly.

On that occasion, the scholar gave them good news as well, telling them that the journalists from the *Românul, România Liberă, Timpul, Telegraful,* and *Războiul* newspapers, when they founded the Society of the Romanian press, chose him as the president with the majority of the votes, against C.A. Rosetti who'd lost. After more news, he ended his letter with the same theme:

"Lilica must stay healthy and study..."

They moved into a new apartment that was closer to the school. Rue de Condé, a street neighboring Saint-Sulpice Street was equal in length to Tournon Street where they had lived during the first year, but there were no military barracks there, and Lilica was straight across from Sevigné High School.

This high school had been established in a historical building. The street named after the great state politician Condé used to be the place where he had many of his properties, and the school used to be the home of the French man. At the time the high school was established it belonged to a countess who was a direct descendent of Condé's.

The neighborhood around St. Sulpice Cathedral was Catholic, with stores selling icons and various other religious merchandise.

That's why Hasdeu was glad "Condé Street was not in the way of anarchists (??!) and if you need you can find refuge at the Sévigné College…" On the occasion of this letter, he told them the International Society of Painters in Rome had released a splendid album resembling the "Paris-Murcie Album" to celebrate 400 years since the birth of Rafael, and he had been asked to send something in Romanian for the occasion:

"…Because Alecsandri only asked me and the Queen, and not people such as Ureche, I sent them a page. I sent it to you; read it and let me know your opinion: *La Madonna Velata...*"

But this Madonna (who sounded widowed most of all) who was supposed to be Romania after losing Bessarabia, is not worthy of being reproduced here, because it's far from Hasdeu's usual works. But from the lines above we understand three things. First, there was Hasdeu's ego, then his resentment towards Ureche, and finally his consideration towards Lilica, because her opinion was very important considering he saw her as a colleague, as he'd shown before.

Lilica's friend, Florica, was gravely ill. She sent her a long letter full of sweet talk and jokes, a true literary piece to cheer her sweet childhood friend up, especially since she missed her greatly and Florica had refused to join her in Paris. At the same time, Lilica sent letters to her other friends, Marie whom she loved with all her heart and who was the recipient of some of her morbid-romantic poetry other high schoolers were not capable of writing, also to her teachers to whom she sent true love declarations. For Lilica Hasdeu, this type of love was some kind of windowsill on which it rested as a dove that had escaped from its sad cage. The love rejected by her subconscious for a young man that would soon come into her life was first unchained towards her friend Maria, whose gentle and understanding soul, and moral and physical beauty had captivated her for so long at a higher level than Florica's and in another way.

In a draft that she had probably written a few years prior, after the work in 1877-1878, that took its final form in the summer of 1883, Iulia Hasdeu wrote the gentle love tale of the soul sister of a soldier that went to war, the sacrificial, heroic love as she saw it. Păuna, the girl, even though she is destined for the monastery, can't suppress her love for Bujor, but the boy is in love with another girl named Sultana. Bujor opens the girl's eyes to the sin of love and makes her resign herself to her fate.

"Thank you, brother, and I'm sorry. Without me realizing it and against my will, the subtle poison of love has sneaked into my heart…Forgive me…!"

After Bujor goes to war, Păuna becomes a nurse only to protect the life of her beloved. Fate takes her to the front just before Bujor is about to get shot, but before the bullet touches him, Păuna jumps in front of him and falls to the ground, saving the boy she loves.

"Now," she murmured, "you are free, brother; marry Sultana…"[7]

The "subtle poison," the "bitter filter" had truly crept into her compressed soul.

In the apartment on Condé Street, Lilica and her mother lived in two rooms with a hall in the middle on the second floor.

In the apartment on Saint-Sulpice Street, Lilica didn't have peace to read, and her mother couldn't sleep because of the neighbors living on the floor above. The neighbors at their current residence were an artist and a man working in a store, so it was completely quiet. The building administrator had let the mother know some foreigners were living there, but she didn't know their nationality. They seemed to be English because mother Iulia couldn't pronounce their names. One of them was an old man suffering from palsy, the other was his son who was a university student, but they didn't know at which university.

A few times they saw him going up or down the stairs with a worried look on his face. Lilica saw him from afar and she didn't know what he looked like. He must have been a very well-raised and gentle young man since he didn't seem to know anyone besides his father.

"Just like me! Poor boy!" said Lilica when she heard that.

One morning, at the end of February, Lilica left her apartment dressed in a high-collar coat and a scarf, closed the door, and started down the stairs to go to school when she found herself face to face with the young man. He greeted her and moved to let her pass. He had a wide forehead, his hair was combed back, and his bright eyes were bright blue. They both went down the stairs in a rush and each went their way in a quiet, respectful manner.

---

[7] (*Idylle Moldave*, Theatre)

"Was this the son of the paralyzed man?" Lilica asked herself. She answered herself indifferently. However, his unique features and the gentle manners in which he let her pass and greeted her respectfully didn't leave her mind.

But as the days passed her neighbors became quite absent. They didn't hear them leaving or coming home. Lilica knew to only play the piano quietly; maybe her neighbors didn't like music, maybe she was not very good at playing, maybe the young man was busy. The blue eyes were burning in her mind.

"No, none of this!!"

A few days later the administrator came to bring a few letters, entered Lilica's room, and confided in her. The night before when she was playing the piano, the young man had stopped in front of her apartment right next to the door listening, and when the administrator passed by her door the young man pretended to be just passing by and asked her if he'd gotten any letters.

"No, these are for Ms. Hasdeu," she told him.

"What?" he asked in French with a strong foreign accent.

"Has-deu," she emphasized to him.

"Thank you," he said. "I thought they were for me." He then walked up to his apartment...

During classes, the girl did her best as usual. Her lessons were prepared with diligence, but the rhythm of her studies slowed down. Her pen was often stopping mid-writing, the lines in books were becoming blurry, and her eyes were staring into space. Inexplicable tiredness was stopping her workflow. It might have been the spring approaching, a reflex of blue hues... maybe a reflex of past suffering that was hiding in her heart... Who knew?!

"What a beautiful thing sacrifice is, Mother!"

"It's beautiful if you need it. But why do you say that?"

"Oh, it's nothing, Mother! The world would be a much better place if everyone would sacrifice a bit for a loved one."

"For example, the sacrifice a child makes for his parent, such as the boy on the floor above."

"This sacrifice might also be duty, Mother," said Lilica in English.

"What?" asked the mother.

So Lilica repeated in their language while working on a translation from Homer that had never gone slower as it did that spring night in which the sunset rested a bit more above the towers of Paris…

Her fellow students noticed that Iulia Hasdeu was not paying attention in class, and aside from her good friend, Jeanne Créhange who loved that uprooted flower dearly, that Romanian girl with rosy chubby cheeks that seemed to be paler than usual, and her classmate, Marie Mavrodin whom Iulia loved, the others enjoyed when the top of the class became slow in answering questions. One of her geography tests was graded with a four and a question mark, which the professor brought up in class:

"Ms. Hasdeu, I graded you with a four only for your past work, because the test was worth less than that…"

Lilica blinked rapidly with red eyes and her chaotic answer echoed in the classroom: "I'm a little ill, Professor; I assure you I will make up for my grade."

"I hope so!"

"I assure you, I assure you, I assure you…"

That "I assure you" would have probably been repeated ten times if tears hadn't flooded the girl's cheeks and lips…

Her grades started dropping even at subjects in which the girl was better or equal to many of her classmates, such as Latin, Greek, history. The professors talked among themselves in the office and the word reached her mother as well.

"How could this happen, my girl? What's happening to you? I saw you reading every night. What are you reading? Why are your grades so low?" asked her mother a few days later.

"I don't know, Mother. I feel weak. I'm trying just like before…but…"

"You might be studying but I suspect you're writing poetry like you were doing in Bucharest when you were hiding away from us."

"No, Mother, I'm not writing, however…"

"Then I'll call for the doctor tomorrow… to check what ails you."

Often people's eyes that only see what is tangible, concrete, something concrete can be reduced to four or five current events, suffering must be manifested by the sixth one: "What ails you? Why don't you want to eat? Do you have a fever? No? Then what's wrong? What could be wrong? Be good and do your work!"

Scope of the soul!... A chroma that few artists can represent in its small and difficult shades, and which, however, together make an angelic melody!!

A few days later she received a letter from her father, the man whose understanding was amputated by distance:

"Dear Lilica, I was shocked to find out you stopped studying, and from the top of your class, you became the rear! I am so nervous that I don't know what to say and what to write. Now, when you're fourteen years old, when you're supposed to make your judgment, when you shouldn't be asked by your parents to do your work, when your country gave you great honor and the unique exception of a scholarship without having to take an exam for it; now you forgot who you are? I won't even mention my pain and the pain of your mother to whom you owe so much. Lying and laziness will make you lose ambition and dignity, it's only hard for someone to start because after that they'll start tumbling down lower and lower. Dear Lilica, think about it. I send you a kiss hoping that when you receive this letter you would already have straightened up your behavior and taken the right path. I eagerly wait for you to assure me of this by sending me your grades. The love of parents for their child is proven through sacrifice; the love of a child for their parents is proven through learning and respect.

Prove to us that you love us...

Your loving father, Bogdan"

(7/19 March 1883)

The harshness of those lines, full of bitter accusations, as well as the final note, hit sharply and bluntly at the same time in her young soul. The child was shivering with the letter in her hand wanting to hide it, but her mother was the one to open it first. Lilica sat motionless with tears in her eyes, humiliated, crying more inside than outside, and she was strongly affected for the next few days. She wanted to reply to his letter immediately, but her pen wouldn't obey her.

How could she talk to her good, understanding, and superior father of lying, laziness, and the loss of ambition and dignity? About "lying" especially? What was she lying about? How can someone be lying when they don't make any statement when they are chained by unknown titanic powers and their inner energy becomes sluggish? Laziness? What was this laziness? Was it an activity done willingly or against one's will, or was it a rebellion against working? How? Was she lazy? Did her philosopher father believe that? Her? "Have you forgotten who you are?" When did she forget this addition, this so-called pedestal that was always keeping her anchored like an obsession, which Papà kept reminding her about so often?

Lilica was desperate. The whip lashes left bleeding marks on her. They were burning her horribly... Her mother, instead of healing them, deepened them. Who could she talk to? And what could she talk about? What did she have to confess? She didn't know anything about what was causing it... She was feeling a vague nostalgia for the unknown, for a finality that made her shiver: death maybe!

The following Sunday the girl took advantage of her mother being out of the room, put a coat on, and went out alone. To where? Often these movements are reflexes, against our will, and our steps take us directly to safety; nobody can tell if these reflexes are impulses of our subconscious mind with precise but unknown goals.

Paris was burning under its seething furnaces. Spring had invited waves of people, carriages, and horse riders out on the streets and boulevards... The air was thick with a foreign, unusual feel. It smelled like buds, just as in the far garden of the Archives! Oh! The garden of the Archives was full of white lilacs, beloved, fragrant white lilacs whose shadow seemed white as well. They may have been the buds that had blossomed already from their thick glossy petals, bringing out small heads as a remembrance of the long-gone childhood...

Lilica didn't see almost anything of what was surrounding her; she was only careful not to bump into people. She was walking among lilac trees, among her friends Florica, Maria, Hermina, and Xida, who was now married... She felt new impressions in her soul... The sweet taste of freedom was overpowering the threats! Alone! She with her memories wider than any other view! Alone! Free! She walked ahead free. She had escaped!

She involuntarily stopped before two great gates. She gazed up in astonishment. Two lacy gates between great poles gave way to a row of stairs from where she could hear wide waves of harmony. She could hear the music of an organ. What was it playing? Oh, yes... Ave... Of course! This was the St. Sulpice Cathedral! She had not walked that far. Her feet took her up the steps and her soul complied... The Gothic arches were welcoming. Enormous Corinthian pillars were aligned on her right side, and two of Delacroix's frescos captured her attention for a few moments.

Everyone inside was praying and reflecting, but she could hear whispers, murmurs, and litanies... Once in a while, the devotees received notices after the sound of a bell. Suddenly the masterpiece of Cliquot, one of the greatest organs in the world unleashed its majestic song through the infinite hall... Lilica felt small, closed her eyes, tried to cross herself, and her soul crumpled in her chest in those echoes...

God was singing!

Everyone around her disappeared somewhere far away... It was hot in there but pleasant, and the air smelled like the myrrh that embalmed the altar and their hearts. Lilica listened, felt everything, touched the whole world. The world was now better, just like Florica, like Maria... She wanted to cry from relief. She wanted to forgive. Forgive who? She wanted to ask for forgiveness. But from whom?

Her feet took her running again.

"Forgive me, Mother! I left without permission! I was wrong! I know. I should have told you I wanted to go out. Enough, Mother! Yes, yes, you're right. I'll try to straighten myself, I already started... I'll do as Father says... As you wish... Trust me..."

"But where were you?"

"At St. Sulpice church."

"If you wanted to go to church I would have taken you to our Romanian church. Since when did you start going out by yourself?"

"I won't do it again, Mother. I'm crazy... But I'll better myself. Trust me! You'll see! Lilica was wrong. Lilica needs you to forgive her..."

The nearby table full of books and notebooks received her and she became its prisoner again. Her poetry came again after she called for it... She hung on to it with her nails, calling to it with deaf screams.

And Lilica got better. Became a diligent student again with superhuman powers. Her strength was fighting against the torment of dreams and inspiration that tried to break into her closed mind daily. She fought against it and succeeded.

But every war takes its toll...

She didn't raise her gaze anymore while going down the stairs and she didn't answer any more greetings. And she especially stopped playing the piano. It was the best thing to do. This secret chest with dozens of keys contained divine voices, passionate callings, echoes that tried to escape out the door or out the window... and that wasn't good for her.

The room of a schoolgirl must be a prison, with its isolation, equations, translations, homework, and fears. The room of Hasdeu's daughter especially! A cat should be the only companion...

Weekly she received care packages from Bucharest with caviar, halva, olives, and other delicacies the small patient appreciated. She also received a medicine book about myopia, and the anatomy and physiology of the eyes, about deformations the human eye could suffer, the causes of myopia and its treatment, a book that she had to read despite that disability, as her myopia could simply be fixed by hygiene. In a letter, her father informed her about the growth of his beard, about the money she was going to receive, and other benefits the schoolgirl was about to get:

"...I'm waiting for a letter from your mother to tell me you're doing well in school again...

The election for the Deputy Chamber has started. I have a lot of support in Craiova. If I win, your mother will be glad to know I could choose to be a deputy in Paris, so we'll be able to stay there together until you obtain your Ph.D., and that gives me peace of mind..."

Ph.D., bachelor's degree, but before that she must first graduate high school! And Iulia was barely in the fifth year! Yes, but her strength must be trained daily. The race was too long, the finish line was too far, and her horse was not a fierce and noble animal, but a Pegasus...

But aside from his psychological activism, Hasdeu was sure of the physical one as well. His value and work stamina must be reflected in his child as well. She was Hasdeu's daughter! And that was enough!

The physical changes of puberty, the vague soar towards an ideal, the natural questions about the world, the spring breeze, all these auras of the teenage years had skipped the minds of her parents and her professors. Hasdeu didn't realize it either. The laziness some children feel during this delicate stage of youth is not real laziness, loss of focus, or lying. No! Maybe this was the cause of her problems.

The child lied because she couldn't tell the truth about what she was feeling. Truth be told, she didn't quite understand what she was feeling. But her parents and professors were guilty of discarding unknown causes when it came to a child they knew well. Their lies were often fatal.

"Pay attention to puberty," said some unknown scholar. Was it possible that Hasdeu never read this warning, even though his daughter was approaching this stage in her life?!

Besides her everyday schoolwork that was taking most hours of the day, including private tutoring and barely keeping her Pegasus in control, Iulia had to write letters to her father constantly, a few telegrams as well to let him know she was well. She also had to send letters to her friends that she missed so much, here and there a letter for a former teacher… However, she became the top of her class again thanks to her fast-paced lessons.

She carefully avoided the blue eyes… but she couldn't avoid her memory of them; she tried to compartmentalize her mind.

That's why in May of 1883, Hasdeu wrote to his family to complain about physiological laments: "I'm very worried about Lilica's migraines. They are connected to her myopia… She must not overdo it because she has plenty of time in the future…"

His letters produced genuine amazement. How could they not mind the effect when he was the main cause? Migraines? They were related to something other than overwork, maybe that obvious asthenia related to her age. And why would anyone believe that myopia produced migraines when it was obvious it was the other way around? And nobody would talk about glasses.

It was true that the child was suffering from terrible migraines, but sometimes she didn't even mention them. Her mother was very worried about her… Sometimes, when the migraines surpassed her teenage patience, she dropped her head, the pain thumping, and she stayed there, holding it in her hands. The pain was unbearable, and she couldn't see clearly.

"What's wrong, Lilica? Is your head hurting again?"

"Just a little, Mother, don't worry. Bring me a cold compress and it will help."

"Shouldn't I make bring you some potatoes and vinegar?"

"No, it stinks and I can't handle it," said the powerless girl.

"Then put the book down! Should I bring you a sour lemonade?"

"No, it will go away with a cold compress," said Lilica, losing her patience, knowing her exams were getting closer, and that she had to be better than everyone else, just like in the past because she was Hasdeu's daughter. Bréal, Gazier, and Picot repeated to her that she was lazy while she was going through this crisis. Even though Hasdeu was very worried about her migraines, he was involved in politics, in the Craiova elections where with Chițu's and I. Brătianu's help, he was elected as a deputy because of the success of young Romanescu, the son of a doctor and leader of the city. So the Romanian scholar walked off the train triumphantly, was cheered and very proud of the "triumphal march" in the capital of money, in Oltenia. When I.C. Brătianu asked him how his goddaughter was doing, he replied: "She will make you proud through her studies and morals."

So, Iulia was not just Hasdeu's daughter, but also the goddaughter of I.C. Brătianu…

The great philologist would one day admit that all these were equal to "a girl transforming into a boy," and it would have been better to bring the girl to her father's home where she could have graduated university slower but more effectively. If that had happened, Iulia Hasdeu wouldn't have been any less a genius than she was. She was a compressed genius patented by a rushed system, but one affirming slowly, healthy and viable.

Chapter VII

The Blooming Flowerpot

A few days later the mother left to pay a visit to her friends, the families Odobescu and Popovici. Shortly after that, the administrator walked up the stairs, knocked at the door, and entered holding a small box in her hand.

"Here, miss, I know you suffer from migraines. I got some medicine from someone. Let me give them to you."

"Thank you, but what medicine is this?"

"They're pills that will help with your migraines immediately. You must take one when you feel them coming, lie down for ten minutes, and that's it. It will pass! The person who gave them to me also had migraines, and this is what helped them."

"Oh, thank you so much, madam!"

After she left, Lilica took the box, opened it, and saw four white pills inside. The writing on the box was in English: "for headache." It was a man's handwriting. Who could she have gotten them from? Was she the direct or the indirect recipient? "The person who gave them to me also had migraines." Lilica stood up and ran to the administrator's office.

"Who gave them to you, madam?" she asked in a whisper.

"I can't tell you. All I can tell you is that they gave them to me for you because they found out you were suffering… Goodbye, miss," she said, going out the door.

Lilica made a plan to find out. She had the perfect way to learn if the pills came from the person she suspected. Just then, she felt another migraine coming. She took a pill, drank a bit of water, lay down on the sofa, and lay there with her eyes closed and her mind wide open. Waiting…one to two minutes. Nothing! Five more minutes! Nothing! She opened her eye wide. Her eyes were clear… A weird feeling was flowing down her nasal bridge that opened her airways, evacuating them of some sort of congestion and pressure. Five more minutes. Lilica jumped off the sofa and sang. What? Something that had come to her from far away, seas and countries away... Her head wasn't pounding anymore... She started studying again and everything went smoothly.

The next day when she returned from school and walked up the stairs, she met the young man from the floor above who was coming from the opposite direction. It was the perfect time for her plan! She would only thank him in English when he passed by her. If he didn't ask her anything, he was the one; if he asked, she wouldn't say anything and would just run up the steps. Her jaw was clenched and the moment was approaching. Oh, why did she have to be so shy? They were on the same flight of steps now. *Come on, say it!*

"Thank you!" Lilica blurted out...

The young man stopped quietly for a moment, but Lilica was already running up the steps; she unlocked the door, entered, closed the door, and stuck her ear against the door listening. Nothing... Nothing! Her pounding heart was now starting to slow down.

Mignon, the dog, was at her feet. Lilica picked her up, cuddled her, talked to her, gave her some sugar, and the tail of the little dog was wagging happily.

Shortly after, the image of her father appeared angry in her mind. What would he say if he found out about her behavior? He would surely scold her. She was forbidden to go out alone except for going to classes, and she was especially forbidden from talking to strangers. "Men are dangerous and malicious!" And much other advice... But what harm had she done? She was just being polite, nothing more. Yes! If he was not her benefactor, then who was? He was silent! What if her mother found out from the administrator? What if Lilica told her? Would her mother understand? No!! She couldn't tell anyone. Nobody would ever find out anything! Why was it that important? It was simple neighborly help and a simple gesture of gratitude from her. Was that all? Lilica, Hasdeu's daughter, couldn't be neighborly or grateful.

But her father was caught in the chains of politics and completely forgot about glasses or migraines; traveling, giving speeches and conferences to gain electoral popularity.

"I am convinced again that I'm very popular among my people in Oltenia."

Her grandmother was finally sent to the Ciorogârla Monastery. Mrs. Svârlescu was now in charge of the household and the garden. The dogs were guarding the house and livestock...

Lilica felt the need to talk to her father more than ever. Seeing his absence was longer than usual, she decided to write a pathetic letter: "What did we do to deserve being abandoned in a foreign country?"

Hasdeu replied to her letter talking about politics, their home, but he also informed her he would join them in Paris for the summer, from where they would travel together to Copenhagen or Lisbon because they haven't visited Spain or Portugal yet…

And again: "How are Lilica's migraines? I'm very worried about her."

At the beginning of June, he sent them another letter, telling them about his trip to Iași where he had represented Oltenia at the inauguration of Stephen the Great's statue. His speech had been published in *Românul* and had been greatly appreciated by the public in Moldova's capital and the rest of the country.

The mother was working on sewing dresses for the school she'd been caring for in Bucharest and sent them to Hasdeu to offer them as graduation prizes. Finally, Hasdeu let them know that Bucharest was going through a terrible heatwave:

"It's horrible! I'm not surprised that poor Eminescu went crazy from the heat, the day before yesterday they took him to the nuthouse."

(July 1st, 1883)

So Hasdeu thought Eminescu lost his mind because of the great heatwave of the season… and not because of the coldness of the ungrateful public and the officials towards his suffering that had precise and deep causes that had required their attention to save this genius representative of the Romanian nation… Again, the science of human biology showed its force in the titan of all the other sciences that Hasdeu was. The letter didn't come as an attempt on Hasdeu's part to insult the poet, even though he didn't value him enough.

Lilica was working hard for the fifth-year exam. Paris was under intense heat as well, and people were getting bored. She had her issues that didn't include speeches and conferences, but silently concealed her fears. However, algebra, geography, and classic languages were equally important. They knew how to mercilessly impose in her mind. Lilica didn't hesitate. She refused to suffer but relied on patience. She was Hasdeu's daughter after all, and Brătianu's goddaughter. And so she passed the exams just like in the past but she only ranked second in her year.

During the French exam, she almost fainted. She felt a sudden void in her mind and seemed to sway. But the strong young arms grabbed the desk and held her steady. She confused two works of Georges Sand with the ones of Mrs. Necker of Staël. A daze! But she came back to her senses, corrected herself immediately with strength she didn't even know she had helped by bright images in her mind. The professor listened in amazement to the way she corrected herself, the details and explanations of the works of the writer she had read over and over again, interpreted by Iulia Hasdeu: Indiana and Lelia on one side, Delphine and Corriene on the other side.

Once the exams were finished and the prizes were given, Lilica and her mother went out for walks every day to visit Versailles, le Bois de Boulogne, Auteuil, and Luxembourg. After resting her soul in museums, they went back to their routine. Aside from writing a bit of poetry, Iulia managed to finish the story *Idylle Moldave* (the skeleton of a drama or a novel) and *Le Fils de Frédégonde* (a drama). By the end of summer, she finished the proverb *Buvez de l'Eau* (drink water) and came up with ideas for other stories, novels, or theatre plays.

The first one mirrored her memories of the war in 1877-1878, and the sacrifice of true love portrayed before in the novel about Bujor and Păuna, but the beginning of *Idylle Moldave* is worthy of being mentioned because it showed the mature thinking of a thirteen-year-old when it came to the true noble character and the respect the author had for peasants:

> "A nobleman does not claim to be noble because of his lineage, but for being the one who puts his dignity above lineage; a real peasant, crude, uneducated, simple, naive, but noble though his connection to nature, and through nature to God. Simple men are ennobled by the way they behave with one another…
>
> The scene takes place in Romania…"

In *Le Fils de Frédégonde*, Iulia Hasdeu aimed to portray a historical theme from the beginnings of France, featuring Chilpéric, Frédégonde, Sigebert, and Mérovée, with crimes, revenge, monasteries, and more, and *Buvez de l'Eau* that we mentioned before, is a love story centering around a young girl who was in love with a boy, but she was betrothed to his father… The story is naive, ironic in parts, and aimed to show how normal love was supposed to be…

The naivety of the thirteen-year-old girl reflected, however, a true literary balance.

Meanwhile, Hasdeu finished his classes in Bucharest, prepared the future issues of *Columna* that had to be published that summer, and obtained the money necessary to travel to Paris and to the resort where Lilica had to go following the doctor's recommendation. He arrived in Paris with everything required for his vacation. They decided not to travel to Sweden. It was too far and too cold. They also gave up on traveling to Spain or Portugal since the weather there was unstable.

Lilica needed to be in a mild Nordic climate, with not too much heat, but where the temperatures didn't oscillate too much, a resort near the sea where she could do heliotherapy. After asking around for advice, they decided to travel to the Netherlands, a country with a beach in the northwest, a healthy ambiance, and friendly locals.

Hasdeu was thrilled to find out from the professors that his daughter had started working hard again after her moment of confusion, which might have been caused by some physical illness, and he was very excited to be able to watch her closely. She was forbidden to read, but Lilica only half listened to him. She had some leftover space at the bottom of her suitcase, where she hid some books between clothes, such as books by Molière, and the novel of Ms. Scudéry, *Clélie*, and *Le Grand Cyrus*, a novel she had recently heard about from Professor Albert.

While everyone was packing, the administrator rushed to bring them news in the form of two letters for Mr. Hasdeu, pronouncing his name in an archaic Celtic accent, as suited a magister of his rank, and she took the time to whisper to Lilica that the young man was also leaving for England and that he had asked where she and her family were going. She had told him she didn't know, but she wouldn't have disclosed it even if she knew, because she was a very discreet woman. However, Lilica took a walk outside in the evening and met the administrator again, who was more than willing to give her more information about him.

"The young man speaks French poorly, not like you, dear Miss Joulie. You speak like a true French woman!"

Lilica didn't go. She was not being called by something precise. Maybe she was, but she heard another call that was louder and more demanding!

The train sped along the railway. The north of France was seen in passing but she glimpsed interesting aspects, especially the Loire Valley with its hills, small castles, and people working the fields. They stopped for a couple of days in Belgium, in Liège, then Anvers, Rotterdam, and the Hague. The family spent a week in Scheveningen, a small harbor with a beautiful beach, and finally, they traveled to Zandvoort where they rested for a week under the bright sun of the North Sea. Hotel Curhus housed them warmly in two rooms with a view of the sea. A light headache urged her to look in her bag for the pills…

Lilica lost her gaze over the infinite water. She saw seagulls with wide wings flying in circles, diving in the waves, spotting the blue waters like the petals of a dahlia.

Sailboats with fishermen at work were barely visible in the distance. Under her windows, there was a park with flowers in many colors that invited her to lie in the shade and dream. The family of three drank their coffee quietly, in a relaxing meditation. When Hasdeu finally asked his daughter something, Lilica's eyes stopped on two blue reflexes on the surface of the water…

"Your migraines are gone now, right Lilica?"

"Yes, Papa! I'm rested. The sea relaxes me. How about you?"

"Me and your mother both! Right?" Hasdeu leaned towards his wife.

"I feel immortal," exclaimed Lilica lifting her arms towards the sky and making a wide gesture towards the water, feeling like she could hold it in her small rosy hands. "Yes, immortal like this sea, like God who speaks through the music of the waves. Immortal like love itself…" she stopped for a moment, "love that God used to create us and that I feel for both of you. You believe in God, Papa, right?"

"Did you ever doubt this, Lilica?"

"I didn't! Others did…"

"How about you, Iulia? Do you believe I do?"

"What do you mean?" asked his wife. "I know you don't go to church."

"I'm too busy, that's why! But I do pray, and God helps me. If only you knew how much I prayed when Lilica was sick! And during these past few months when she was suffering from migraines… Especially when she had trouble with studying… I still can't understand what happened to you."

"I don't know either, Papa! I don't know either… It was something like… an imbalance in my heart… It was hard to breathe, my hands were heavy, my head was heavy… An accident? Who knows..."

And the girl's eyes went back to the blue horizon where the two reflexes persisted.

Her parents had discussed it the day before, trying to reach a conclusion.

"Iulia, do you think she might be suffering because of too much work?"

"I don't know, but I think her eyes have something to do with it," said the wife.

"I think so too, but do you think there's something else?"

"What else?"

"How am I supposed to know? I thought you as a woman understand her better... Don't you think she's precocious when it comes to...? You know... Do you think we should get her married?" asked Hasdeu.

"Oh my! What's with that idea? Are you a child?"

"Maybe it's genetic! My mother had to get married at thirteen... I'm just saying. My thoughts are scattered. Classes require work, and if her head will keep hurting... Listen, Iulia. You must watch her closely. If it's a sentimental nature, then..."

"What do you keep saying, dear? Does it look like that to you? I'm here too."

"I'm serious, dear Iulia."

"I'm serious as well!"

"Listen, dear. What do you think about young Ionescu-Gion?"

"I like him."

"I'm glad to hear that. Don't you think he's a suitable match for our daughter for when the time comes?"

"I think we should mind her health for now... that's what I worry about! Leave this nonsense about marriage for later."

The following evening found Lilica in her room, thinking about the past. Her parents were asleep in the other room, happy about her improving health. Improving health? Sometimes she felt it, sometimes not... Her breathing seemed to slow down from time to time, her lungs seemed to struggle. Oh, no! Her breathing was surely changed by some internal struggle. Maybe it was an inspiration! She opened the window. The salty breeze and the smell of the park entered the room and kissed her eyes, her cheeks, her palms... Who sent it so generously?... Who?

Did you ever listen when the night is clear,
The sea's secret hymn rising to the stars?
It's God's voice, my friends, from the divine sphere;
A voice the Creator of blissful charms
Lent the waves to teach us his laws and his will.

These verses she wrote at that time later became part of the poem *Au bord de la mer* (*On the Seashore*), with the motto: "It's the Lord, it's God" of Hugo, a poem that she would write two years later in Paris.[8] Iulia Hasdeu's poetic soul of transcendental essence and amazing divine intuition was clearly reflected by it, despite her being only thirteen years old.

The days flowed smoothly, relaxed, and dreamy, in a quiet understanding among the three souls that were bound by the same love. And so the vacation ended. It ended just as it had begun, the moments flew just like the past years and centuries... with memories and forgiveness.

The end of August found them back in Paris, and Hasdeu was forced to leave his dear family yet again and return to his home country. He had detours in Florence and Rome for studies, in Vienna to visit his uncle, then in Budapest to finish his manuscript *Anonymus Lugoshiensis*. Once he returned to Bucharest, he went back to his work. That was the time when he realized how dangerous his journey on the train with his girls was when they had to travel with three men who pretended to be Turkish or Greek but were, in fact, gamblers and adventurers. Passing through Craiova, he stopped to visit his good friend Gheorghe Chițu.

Around the start of the new school year, mother Iulia took her daughter on carriage rides through the wonderful forests surrounding Paris. During one of these rides, when Mignon the dog joined them on Lilica's knees, they assisted in a comic-tragic event. At the sight of another dog that was barking, Mignon jumped out of the carriage and attacked its rival. Lilica and her mother called for her, and also called for the driver to stop, but that rude man pretended to be above everyone else and said, "For a dog!" as he didn't feel like stopping for two fighting mongrels. The mother stood up, shouted again, and seeing a tuff of Mignon's fur in the middle of the road she jumped out of the carriage. Lilica screamed, and finally, the carriage driver stopped. However, the mother ended up with a sprained arm and Lilica with a terrible scare...

Hasdeu found out about this event from one of Lilica's letters and replied, upset with them for not grabbing the driver by the arm and forcing him to stop, giving them as an example a similar case from Russia when the passengers decided to take down the one holding the reins... In that letter, he informed them of the fact that Frățilă, his devoted helper at *Columna*, had received a scholarship to study in Gratz with the great Schuchardt for a year, after which he would go to Paris. The mother

---

[8] "Au bord de la mer," in Julie (Iulia) Hasdeu, *Oeuvre poétique / Opera poetică*, ed. I. Oprișan (București: Editura Saeculum, 2017), pp. 180-181.

and daughter read the letter again and commented on the news. How could they have grabbed the driver? That was ridiculous!

The fall of 1883 arrived with its usual signs, with a rich harvest, red-cheeked children walking happily with the memory of vacation and the worry of a new school year, with piles of books and schedules. Jeanne Créhange, her bench mate, Marie Mavrodin, Berthe Horsh, Marie Meyer, Elli and Margaret Scott were gathered before the school rekindling their friendship abandoned two months before, and recounting small adventures from the summer vacations, confessing things that nobody else knew aside from those classmates that protected each other's secrets... Iulia was more flushed, Jeanne was skinnier, Marie was chubbier.

"Did you compose anything else, Iulia?" asked Jeanne.

"Nothing, or almost nothing," said Lilica. "Plans, projects, this type of stuff... I have enough ideas in my head for two lifetimes. If I could only live a long one! Poems, novels, plays... so many, barely sketched... When would I have time to write them down? My parents on one side, Bréal and Gazier on another side... exhaustion above all else."

"And Albert on another side...," added Jeanne Créhange.

"Albert is the only professor who is close to our young souls," corrected Lilica.

"Maybe to yours," interfered Marie Meyer.

"Maybe to yours especially, dear Marie, since you follow the same religion," said Lilica.

"That didn't stop him from grading me with a six in French," added the Jewish girl.

Other confessions were being shared in another group, among which was Margareta Talois, Lilica's rival when it came to prizes, who had received the first place the year before, and who was throwing side glances her way.

That group had managed to start protests and comments regarding the prizes, which resurfaced at that time. Lilica didn't hold any resentment toward that girl, but she decided to do her best and surpass her. She had sworn it to her father. She was going to be at the top of her class in sixth grade. Yes! Hasdeu had not forced her to promise she was going to achieve that, realizing that placing second was a great accomplishment on her part after the illness in January and February. He also tried to restrain himself from scolding her.

Another thing happened that year. Ms. Salomon, a professor for the Superior Grade became the principal of the school, and she was not very fond of this student considering she was the daughter of a notorious antisemitic Romanian.

The start of the school year was nerve-wracking for Lilica and Marie Mavrodin, who became a confidante of the Romanian student. Lilica wanted to switch schools, but Marie didn't let her. They would make it. They had to.

Lilica wrote a letter to her father trying to explain the situation by using humor. Hasdeu replied to her with an appreciation for the style that showed "liveliness and variety, I confess that Lilica is victorious." He also advised her not to switch schools despite all the "Jewish airs of Ms. Bréal," the daughter of the former principal, who was even more insolent than in the past. Regarding Lilica's diligence with the ambition of surpassing the "terrible Margareta" at the start of the new school year, Hasdeu advised her not to exaggerate after remembering his behavior from the previous year and probably feeling some regret.

> "...I don't want you to overwork yourself and leave your health in the second place, because your chest and eyes will suffer. You must always keep this in your mind. It's better to be in second place after Margareta, healthy and lively, rather than to be at the top of your class, but sick and broken.

> If you study too much you will start to resent it. You must always measure your work in such a way that you will never lose the pleasure of working and not damage your health.

> You two should consider my words and deduce how far can the physical build of a thirteen-year-old can go when fighting against a sturdy girl such as Margareta, whose intelligence will always be inferior to Lilica's anyway. Don't forget about your myopia, which needs special care, especially rest and avoiding books printed in a small font.

> Other parents need to push their children to get them to study. I'm such a happy father to see myself required to ask my daughter to rest more..."

"Other parents"? Which ones would those be? Hasdeu's voluble spirit tried to create diversions; of course, his excellent memory had whispered something else in his ear... Only a few months had passed from that terrible accusation: "Now when you're already fourteen years old, you must make your own decisions, your parents shouldn't force you anymore...," a phrase that had injured the girl's heart deeply, and that had brought scattered energy that hurt the depths of that small chest. She had felt it even stronger since she was still recovering from the measles, and Hasdeu was trying to fix what he had said. Wasn't it already too late?

Invigorated by sunbathing on the beach and the salty air of the sea, Lilica couldn't contain her excitement. Her success was very likely, which made her father write her another letter.

"Lilica's success makes me very happy and proud…"

Without his knowledge, however, Lilica had managed to catch a cold that had turned into bronchitis; nobody knew when it started or when it was going to end…

On the 14th of November, when Lilica turned fourteen years old, she received a letter from her father who was very worried about her health.

"Happy birthday, my baby! Many happy years to the one who is the happiness of her parents and the pride of her country! But take care of yourself, mind your health, your eyes, and your chest. The bronchitis you've been suffering from upsets me and you shouldn't let history repeat itself because your chest is delicate…"

Perhaps as a result of guilt, Hasdeu found more jobs to work on so he could send more money to his family and their friends, especially to Ghiuri, who was his wife's protégé, who was also studying in Paris.

At her mother's advice, Lilica found ways to entertain herself by playing pranks, playing with her dog, annoying her cat, singing and dancing through the house.

On Christmas Eve, she found a nicely illustrated magazine in English among their correspondence, which told her the Englishman had returned recently and he had "forgotten" the magazine with the administrator. She spent time browsing through the pages of prose and poetry. Among the verses, she found some that were signed as "Albert James," a name that was underlined in red. Who could that poet be? It was an idyllic poem, quite well-written, and with an obvious emphasis on honesty; the love of a Scottish shepherd for his shepherdess…

But studies kept her anchored at her desk. During the first few months, she had great grades, superior to even the ones of "terrible Margareta," the daughter of some merchant… Lilica was studying diligently and rampantly.

Her mother started having strange dreams, including reliving the dream she'd had before giving birth to her daughter. She wrote to Hasdeu about them, even though according to Lilica they were not bad omens. But her last dream proved to be one. Hasdeu at least confirmed it in his letter from the 5th of December 1883. He had been seriously ill, with a severe sore throat and chest pains, and his doctors were advising him to quit smoking:

"You couldn't even imagine what was the result of my illness, but the good news is that Hasdeu has stopped smoking…"

His dear family was extremely happy about it as well as the new Swedish housekeeper because Hasdeu had always had "great sympathy and admiration for Gustav Adolf's country…"

However, quitting smoking was short-lived. A doctor, or better yet, a friend had told the magister not to smoke a full cigarette, but to smoke two or three puffs and throw it away, because of a harmful chemical reaction between carbon dioxide, nicotine, and the other components that happened only after the first few puffs. His office was now littered with different-sized cigarette butts, sheets of paper, crumpled paper, and cigarette ash…

He was not able to visit them for Christmas, but he asked them to have patience until Easter. The main cause was the financial difficulty. Hasdeu was putting his needs in second place so his family had everything they needed for winter.

"I'm very worried about Lilica's migraines…

Bismarck got word from Schuchardt probably that Lilica hates German…

She can hate a German man or another, but when it comes to science, especially the ones dealing with history and philology, there's no progress possible without speaking German…"

17th of December 1883

Meanwhile, I.C. Brătianu and his wife arrived in Paris. Hasdeu's wife and their daughter greeted them at the train station, knowing about their arrival from a previous letter. Hasdeu was glad about the way they had been received by his family, especially since "Mrs. Brătianu is an exemplary mother just like Mrs. Hasdeu and, at the same time, a pure Romanian and a very modest woman."

Finally, "the mother's second dream about me didn't come true. I'm healthy now and I'm grateful, not for me, but for you. Now, my angels, I send you thousands and thousands of kisses and wishes for happiness…," said the father in the Christmas letter of that year.

It was curious the godparents spent a whole day with their relatives and didn't mention the rumors about Lilica that had been spread by Bismarck.

Iulia's aversion towards Germans didn't take a bad form except in the mind of her father, as he would later admit since the mother and daughter would often pay visits to the parents of one of her classmates, who was German. Regarding Bismarck's remarks, Lilica replied with a funny letter full of caricatures among which was a drawing of Mignon's newborn puppy, born under the bed after the incident with the carriage driver. Hasdeu read it, smiling at her clever words which had just confirmed again the genius line of the family, after which he replied in the same manner with news from home. He said "the old women are well, the animals as well but we can feel Frățilă's absence because nobody is here to help me with *Columna*. I don't know whether to categorize Frățilă as an old woman or an animal. He's something in between..." The devotion of the apprentice that was now studying in Gratz was explainable. One of the old women was his annoying grandmother who was half a nun and half a lady.

Among the visits they received in Paris was one from another of Hasdeu's true friends, the Jewish philosopher Șăiteanu Lazăr, a man truly treasured by him. After he returned to Romania he visited Hasdeu to bring news about his wife and daughter, telling him his daughter worked too much. During the discussions between him and Lilica, he was surprised by her knowledge of literature and philosophy, but she didn't know what to make of him, since he was significantly inferior to her when it came to literature. Șăiteanu also told Hasdeu that his daughter had started to forget her native tongue. Lilica might have just preferred to speak to him in French because he was skilled at it as well.

Around Christmas 1883, on the 23rd of December, Lilica had a weird dream that she wrote down. She was in the cave where Archangel Michael had come to teach Mohammed about the laws of God. There were other people holding torches there: Turks, Arabians, Persians. At the signal of one of them, all fell to their knees and started praying to Allah. Choking on the smoke from the torches she looked for a way out, but the only one was above her head. While climbing towards the exit she heard a terrible voice saying "cursed be the wicked who leaves the holy cave during prayer." But she got out nonetheless. All around her was just water, the sea. Lilica jumped up, feeling wings sprouting on her back and flew like a small bird. The priest who had shouted behind her also turned into a bird and followed her. She shouted to her God and suddenly the priest lost his wings and fell in the waves, while she sat on a glowing cloud looking down. On the cloud was an immense golden palace, brilliant and calming. The girl was dressed in all white, and her hair had an intoxicating scent. She was an angel. A flock of small birds led her to a crystal-clear pond inviting her to bathe in it. She replied, "No, I'd rather sleep!" So she was transported to a room full of flowers. She lay down on a bed of lilies and roses, and the birds put her to sleep with their chirping. Lilica dreamt of herself in Germany with her mother, near Munich, in a beautiful house with a garden. While walking on a nearby field they saw a carriage pulled by four horses, and Bismarck was traveling inside it. The girl was sitting in the grass and a peasant shouted at her to stand up. However, she replied, "Shame to Bismarck! The Latin people mock him, because his kingdom is in hell, while ours is in heaven!" And after saying these words, she woke up.

This dream was caused by the dispute between her and her father regarding her phobia of Germans. In the next letter, Hasdeu quoted from *Sic Cogito*, using it as a document to talk about the border between time and space, and show how "the border between space and time is completely erased while dreaming."

1884 brought many rewards for Hasdeu but also worries. His family received an exceptional letter from the ambitious and proud man, as he often appeared.

It was incontestable that on the chart of intellectual values, modesty didn't deserve Cinderella's fate. But if it was left aside by the majority of those who feel like they're above it and replaced with egocentrism, which is the domain of every mediocre person, the trite values which are high on that chart are allowed to show a bit of vanity which looks good on them anyway. Hasdeu's vanity was notorious, but not the cerebral abundance that God had bestowed on him. That's why he wrote with sincerity and balance:

"I was given an honor I didn't expect, even though I'm a very ambitious man. You know I'm convicted to exile in Siberia for being viewed as some sort of a nihilist in Russia, ever since I was in Bessarabia. Well, the Imperial Academy of Sciences in St. Petersburg chose me as a member in its meeting on the 10th of January.

At the same time, they named two illustrious Frenchmen as members, Fisserand the astronomer and Jules Oppert the orientalist. This membership raised my rank which will allow me to ask for my father's fortune at the right time, even though I'll sacrifice it if I must just as I always sacrificed everything for Romania. The most valuable treasure is a man's head and heart, knowledge, and conscience…"

His wife was flattered, and Lilica was extremely happy. They shared the news with Odobescu and Ghiuri. The girl bragged about it at school despite Ms. Bréal; the administrator didn't ignore the brilliant news. The "discreet" old woman had people to share it within the building… Shortly after that, Lilica shared it with excitement with a bard she admired, Vasile Alecsandri, but he had already learned about it back home. Do we even have to mention the letters sent by Lilica to her father? They are worthy of the daughter of a great poet.

A few days later, on the occasion of the name day of her father, Lilica played a prank on the French telegraph, and instead of two words she only wrote one, "*Happybirthday!*" Seeing the post, employees fell easily fell for it. She repeated it to inform him of a school party organized by the principal of the school, where aside from music, games, and recitals, the girls were also allowed to dance. She telegraphed only one word again, "*Ballattheschool*." Both those telegrams were passed around their friends in Bucharest, and especially Lilica's friends who were greatly amused by the cleverness of their friend.

In school, Lilica stood her ground and didn't try to hide her hostility toward the principal who was trying to make her life a nightmare. And Hasdeu advised her not to give up.

> "I suffered a lot in my life and I still do, but with zeal and willingness, I defeated my enemies or my adversaries. Regular successions of pleasures and hardships sharpen one's mind and harden one's heart…"

In truth, Iulia Hasdeu didn't crumble before hardship. She only cared about school, the voices of the muses, and the sweetness of art. She was always studying until the late hours of the night, especially since Aumont and Chalbot, her tutors helping her with Latin and Greek for her final high school exams expected her to do extra work. Her piano was not neglected of resonance and gifted the small pianist with great accords and gracious melodies. The color palette was not passive either, and the colors were laid out on landscapes reproduced from the originals or from nature itself. She sent a few drawings and canvas paintings to Bucharest. Matilda Constantinescu and Florica Zaharescu didn't waste any time requesting them from her father. But there was one event that she couldn't wait for.

Easter was not too far away, and the child wanted to show her creations to her father as a small reward for his significant sacrifices.

One day, Mignon was taken for a walk by the Swedish housekeeper, who even though she was related to Gustav Adolf had not inherited any of his intelligence. The interior court of the building was the dog's favorite place to promenade, but unfortunately, it wasn't only hers. And that's how the delicate four-legged creature that had been brought with such care from Bucharest, saved from an aggressive incident in the forest not long ago, was compromised by the fangs of a pug who was already taking its walk in the park. The yelping was so loud that every neighbor was leaning out the window. Lilica heard, rushed down the stairs, and barely had the time to save her friend whose fur covered a quarter of the courtyard. A gentleman intervened immediately and Lilica, who was ready to protest at the wickedness of the pug, received a delicate apology from its owner, who was none other than her neighbor on the third floor...

"I'm sorry, miss," said the young man in Byron's language.

"Is this your dog?" asked Lilica in English, visibly flushed.

"Yes. I apologize... this is my father's pug and he can be quite insufferable. He's my father's only company for most of the time... Please accept this apology in the name of my father."

"Thank you!" said Lilica, studying the blue eyes of her neighbor. "Are you a poet?"

"I'm an architecture student, but in my spare time I do like to write some poetry... just like you, miss," replied the neighbor, a bit daring.

"How did you know?" asked Lilica, pretending not to understand.

"What doesn't a poet know? He also knows you're a talented pianist, as well as the daughter of a great scholar who's a member of so many Academies. I congratulate you, miss!"

"Thank you, sir."

"I'd love to read some of your poems in French..."

"You know I write in French?"

"I'm informed... I believe you like Shakespeare."

"Me?" asked Lilica, suppressing a smile. "I believe I understand him just like the English do. He's one of my favorite writers... just like Byron, Shelley, and Chatterton. I regret that your pug didn't know this... Goodbye!"

And after snatching the small dog and throwing a last look at Shakespeare's countryman, she ran up the stairs, leaving the blue-eyed man visibly disappointed.

"Slow down, Lilica! Why are you running? Who's the gentleman you were talking to?"

"An insufferable Englishman!" said Lilica.

"But what did he do to you?"

"Nothing. He's the owner of the pug who bit our dear Mignon."

A raspy cough stopped her from speaking.

"See? You're coughing again. Who made you run? Was he about to eat you up? To hell with that Englishman!"

"It's nothing, Mommy, it's going to pass shortly! Don't scold the Englishman; he's very kind," said Lilica.

Her cough didn't pass shortly, only later, once she remembered the eyes of the poet known as Albert James by his signature, but his name was another according to the administrator.

The running out of air every time Lilica walked faster started repeating... She didn't mind it though. If only her mother didn't find out because she didn't want the prescription syrups again. It often happened during classes if she was involved in serious debates, but she knew how to cover this problem with a smile or with a joke to distract her classmates that knew her as a cheerful girl.

One of those days during Latin class, after Cicero, Iulia Hasdeu quoted something from Tibul, who was not considered as a great Latin example by the school curriculum. The professor was not upset, but he asked her where she'd heard of him to which she replied quite declamatory...

"I've been reading Latin authors for a long time. We Romanians love Latin more than other nations."

"Like any other nation of Latin origin," corrected the teacher.

"As any other Latin nation and more. In the part of the world that my country is in, Latin is a refuge and a means of support."

"Very nice. I'm glad to know that. The French, however, have the same means of support."

"Obviously, Professor, but for us Romanians this is vital. That's why learning Latin is very important for us," said Iulia, emphasizing the words.

The topic was brought up again during recess between Margareta Scott and Lilica, starting a small intellectual battle witnessed by the group of students gathering around them.

"Yes, yes, Marguerite! We are more Latin than you," stated Lilica.

"Allow me not to believe that Julie!" replied her classmate. "Your language is mixed with Slavic and it sounds very odd. I can't hear any Latin word when you speak to Marie Mavrodi."

"If you had more Latin blood and finer hearing you'd hear a lot," replied Lilica to the classmate she suspected wasn't pure-blooded French. "I'll give you some examples that are almost identical in both Romanian and Latin! For example: tort, not the French pastry, but the spun wool is the Latin tortus. *Arbore* (arbor) = arbustum, *Alb* (white) = albus, *animal* = animalis, *aproape* (near) = prope, *argint* (silver) = argentum, *a arde* (to burn) = ardere, *ram* (branch) = ramus, *spirt* (spirit) = spiritus, *a tunde* (to trim) = tondere, *forma* (form) = forma, *a limita* (to limit) = limito, *permis* (permit) = permissu, *a perde* (to lose) = perdere, *piele* (skin) = pelis, *pictor* (painter) = pictor, *scena* (scene) = scena, *regina* (queen) = regina, *rege* (king) = regis, *fals* (false) = falsus, *demis* (demited) = demissus, *infirm* (cripple) = infirmus, *statue* = statua, *a sta* (to stay) = sto, stare, *secure* (ax) = securis, *cute* (folds) = cos, cotis, *a șterge* (to erase) = abstergere!"

The words kept pouring out from the vocabulary of the annoyed Romanian girl in the voice of three members of the Hasdeu family, many centuries, and millions of Romanian scholars, ancestors, and grandfathers now resting in the ground in the land of Trajan...

"But for us, my dear, we have original words as well, which cannot be translated. For example the word *dor* (longing). It's something between *désir* (*desiderium* in Latin), *envie* (envy), *tendance* (trend), or maybe all of them together, but with very poetic meaning. Next to it, we can put the word *poftă* (that has a Slavic sound) but which is the Latin *cupidas* or *apetitus*, not the French *apetit*, or *envie*. It is more than that... more expressive. Then we have the word *doină* which is not translatable and many more!"

"I'd dare to show you that Romanian is the richest Latin language, even richer than French which is full of foreign influences, such as Celtic, barbarian, Saxon, Flemish, etc., just like all the other romance languages."

The bell stopped the modern philology lesson that Iulia Hasdeu held with inspiration, without pause, cutting interruptions, chocking from time to time on a dry cough...

She proudly told her father about this when he came to Paris for Easter; she saw the class as an arena, and herself as an unbeatable gladiator.

Hasdeu embraced his small philologist but advised her to temper her linguistic soar around foreigners who would use occasions such as that to dislike her even more.

During the ten days he spent in Paris, Hasdeu forced her to take a break. He made her laugh, avoided any scientific conversation, took his family on carriage rides almost daily to visit le Bois de Boulogne, Buttes, Chaumont, and le Bois de Vincennes. Then, on the Saturday before Easter, they visited the Pére Lachaise cemetery.

The day seemed fated for a visit. April had brought the gifts of spring among the graves and monuments: sun, butterflies, and aromas. People in mourning were kneeling before graves, and the whispers of their prayers were floating under the budding branches.

Lilica and Hasdeu stopped in front of the graves of the writers Rachel, Abélard, and Heloise to pay their respects, then they visited the resting places of La Fontaine, Béranger, Beaumarchais, Balzac, Delacroix, Bellini, Bizet, Champollion, Ingres, and spent a bit more time with Thiers, as well as other stars of French culture that were still shining in the world.

The sponge cakes sent by Mrs. Svârlescu were gone by the time the vacation ended, and after advice and embraces, the father returned to his country.

Chapter VIII

Petals and Fragrances

Lilica was back among her books, notebooks, exercises, and homework. She felt pulled between the two Maries that she loved equally, her classmate and her childhood friend in the country with orchards and meadows, with birds whose song brought forgotten dreams from childhood. Lilica longingly sent her thoughts to that land. In the weak lamplight, the books were closed, the notebooks were put away, and the poet was writing on a fresh sheet of paper.

Romance for Marie

Marie, have you forgotten
Those charming old days past?
We made oaths to each other,
Our hearts were merged at last.
Our love was true and candid...
For that, I still shed tears!

Like soaring birds to heaven
Joyful and without fears
We ran through our Eden;
And in your long black tresses
I whispered loving nothings,
And adorned them with roses...

Those times are gone forever
Our essence we loved so,
When we were being treasured.
You were glee, heart aglow,

I, in my sad existence
Was charmed by my Marie.

Alas! It was astounding
To love you as I did
Your arms that were surrounding
My figure. Fleeting dream...
Beautiful moments vanish
Leaving me here to weep...[9]

The Marie from far away, whose love she always carried in her heart, but who became estranged because of her new life, was the recipient of the poem *À quoi bon? (What's the Point?)* written around the same time, and where accusations are shown in the following verses:

In the end, with extreme sorrow,
With ardor and missing your touch,
I would just tell you that I love you
That you wounded my heart so much;
But what's the point? You know it well too...[10]

The same Marie was the recipient of another poem written by Iulia Hasdeu in the same year, one that was not dated, named *Sur un Album (On an Album)*:

You like my poems, right Marie?
Should I bestow you with more lines?
But what is the point of poetry,
When you know what my heart confines.

The life and the literary work of the fourteen-year-old poet were visible in chronological order, as her verses were honest, displaying the state of her mind, her private thoughts, her sensible progress, but also her pain. That first year, during which the drafts of her poems and stories started to take a definite shape (but, we have to repeat, not a final shape, because she was hiding them from everyone and never thought about publishing them), was marked by love declarations, by her sentimental side, by songs of her poetic nature, but also of deep studies on literary criticism.

---

[9] "Romance à Marie," in Hasdeu, *Oeuvre poétique/Opera poetică*, pp. 204-205.

[10] "À quoi bon?" in Hasdeu, *Oeuvre poétique/Opera poetică*, pp. 184-185.

That was also the year in which Iulia Hasdeu wrote the comedy *Tante et la Nièce* (*The Aunt and the Niece*) published in the volume *Théâtre*, which was not dated but holds the subject and the approach of that year, or the year before through its simplicity. The plot revolves around a married aunt, the Baroness of Villemont, whose husband left a long time ago and was considered to be deceased, and a dispute between her and the niece she was raising for Germaine, the Count of Almaby. Scene after scene brings the reader to the normal conclusion when the aunt is forced to accept the fact the young count is in love with her niece, especially since her husband sent word that he had been stranded and was returning home.

The legend that wasn't dated, *L'ange et la Primevère* (*The Angel and the Primrose*) was inserted by Hasdeu's friend, Count Angelo of Gubernatis, in a public conference in Florence, five years after the poet's passing, which was then translated into Polish and Hungarian and published. The story starts with "One day flew into the pure sky, embraced by the stars…" and it's filled with gentle poetry. The angel flies down to earth, picks up a flower, and takes flight towards the sky again to the confusion of all the other flowers. Why was their sister chosen? Later, they heard a voice from the sky. He had chosen the primrose because it was the first one that bloomed at the end of winter. "The first flower that smiles at us after the gloomy winter, it's white as if it still bore the imprint of the holy tear."[11]

If only her father knew! If he found out about it in time, while she was rapidly blooming! Oh, if only he knew! If he heard this wonderful legend in which the virtue that was bestowed to her during her baptism on the tray with gifts was so brilliant, he might have allowed her to follow her calling, which might have brought her father more than a mausoleum, and which might have brought her nation more than a few scattered notebooks with sketches.

Hasdeu wrote:

"The main thing that matters is the baccalaureate. Greek and Latin must be given at least two hours a day!... And my advice for her is not to joke with Aumont, but to take advantage of his teaching, otherwise, we're paying him for nothing…" (Thursday, 3/15 May 84).

That was the echo of absence! It was the effect of telepathy from this great scholar who had ways to tell the future and to understand the spirits floating around, sent by the loved ones who had passed!... "Baccalaureate!" Not "the angel that flies in the pure skies, embraced by the brilliant stars." Hasdeu the philologist didn't

---

[11] *Théâtre* 315.

give two cents on the opinions of Hasdeu the poet! That was the fatal seed of that tragedy. The flower dried by the breath of death was found too late, when Hasdeu stumbled upon the school notebooks, and learned that beside conjugations and Greek translations rested the poetic values of her daughter.

However, the father was too busy with his literary work about the army and too busy with *Magnum Etymologicum*, so his aura was shadowed by Greek, Latin, derivations, word transformations, rhotacisms... Everyone was between the beginning and the end of his work of great proportions.

On the other side, the mother was focusing on brewing tea, feeding Lilica extra portions, overseeing the tutors (three by that point), staying by their side the whole time, so she didn't know what her daughter's mind was imagining during the late hours of the night.

During spring break, the parents discussed Lilica's cough and exhaustion, and they taught about taking her to the mountains during the summer, but that her face was bright as a day of May. His father wrote again, insisting on how important the final exams were. Lilica had become a true lady.

Her hair was braided and coiled at the back of her head, with two curls resting on her forehead. Her round cheeks were pale under the lamplight, but rosy when being kissed by the sun; her lips were always adorned with a smile, her chin was round and gracious! And her eyes! Those clear eyes showed the goodness in her heart and her intelligence; those eyes were worthy of a poem written by Eminescu. Her earlobes ended in two pearly beads. The young body was round and curvy, with a rich bosom and a thin waist, gratuitous like a lily in spring. Any neighbor or passerby with wandering eyes would have admired this creation of nature.

The only thing Hasdeu could do was to contribute with books, prizes, and loans opened by Mircuș for the well-being of his dear family.

Lilica replied to his letter with gratitude in polished and spiritual phrases, which were indications of true literary talent for any parent, not only for a poet or a scholar. Odobescu was moved by the attention of the two women, and he tried to rekindle the lost friendship with Hasdeu. But the philologist avoided him when visiting Paris. He wrote to him politely but coldly, because he didn't believe in his honesty.

He also wrote to his family, telling them he was saving money to take them to Switzerland in the summer, which was a place favorable for his studies. He informed them that his grandmother had been sent to the monastery again, after insisting on leaving. "Both the gardens bloomed and they're so beautiful, especially

Lilica's garden that has grapes too." He talked about the political campaign in Craiova for the following fall, telling them it was going great because "Craiova was not influenced by Brătianu, nor by Rosetti, but by common sense and nationalism!" "My dictionary is going as planned…" "I can't wait to see the oil painting of Ms. Iulia Hasdeu…"

Finally, he expressed delight towards the week-long vacation that Lilica and her mother had spent in the countryside near Paris, breathing fresh air before the exams, just as the doctors recommended. Fresh air, as much fresh air and sun as possible!

Hasdeu embarked on another journey in the middle of July 1884. The Government was not only making mistakes but appropriate actions as well. The Ministry of Public Instruction led by Gh. Ghițu ("baba" as his friend Hasdeu was going to call him) had obtained the funds so the great philologist from the Archives could travel to Switzerland and study the organization and functionality of the Swiss school system. Hasdeu was supposed to return with documentation and proof of expense.

He was loaded with lots of things (excluding halva which wasn't in season), such as olives, caviar, a basket of apricots, a bouquet wrapped in cotton to impress his wife and prove his loving thoughts, so she would realize he wasn't unfaithful during her absence from the home. Her friends had been eager to tell her that her husband was not quite done with his habit. Hasdeu had trimmed his beard, groomed his hands, his hair, and arrived in Paris with his plans set, and hugged his wife and daughter who had been on his mind every day and night.

He kissed Lilica twice for her accomplishments, after being awarded first prize for her studies despite her rival.

Before traveling to Switzerland, the parents consulted the doctor and decided to go to Montreux, which was recommended for those with lung illnesses.

As always, the father banned every type of reading material, and as always, Lilica found ways to hide some French volumes between her clothes, books written by Prudhomme, Belleau, d'Arles, Froissart, etc. She was allowed by her father to take her palette and paint, and her drawing pen.

On the morning of the departure, when the carriage loaded with suitcases, blankets, and umbrellas was about to take off, Lilica observed someone waving at her discreetly from near the apartment building. Noticing her parents' confused looks, she made a small greeting gesture while holding Mignon that could have been interpreted as her switching to a more comfortable position. That's how the blue eyes followed in her mind during her train ride to Switzerland.

They got off the train in Montreux on the same day, on the shores of Lake Leman, the town renowned as the haven for those with lung illnesses. It was composed of several neighborhoods with charming names: Chatelard, Les Planches, and Veytaux. Hasdeu stopped in the center of the city (in Les Planches) dominated by the harbor, with a wide view of the lake, and with a breeze of fresh air coming from the Bernezi mountains. Other smaller towns were connected to the main city from every direction, each serving as a resort. Towards the harbor, there was Territet from which a cableway was transporting visitors up to Glion. Each part of the city was used for different treatments and Lilica visited them all in turn during this vacation, and in the following year.

Her vacation started with relaxation, treatments, baths, and lying in the sun. Her mother was watching over her day after day. Hasdeu was with them for the first few days, but he was required to leave and complete his mission in various other Swiss cities. Before traveling too far away, he organized a boat trip across the lake to Ferney, the northern shore, which was Voltaire's refuge.

The small boat set sail in the chilly air of the morning, filled with happy but relaxed people, each on a trip to relax and heal. Lilica, dressed as a tourist, was standing near the railing with her father, ignoring the rest of the people but admiring the sunrise, the white lights in the distance, the sailboats flying on water like the hope of the ill and lively like nature. Hasdeu had wanted to visit Ferney for a long time, a town that had become famous for the twenty years Voltaire, the great poet, philosopher, and historian had spent there, after visiting every royal court in Europe, and being exiled from France.

Between the "patriarch of Ferney" as he was known and the "mage from Câmpina" there were many similar points regarding political ideologies, genius literary production, philosophy, and history. Both of them had wide minds full of ideas, culture, intelligence, encyclopedias, just as many other scholars of that century. They were both poets and scriptwriters, documenter historians, revolutionary spirits defending individual freedom and democracy, burning with vitality, sarcasm, and mockery against those times' power that oppressed and shared injustice. They were both anticlerical without being atheists, they were free-thinking, and at the end of their lives, they were preoccupied with divinity. Hasdeu had a more mystical way of approaching this topic, but his views were still close to the eighty-year-old Francois-Marie Arouet (known as Voltaire). It's possible this trip Hasdeu took with his daughter to the house where the patriarch had lived in isolation greatly influenced his decision to retreat to Câmpina later on. Both of those bright men turned their homes into altars, Voltaire building a small church in

1761 near the gate of his house that was inscribed with "Deo erexit Voltaire MDCCLXI," while Hasdeu set his altar in the main hall of the castle in Câmpina. That was how two misunderstood men, that were faithful to the Lord, knew how to live their last years in recollection and piety.

"I will never forget the two hours I spent with my daughter in Ferney, in the park, in the home, in the work office of the great scholar…" (*Sic cogito*)

There, the father and daughter relived the life, work, and sorrow of the patriarch, whose spirit was still overlooking the whole area.

"Suffering for an idea made it come to life so much brighter."

"And Voltaire suffered so much!" explained Hasdeu before entering the memorial house.

"But he made others suffer as well, dear Father."

"It's true! He was a fierce warrior. A creator! A professor of humanity. Professors often make their students suffer! And what a teacher he was!"

"And what a poet! Father, do you believe science gives people more than poetry does?" asked the young poet.

"Dear Lilica, poetry gives just as much science does. However, it brings suffering to the poet. Ask me about it! Ask his spirit! What did poetry offer us?"

"But still, Father… Poetry gave other poets glory and immortality!"

"Yes, but after death my dear daughter…"

"What you're saying is too upsetting…"

"Upsetting, but true. Voltaire knew glory during his life. Look, here in Ferney, the genius old man was a true emperor. Here, away from the rest of the world, in the company of his niece Marie Denis, he was visited by all his admirers from all over the world; he gave advice, programs, wrote pieces for the less fortunate, and wrote the remarkable literary works *The History of Peter the Great, Emperor of Russia*, *The History of the French Parliament*, many theatre scripts, many letters, all that was given to the world as a testament."

"He wrote that wonderful novel here, *Commentaries on Corneille*," added Lilica.

"True! I've forgotten about that one," said the father. "Anyway, he had a beautiful life."

"And a beautiful death… he died when he was eighty-four years old," concluded the child, lost in the mystery of life.

A few days later, the girl got inspiration from reading the verses of Lamartine in *Le Lac*, and her hands looked for a fresh sheet of paper. A stanza one day, five stanzas on another day, until her poem was almost finished close to the time her vacation ended.

That's how the poem named *Au Lac de Genève* (Geneva Lake), with a motto from Lamartine, was born:

"The sun shines with its golden beauty
To the horizon, on the dormant waves;
Setting the sky ablaze in tones of ruby
With shades of purple and fiery hues.

The sleeping waves are not great beauties,
The mountains all around are not quite tall
But all the barren cliffs look like stone sentries
They are alert, and proud, watching it all!

But why, dear lake, can I not stay and linger
And live my life here happily till I die?
Your waters have the voice of a soft singer
Whose anguished song is a regretful sigh.

But oh, my charming lake so full of stories,
I must tell you goodbye maybe forever.
I'll leave you all that's good, and take my worries
For you gifted me the pleasure of first love.[12]

The pastoral reflects evocative poetry, despite its author being fourteen with an intimate and proportionate closeness to the poem *Le Lac* written by Lamartine. That poem was written in his youth, however, it reflects the age that was at least double compared to the child who was inspired by him.

"My first love"! Everyone knows poets understand love by instinct, this phenomenon of universal creation, psychological affinity, which almost always embalms the heart before the great views of the generous nature! But the child's "first loves" are believed to be entangled with that vague breeze around her heart.

---

[12] Bourgeons d'Avril 40

Was it love for a definite being or an imaginary one, or an obsession that she always tried to cast aside? Who would know?

The young poet confessed the feelings she'd felt around the same lake in another poem called *En Suisse* (In Switzerland), with a motto belonging to A. Chénier: "Come! Everyone loves spring, and I always love it."

A light breeze gently flows about,
Bending thick reeds over the water;
A nightingale sings from its secret hideout;
Nature is sweet, and I'm its loving daughter.

The jasmine, the lily, the majestic rose,
Take turns in gifting us their fragranced breath;
A delicate moth lands on them and it knows
Their nectar is pure love shared till death.

Oh, my friend let me sing you a song
The same song that birds thrill in the mountains
The one shepherds sing to their lambs all day long;
It's the love that pours from my heart like a fountain![13]

Meanwhile, Iulia Hasdeu painted some of those views, scenes, and light effects on the mountains and the lake, paintings she would later gift to her friends and her classmates. The canvases and boards painted with respect for art, knowledge of colors, and full interest in the subject proved the artist was very confident in her skills.

While she was in Montreux she wrote and received a letter from her good friend and classmate Jeanne Créhange, who was traveling to Bourg la Reine. It was she that informed her of their best friends, brothers Lucien and Leon Blum (the latter ending up France's prime minister for a few years) had received great grades and prizes in the exams. Jeanne and Iulia were supposed to appear in a social theater play with them. Her classmate also wrote to her the brothers and their other stage partners didn't want to interpret *Le Misanthrope*, but *Les Femmes Savantes* (*The Wise Women*). Iulia, who had an excellent impression of the two fellow scholars, especially for Leon Blum whose wife was her classmate, didn't want to defy their wish.

---

[13] *Bourgeons d'Avril* 195

She also replied to Margaret Scott with savory pages about the beauties of Montreux, informing her that her sister, Elli Scott, and their mother had visited her for a whole day; they rehearsed their roles and took a few strolls. She told her that Elli was reading an "exclusive novel by Iulia Hasdeu," which was very private news, barely mentioned as a secret among friends... (What was that exclusive novel if not one of the Théâtre volumes that only contained a few of the novel drafts).

Finally, after a few trips, they made one to Bourg la Reine to visit Jeanne Créhange and her parents. The rest of the time she spent strolling around with her mother or alone, on the mountain path or around the harbor, with her gaze far away and her soul near, absently passing people, preoccupied with matters of the soul. She didn't have any friends; she didn't know anyone. It was better that way. Her peace was only hers. Sometimes she saw someone that disturbed her peace; it was a mirage that looked like a certain poet. The child kept walking, however...

And so, summer passed. Iulia Hasdeu felt healthy again. She was not getting tired as easily, and she could face the uneasy memories of the unknown and misunderstood blue eyes. The two Iulias returned to Paris accompanied by a housekeeper who spoke French and German.

September came with new worries and new books. This was the final year! The baccalaureate was the most important... School didn't scare her, and museums didn't abandon her. Her classes at school were mixed with tutoring for algebra (oh, algebra!), Greek, Latin, but also with hours of writing drafts and verses in the corners of her notebook. In September of that year, she wrote: *Le Pauvre Roi Fol* (*Poor Mad King*), which was dedicated to that king who had been abandoned by everyone, the only ones near him on his deathbed were his dog and his wife. The King of Bavaria who died shortly after was also mourned by Iulia Hasdeu, because people considered him to be crazy, while he was only a poet: "Live only with poetry, oh king!"

Shortly after that she continued her work on the essay called *Mon Shakespeare* (*My Shakespeare*) that she had started in 1882, and started work on the study *Various Thoughts on Racine and Corneille* regarding the sketch *Mademoiselle Milet*, the girl promised to Corneille. (The plan for a comedy in verses). Those thoughts on the two classic French playwrights formed a study that's worthy of a renowned critic. The essay starts with:

"I got used to saying 'my Corneille,' just like I say 'my Molière,' 'my Shakespeare,' 'my Sophocles.' Well, as much as I'd like to do the same for Racine, 'Mister Racine' escapes me."

Her observations and confessions were full of intelligence. Even though Iulia Hasdeu wasn't original in what she stated about Racine, she knew that he had surpassed his predecessor and confirmed the critiques, but she was original in her phrasing, especially since Napoleon I, the man she admired, had believed the contrary, saying if Corneille had lived during his time, he would have made him a Prince… She disliked Racine.

Iulia studied, character by character, the literary works of the two poets, citing other opinions in support of her own, defining the value of each regarding the unfolding of the drama, psychology, gestures, and actions.

"And the women of Corneille? 'They don't know how to love. We can see Corneille doesn't know much about women,' said M. Sainte-Beuve. So, can we openly talk about the one behind the creation of Chimène, Camille, Pauline, and Cornèlie? Camille has a chaotic and blind passion; Pauline is the pure and perfect wife; Cornèlie is a brave widow in Pompey.

The one who made Chimène speak, encouraging Rodrigue who is going to fight:

'Come and fight to win Chimène as a prize…'

To Pauline he demanded the grace of Polyeucte:

'Two hearts united never separate

And to separate them we have to tear them apart…'

To Camille: 'Everything I see reminds me of the Horatii.'

Does he not understand the feelings and weakness of a woman's heart? Either way, we must not think that Chimène, Camille, or Pauline were any less great than their lovers; no. At the same time, they all have something sweet, graceful, and touching, and they are poetic characters who don't yield to either Monime or to Andromaque of the harmonious Racine. The unnatural women who are not any more natural than others, just like Corneille's Cleopatra, that enchanting Cleopatra who can't be compared to Agrippina, nor to Racine's Athalie, these revolting characters are painted in their true colors. Obviously, Corneille chooses to get our attention with admiration and enthusiasm. If our opinions on bad or terrible characters are negative, he can show us the way a noble soul can tame their habits and their passions. Of all the characters Corneille created, the one I most admire and love is Pauline…"

These pages were worthy of being studied and commented on not just by high school students, but also by some professors. They showed her spirit loaded with romanticism despite her young age, but also her balance in conceptions regarding life and literature, and especially theater, which was fascinating to her.

Once Hasdeu arrived in Bucharest he wrote to them, informing them that he had traveled a long time, that he'd passed through Vienna to see Uncle Stanislas, and that he had gone to Munich. When he arrived in Bucharest, he had six francs left in his pocket. He told them about various gossip and news from Bucharest, including the marriage of their friend Barbu Constantinescu to a girl sixteen years of age. "The future metropolitan went mad in every sense…" said Hasdeu. He added he was working on the report of his studies in Switzerland, as well as on his dictionary, and the comedy with Gh. Chițu, who had lost all his teeth. "I gave him the directions of the Italian Opera in Paris to find an actress for Macbeth and three hags to play the three witches, but he told me to hire him, Zalomit, and Bacaloglu."

The news included the death of Carol Davila.

"You might have learned that poor Davila is no more. His worth is now barely acknowledged. There's no way someone can replace him at Asil. His place was offered to me, but I refused immediately…"

Hasdeu was getting ready for the elections in Craiova, a city he was visiting often to hold conferences and where he was an independent liberal candidate, because "I don't support militant politics, I'm not a party man or part of any group…"

That's how their lives were flowing between eulogies, proclamations, and the occasional tragicomedy that all of us encounter. The news that her father became a deputy didn't leave Lilica indifferent, especially since her mother was content with him being only the director of the Archives. The little girl knew better than anyone what a great person her father was. It was one thing when someone presented themselves as "Ionescu;" it was a completely another thing when they were presented as "Deputy Ionescu." People bowed their heads and their backs, and doors opened for deputies. That was the reason Lilica was so happy; however, the end of October came with news and homages in the newspapers from Bucharest. Marie Başkirțef had died, the twenty-five-year-old genius girl who'd traveled the world after leaving the shores of Don River. She'd been lured by the lights of Paris and decided to study there. She had spoken French, English, Latin, Italian, German, and Polish from the time she was thirteen years old, the same age she'd been when she started filing her journal with spiritual and objective observations. She studied music as well, piano, harp, organ, mandolin, guitar. She was also a painter, learning the art of colors, and only a year after starting she had her first exposition for which she'd received a medal. She had famous artwork displayed in the gallery but under a pseudonym. In the fall of 1884, while painting a street scene outside, she was surprised by a rain shower, caught a cold that turned into consumption and killed her shortly after. The newspapers wrote touching articles about her.

"A genius child has died. As always, geniuses discovered early don't live long. It's the balance of evolution and growth. Whoever tries to defy time, falls. Marie Başkirțef worked too hard…"

Lilica's newspaper fell out of her hands… "Whoever tries to defy time, falls…"

Her eyes tried to pierce the veil between worlds, trying to see the smiling eyes of the genius Russian, eyes that would share advice and confessions…

A few days later Hasdeu informed them of certain political intrigues that had started against him. Stănescu had given him an ultimatum to choose between the Archives and his spot as a deputy.

"I will only give the Archives up if I lose my head" (November 2nd, 1884).

Finally, he won the elections in Craiova, and he was chosen as a deputy. But his fight had to go on! He had many fierce adversaries, led by Kogălniceanu, Stolojanu, and Stănescu. And it was true because Kogălniceanu stood up in the chamber and contested the election, asking for Hasdeu's term to be considered invalid, since he was also the director of the Archives. But since every contestation had to be supported by at least five deputies, it failed because no other deputy supported Kogălniceanu. The President validated the election and Hasdeu got to keep his deputy position as well as the position as director of the Archives. Lilica replied to his letter, and after sharing her thoughts on the possibility of giving up one of his positions she continued in French:

"Oh, no, since you are a deputy because the residents of Craiova chose you, don't insult them like that, don't lower yourself to giving up that glorious role they've given to you. My opinion, as well as my mother's, is that you should make a formal request to the Chamber, offer to keep your director position at the Archives but with an honorific title, without earning a salary from it. In this way you will shut the mouths of those who envy you, you'll remain a deputy, and you'll also keep your position at the Archives. Do it, if it's possible. If not, give the Archives up, a terrible sacrifice, and stay a deputy since you worked so much for it."

The one giving such advice was only fifteen years old, and maybe his wild wife, if she didn't say "your father was a fool for becoming a deputy." We tend to believe that the "mother's idea" was just a piece of armor for the child who dared to give lessons to Bogdan Petriceicu Hasdeu. Lilica also added:

"...And now the most difficult affair: money! I imagine you looking at the sky and shouting like Molière's *Harpagon*: 'What the hell! Always money; nobody can talk of anything else but money!' Well, yes! This cursed subject. But you can't do anything without it. Well, we need money, Father; we need it badly. Think that Christmas is in eight days!!! We mean the French Christmas because we don't think of ours anymore. So, on Christmas, we have to buy presents; I need a dress and I don't have one. I need money for it! I'm angry but I need it. How much we need, only God knows. It's unheard of..."

Your respectful and loving daughter, Lili.

December 18th, 1884

Hasdeu replied to her letter with great appreciation for how wise his daughter was, promising he would do it. He did, and from the money he didn't have, he sent them money for Christmas along with a significant amount on the side.

Meanwhile, the *România Liberă* newspaper attacked Hasdeu with a news article describing an acute conflict between him and Gh. Chițu. Mother Iulia, who had great esteem for their benefactor in Craiova, found out and wrote a long letter to her husband, a letter which reflected her panic, where she made accusations, but Lilica wanted no part in it. Hasdeu replied to her:

"...I've never been an ingrate and I'll never be one. Regarding Chițu, gratitude should be mutual, because if he helped me financially, nobody gave him more moral support than I did, always sending him letters, speeches... More than that, he could have never become a member of the Academy without my help. That being said, I'll always avoid bashing him, even though he wouldn't do the same..." (December 1884)

Iulia Hasdeu's literary contribution was written between 1882-1888. In that category, we must take into account the essays written in 1884, which were grouped by her father in the third *Chevalerie* volume, in the chapter entitled "Canevas," a name probably picked by Hasdeu. The reason we feel compelled to mention them is their spiritual climate that reflected romantic-idealist and fantastic attitudes and dreams. For example, *La Lune* (*The Moon*, p. 204) is a sketch, a poem in prose, followed by a few verses, similar to a school composition, or a dissertation on the nights with moonlight, nightingales, months, and bats. She hadn't started on the mystical and philosophical meditation found in her works from the later years. In *Christine*, Iulia Hasdeu noted her impression on balls:

> "Oh! I don't care about the ball. Come girls, come dance. The beautiful girls just turn and turn in the arms of their lovers.
>
> Christine cries at home; she cries for the youth she lost in isolation and sadness. But that doesn't matter! She had to work…"

It wasn't a joke against balls, but more of the girl rebelling against being forbidden to dance, having to work as much as she could to forget about it.

She followed with a few sentimental compositions, such as *Lilas Blanc* (*White Lilac*) and sad tales like *Chevrefeuille* (*Honeysuckle*) that speak of shepherds and their lovers, *Le Berger Roumain* (*The Romanian Shepherd*) talking of the fairy Cosânzeana who inspired the shepherd's flute, or *Berger et Bergerè* (*The Shepherd and the Shepherdess*) full of love between Ionel and Păuna. Hasdeu believed Pèouna, the French writing of the character was derived from Paulina, a name often found in Iulia's literary compositions. We believe that Pauline was a different name than Pèouna, which was the French name for Păuna, a popular name in the Romanian countryside. Another story is Alba meaning White, which is about a love affair in the countryside, under the blue sky among flowers, between her and Andrei. A witch named Kira comes before Alba with a full jug, which was a bad omen. Alba spills the jug so the curse of the gypsy won't come true.

It's not possible to date exactly the time when these works were written, because even though Iulia Hasdeu sometimes noted a date at the end, they were usually the dates when the poet revised them and finished them.

Starting in 1885, Iulia Hasdeu began her first year of true poetic productivity. From over 130 poems collected in *Bourgeons d'Avril* and *Chevalerie*, volumes compiled and published by Hasdeu, the poet wrote almost sixty in that year, next to sketches for plays and novels and essays, compared to the forty written in 1886, twenty in 1887, and twenty in 1888.

This small statistic shows the influx of inspiration she had, and especially the leniency life gave her during those two years (1885-1886), which decreased in 1886, and was smothered in 1888, right when her talent was rising.

The two months she spent in Montreux during which she took relaxing trips, sunbathed, and ate well, brought a visible improvement to the girl's health. Fall passed with her health still strong, especially since fall came with difficult exams for her weak lungs. Sometimes the exam was not tolerated, and the candidate fell without a chance to retake it. Lilica still coughed from time to time, but because she was gaining weight nobody paid attention to that. She was working diligently for the real exam she had to take in the summer. It was the year of the baccalaureate! Her three tutors were arguing about the hours she needed to allocate for each subject; another child would have used those hours to rest. Trigonometry, algebra, geometry, and geography were racing in her mind next to Greek and Latin, and her struggles seemed normal to those who witnessed them. Her father was being very serious about the final exams.

On Christmas, after the administrator of the apartment building was paid for her care, she arrived at their home with a big bouquet of big white daisies for Ms. and Mrs. Hasdeu, without a note. Those were Lilica's favorite flowers.

"These are from me for your kindness and attention."

"Oh, thank you, but this is too much… maybe they were too expensive for you," said the mother, astonished by the gift.

"Don't do this, Mother, you'll insult her."

When Lilica walked her to the door, the old woman whispered in her ear.

"They're from the gentleman… He just left…"

"Where?"

"I don't know! His father left as well."

"What is the old woman saying?" asked the mother.

"She asked us not to be upset about the gift," lied Lilica.

Her heart was beating fast. That was her only Christmas present from her only friend. Her Romanian friends were spending time at wild parties in the chaos of Paris. Lilica and her mother didn't belong there. It was good as it was. But even small attention from the ones that would sometimes join them for tea, for a glass of Bourgogne, or a modest dinner was appreciated. Christmas was lonely and empty, something her father had suspected would happen, as he always advised them to save money because they had no friends and generosity was unheard of. The man had lived a full life, he had learned a lot and he knew what he was talking about. Friendship was not real! But there was something else. There was something that could turn a lonely Christmas into a generous one with songs, smiles, and warm feelings that asked the heart so many questions to which it couldn't give a precise answer. What? Lilica didn't know what to answer to that. Her hands rushed to the keys of her piano and suddenly revived the notes of Godard, Rameau, Padre Martini, and Scarlati, the melody kissing her fingers with its sensibility and majestic sounds. The daisies were watching her from above the piano, each petal resembling a piano key, and the flower itself was a lullaby. Lilica's eyes looked up and down in a confusion between the soul of a child and the ecstasy of Cupid.

One of her hands suddenly stopped mid-air, the other was pressing down on a sharp and distorted chord. Had she made a mistake? Had she forgotten the melody? A face suddenly appeared reflected on the white petals. The blue eyes, the hair combed back, the pale skin, the sad gaze. Just as she'd seen him in Montreux? Was that him? One day when she was slowly walking up the stairs, coming from Gorges du Chauderon, a gentleman came from behind, slightly turned towards her, greeted her, or maybe it was an unrelated gesture, and his outline was lost in the distance. Lilica shivered. It was an illusion. A few minutes before that she had been thinking about him while watching the sun setting behind the mountains. She had not given any more thought to that.

But when the last note crumbled on the piano key, there he was again! Watching her with the same look, with the same expression. Was it accusing? Why? Was he charmed by her playing the piano? How could he?

He left! And his father as well! The administrator told her! But what if she lied? Why if her soul was lying? Memory, focus! What had happened in Montreux? The same thing that was happening now? The same thing that had been happening for a while? What was that syncope from the previous year? So many questions and no answer! Illusions! Imagination! Mysteries!

She stood up, put one of her knees on the stool, rested her elbows on the top of the piano, leaned her cheeks to the flower… They smelled of fields, sun, spring. Oh, poor daisies, delicate and uprooted, destined to bow their withered heads the next day and lose their petals!!!...

There are roses sleeping in gardens,
There are carnations and lilies about,
And jasmines with pale petals and fragrance,
Fresh beautiful hyacinth blooming around;
The white lilac adorns this charming place
Inviting lovers to kiss under its branches;
But there's no prouder flower here than the daisy
Its white delicate head tops them all.

Its name is not a plain, meaningless word,
It's the name of the flower of love:
A delicate name like a serene dove
Like a soft embrace, like a heartbeat.
That name is tender and always sweet,
That invites us to love and to fly
It's your name, dear white Daisy;
And it's not without meaning under the sky!

Your secret talents, oh, dear woman,
Will always be your greatest strength;
But despite your beauty of a goddess,
You'll make mistakes you can't prevent;
Don't worry, this world still has magic
And even though you still might sin
Woman and flower, Rose or Daisy,
Through beauty, you will always win!!

– *Le Lai des Marguerites/ "The Daisy's Song"*[14]

It was February when Iulia Hasdeu wrote *The Daisy's Song*, that ode to the white flowers in which she portrayed queens with the same names, an ode that sings the melody of love. In that month she wrote another similar poem entitled *Le Papillon* (*The Butterfly*), with a Limousin proverb for a motto.

Brilliant chimera
Ephemeral being,
You live for one day.
Being born at dawn
With the rising sun
Won't see it return.
You adore the bright
Rays the first light
Drink dew from the thyme,
Drink dew from a rose

---

[14] Chevalerie

Kiss them only once,
Fate won't give you time.

Let's live without glory.
Let's tell our stories
Before time is up:
Let's talk about love
In a gentle heart,
About naive fun
A blessed distraction
God gifts everyone
Sweet exhilaration.
Don't let love pass by
Because when we love
We conquer the sky!

People would think this was something from Musset. He had been treasured by Iulia and she was inspired by his work. They had the same sensibility, the same connection between the songs they sang and the object of their love!

Almost all the poems that were written in that year and in 1886 bear the same seal of romance and chivalry, of that love that dreamed of a knight in shining armor who would sacrifice honor for love. Longing for life, nature poetry, honesty of a clean heart, sometimes nostalgia for places and her friends, gratitude, the past, and divine piety were the topics that were closest to the soul of the fifteen-year-old poet in those two years of a fruitful but demanding and tiring life.

But in each one of them, Iulia's soul and inspiration floated in the high sphere of idealism. Her world was as she imagined it. She didn't have the time to know it as it was. Everything she learned of the world was from the many books written by Latin, Greek, English, German, Italian, and French authors, or from her imagination. However, reading some of the lines in which the idea of honesty was so strong in every stanza, some readers might be inclined to believe the young poet was sharing her memories and her life occurrences.

For example, knowing of the feelings the fifteen-year-old girl had when receiving the repeated attentions of a young man, why wouldn't we believe that Iulia Hasdeu sung her disappointment in the poem entitled *Au Chevalier Infidèle* — "*The Unfaithful Knight*" — with a motto from Marie de France.

Once you embraced me with tears in your eyes,
With your head in my lap, you gazed at my face,
We lived and we laughed our magical times,
When you called me sweet names, showered me with grace.
You thought I was beautiful and maybe I was,
And you swore to be by my side forever...
Was I naive? Tell me, my disloyal knight, if I was
Alas! Was I wrong to believe you loved me ever?

Now I'm alone since you took your leave,
Oh God, I was punished! And I deserve to be...

When publishing this poem Hasdeu mentioned he had found it in a notebook, without a date, and a title; he believed the date and title were written on a piece of paper, and the poem represented a romance novel the girl was intending to write, maybe it was even the plot of the novel *Séphora*.

The father believed the poet didn't talk about her disappointments but imagined sorrows. We don't have proof to counter his statements, but his own words, "It would seem the primary intention of the poet..." prove it was a hypothesis based on various reasons. Therefore, that love, which was platonic and idealistic, often caused great distress to the young girl. All her love poems reflect the idea, without being able to reach a certain conclusion, that until the end of her short life, she fully knew the feeling of love, privately, conveniently, and true. Iulia Hasdeu might have confessed to it in some poems, such as *Dédain* (Disdain).

No, I don't like love; it's not suited for my age
I laugh at love and its crude face...

She didn't laugh at the idea of love, she laughed at the one with a "crude face," invented by poets, artificial, false. She knew she had to love, and she was afraid that she will fall in love. She believed love tormented one's heart and caused people to sin; that was the idea from the following verses:

Let me run away from a woman's sins
To be beautiful without being aware, without artifice,
To ignore the power of my natural charm,
And live an amazing and beautiful bliss
To keep my heart light and my soul unharmed!

In the same year when she wrote about that fear of love more than the distaste of love, she made another confession in the poem *Etre Aimée* (*To Be Loved*):

Oh, to know you are loved! Blessed happiness
To cry tears of joy whenever you want!
To be loved and to die: a most charming death
When we die in the light, we'll be reborn bright!!

And who were the following verses dedicated to? The poem was written around the same time when the blue eyes, which seemed a dream to her, noticed her somewhere on the street.

Pourquoi? (Why?)

He walked by here a short time past
With angry eyes, with his head bowed;
He didn't smile, and I felt tears.
So why did he even come around?

He's angry, he might even hate me;
His heart — is a block of ice now
And I did nothing to displease him.
So why did he even come around??

He didn't look in my direction;
Was walking slowly and reservedly;
Alas! Maybe he still feels some affection...
Why else would he be walking down my road?[15]

Was this the proof of her imagination about a random passerby? The line "Was walking slowly and reserved" supports the idea this person was real; she crossed paths with someone and he had watched her insistently! But what did she mean by "angry eyes"? Why would they make the poet cry? Was it a lyrical composition? We don't believe that after reading the rest of her honest lyrics.

In another poem (*Quinze Ans* — "*Fifteen Years*") she didn't show distaste towards love, but she showed avoidance toward "that secret love," its "lie." She treasured love, but she was afraid to experience it:

---

[15] Bourgeons d'Avril

Love is the deceitful sight
It's enticing and seductive
But we'll only feel its bite
Later on. Love is destructive.
Weaving lies is your cursed art
And it is also your science,
What you plan no one could say
But we'll watch you with defiance.

Oh, Cupid, with your sharp arrows
You cause only tears of pain:
But at fifteen years no sorrows
Will be running through our veins! (1885)

However, the lines quoted from *Papillon* showed the poet called for love:

Don't let love pass by
Because when we love
We conquer the sky!...

Other poems, such as *Sérénade* mentioned the universality of love.

Everything in nature
On earth, night and day
Chirps, buzzes, and grumbles
Singing Love to stay!!

All of her works from that time show she didn't hate love, she didn't despise it, but the fear of that love she could only barely understand, that she searched for, that called for her; and on the other side she wanted to keep the innocence of her heart.

Angelo de Gubernatis had a conference in 1889 where he reproduced the prologue of *Bourgeons d'Avril* and analyzed the sentimental reality of the poet child. He thought her whole life and work were a mirror of the love she was rejecting. He said:

"Iulia Hasdeu wouldn't have avoided falling into this happy trap. She despised trifling love because in her young girl's dreams she imagined unmeasured love, with sublime devotion. She would have loved as well, without a doubt but her heart was heroic; she needed heroes!"

His observations and conclusions were fully valid. The whole content of *Chevalerie* was dedicated to chivalrousness and heroism, with examples of sacrifices in the name of love, knights fighting for their lovers, or dying with their names on their lips. This was theoretical love, not a practical one.

Therefore, it's plausible the young and attentive man who was affectionate to her, who might have liked her, not to mention, even love her, would have found an echo in the girl's heart, precisely because he was different. But that was not love. She didn't even know him; she might have even avoided him; she didn't know what he felt in his heart, his poetic heart that conjured lyrics about shepherds and shepherdesses from Scotland, but who was not a heroic knight. She was content with the sweet mystery, with the dreams, and the hidden questions he had awakened in her.

It's believable that when the student finished his studies and left, maybe not forever, but to return from time to time, inspired the poem *Il Est Part* (*He Left*).

He Left! What land and country
Will see the one my heart loves so?
He left his timid girl abruptly,
For wealth and honor, he let go!!
Alas! Poor shepherdess! Life's cruel
What's left in her crushed little chest?!
He left her with her tears and sorrow
He left a dagger in her chest.
Oh, France, oh noble and sweet land,
Will my love ever be returning?
Or is he home in gloomy England?
In what castle is his soul burning?
When he returns, deep in the ground
He'll find the one he loved and he'd forgotten,
She will be dead, his pretty shepherdess
Dead from the pain and sleeping in a coffin! (1885)

The last two verses seem assertive, so this was not about an imaginary knight. The presumption of the man who had sneaked into her heart, that cause of her pain was somewhere in France or England is a precious clue, especially since the great "editor" of her work didn't add any footnote for this poem as he did for the others. That's what Iulia might have wanted for her hero; to be far away, locked in a castle, with his mind always on the girl he had left behind. We must emphasize the premonition of mystical sincerity: when he returns, he'll find his beloved sleeping in the ground, away from her brave knight.

In songs, ballads, and fragments she kept coming to the same idea of the heroic, forbidden love of a housekeeper for her handsome lord, or of a hero for the princess in a tower. It was not just once when Iulia felt like that princess locked away in a castle, kept away from society, suffering for her lover…

Oh, noble lord with royal eyes
Give her the freedom and the breeze
And she will pray till her last breath
For your kind soul to be at ease.

Against my will in this big castle
I yearn for the fresh air and sun
I cry, and sigh, and ask for mercy
I wish to live and love, to laugh and run!
I know that you can hear my prayer
So please, unite your heart to mine…[16]

One of the best literary sketches written by Iulia Hasdeu, the story of the *Butterfly Princess*, written in the same year, a story about a king and a queen with only a daughter for a child, was the life story of the author.

The originality of this work was surprising because of its inspiration, symbolism, and stylization, like an autobiography that could serve as a subtitle, by itself, of this great child poet's talent. This is the synopsis:

A king and his queen were beloved and respected by their people. The only heir was their little girl, whose godmothers were the seven fairies of that land. One of them, Darnica (the generous) gifted the girl with beauty. The second fairy blessed her with unmatched wisdom; the third gave her kindness; the fourth gave her a sharp mind and diplomacy; the fifth fairy blessed her with a talent for every type of art; the sixth gave her modesty, and the seventh gave her gentleness. The little girl was named Charmante (Charming). The fairy called Darnica was the girl's nanny at the palace and raised her to be a true princess. At fifteen years old, she was brilliant. She sang like a nightingale, danced, played every instrument, and was skilled in science. The king and queen loved her deeply. They wanted her to get married, so they requested a painter to make a portrait, but none of them could paint

---

[16] La Prisonniere — Chevalerie, 1885

her exact likeness. Darnica suggested the girl paint her own portrait by looking in the mirror, and she managed to create an astonishing portrait. This was sent to the neighboring kingdoms, and princes and kings soon started visiting the court and ended up surprised when they saw Charming. But the princess didn't pick any of them. The king was upset and despite trying his best to convince her, his attempts were futile.

"Why, my girl?"

"I don't know, Father. I might not have the gift of loving any man."

Darnica, learning of this from the king, remembered the fairies had forgotten to gift the girl with love at her birth. But she had a solution. The girl had to become a butterfly, the symbol of love, for a year. After thinking about it for a time the king agreed, and the princess was turned into one.

She became a butterfly but kept her intelligence. The queen was comforted by the idea her daughter would come back, but one of the princes, the Valiant, was inconsolable because he was in love with her.

He was handsome, gentle, and brave, and he had no idea where the charming princess had gone, and he was suffering.

"If I don't see the princess in two days I will die!" he shouted.

And indeed, he fell ill. His father, the king of another land knew what had caused it and asked the father of the princess to bring her to him. Charming found out and flew back. One day, the ill prince went for a stroll in the gardens, saw the butterfly, and asked his page to catch it. Charming let herself be caught.

The prince was working on a butterfly collection, took a pin, and told his page: "Bring me a piece of red velvet; I want to pin this beautiful butterfly on it for a nice effect."

Charming froze! His heart was made of ice. She had to die at the hand of the one she loved. It didn't matter, she'd seen him, and it was enough, therefore, she awaited death with resignation. The page returned with a beautiful red velvet pillow. The prince held the butterfly with one hand, and with the other, he pierced the tiny body with the pin. At that moment Charming felt ice flowing through her little veins; and then she couldn't feel anything. Her body grew, her wings vanished, and she appeared before the stupefied price just as she was before her transformation, as beautiful as ever.

In the end, the fairy godmother revived the princess, and the prince embraced her with that sacrificial love whose sharp spear had fatally wounded the butterfly's small heart…

This story contains the spirit and dreams for the love and life of Iulia Hasdeu from the time she was barely fifteen. It proves she didn't run away from love, just that she didn't feel it by that point. She wanted her love for a brave and handsome man to be white and pure, to allow her to accept the love arrow that could kill, or revive…

Despite her assiduous activity, that year, Lilica had the most charming appearance. Nothing on her face betrayed the slow disease that was silently taking over her chest. She was developing normally, and the word "miss," which her father was using as well, suited her well. She was a lady caught between two forces: the thirst for as much knowledge as she could acquire, and the persuasive instinct of learning true candid love. Her physical build on one side, and her lung illness on the other side, which had just managed to creep into her body, was dormant and somehow going unnoticed, equally contributed to her perpetual wish to know love, the most enticing love.

Her appearance was pure and so healthy that her classmates with whom she often joked, though she was the healthiest one of all. Jéanne Créhange had written to her the past summer saying:

"When are you coming back? I must let you know that even though I want you to spend as much time as possible there, I can't wait to kiss your chubby cheeks.

Don't be offended if I say you have chubby cheeks."

Her classmates were not the only ones strongly believing in her good health, her friends and parents did as well. Before leaving for Paris, after passing the exams at St Sava High School in Bucharest, young Novianu, one of their home's usual guests paid them another visit. After joking around, a fight broke out between the eleven-year-old girl and the young man, whose name was also Silică. We don't know if the joke was started by Lilica or by Silică, or what it was about, but it ended up with them wrestling on the floor and punching each other, a fight in which Novianu was defeated by Lilica. And he was only a few years older than her. Hasdeu reminded Lilica about this fight in one of his letters, and a witness also recounted it for us.

Chapter IX

Polen

April 1885. Partial exams tired her tremendously, and the final one, the baccalaureate, exhausted her completely. She needed new strength. The extra meals served by her mother, who was supervising her closely, didn't help enough and neither did the medicine prescribed by Dr. Percheron. However, something else seemed to help her: her great willpower that gave her an impulse of rhythm and energy. The rosy teenager's fibers were permanently drained of vigor. One day she went for a walk in Luxembourg Park, a place where she liked to go for strolls with her mother or with her friends, during the multicolored days of spring. Lilica sat on a bench feeling worn out, looking around, taking in the realities of life, and remembering the sorrowful past. She didn't know anything about the poet who had gifted her the white daisies. Where was he? What lands were the blue eyes admiring at that moment? She returned home late, and while her mother was asleep, Lilica spent time talking to April and its white flowers that had just showed their beautiful heads from the buds, and writing *Causerie d'avril* (*April Whispers*), with a motto from Belleau: *"Avril, l'honneur et des bois, et des mois…"*

The cheerful birds chirp on the branches,
Their small beaks joyfully kiss their lovely mates,'
The butterflies take their respite on periwinkles;
Blossoming April brings smiles to our eyes.

Beloved April, come, and please come faster!
Revive our lands and bring the song of love.
Dark winter, snow, and frost now leave us!
April revives all on earth and above!

The proud lily with all its gentle features,
Turns towards the blue sky and the bright sun

It is the king of the entire nature
Besides the sun, my equal, there is none!

I laugh at your secretive whispers.
April returns, and with it, comes love.
Why do you whisper, dear naive children?
Everyone's turn comes to feel the love!

Your turn...

That sounded like a threat or revenge.

The following month she sketched a drama called *Les Remords de Madame Audran* (*Madam Audran's Remorse*), which was started but finished in December the following year. The main subject also revolved around love. A man named Gaspard, after falling in love with a mother, also fell in love with her daughter, which was the subject of the intrigue. The mother was stuck between the man's threats to disclose their old affair and her husband's reproaches. He accused her of giving their daughter away to a coward. The mother was tormented by regret, and in the end, she died after being forgiven by her husband.

At the same time, she wrote a tirade caused by the attentions of an old man, which she called *Certain Age* with a motto from *Roman de Flamenca*:

Love is fickle,
Love is childish;
Its beautiful features,
Have a triumphant look.
Alas! You make me giggle,
You are a senile fool,
I have heard others saying
That love was not that cruel.

There couldn't be many reasons for the deep sorrow in her lyrics before she was even sixteen years old, except for the sadness and the inexplicable longing for death that almost always shows up around puberty, especially when the child is too guarded, too isolated, or too austere. Was it that restless instinct of youth that caused her developing vitality to fret? Was she longing for love? Did she have a thirst for that happiness that only Cupid knew how to quench? In seventh grade, her classmates were four to five years older, some were past seventeen or eighteen and enjoyed certain freedom, including balls, flirting, sentimental escapades, and receiving flowers from "special friends" as the custom was in French (and especially Parisian) culture. The girls were confiding in each other (as the following poem in *Confidences* shows), whispering with excitement about small love adventures, but great refuges they felt…

My God!

Young girls, think of the Spanish who are gone with no return!
(V. Hugo)

"My God! Please forgive me, as I have a death wish!"
I am not yet sixteen but my life is too bitter,
My heart is sad, my head is bowed in languish
With no friends, no happiness, at the peak of misery.

I would much rather die than shed tears;
It hurts me because crying feels good…
Alas! What do you want us to wish for
When we suffer and have no more tears?[17]

Without friends, without joy, at the height of misery! It was a true cry of despair, a cry towards God from an expanding soul with restricted indulgence… There were tears, longing, and sorrow. When natural desires called for the young soul, she dipped her wings in ink and flew towards algebra lessons. The young poet didn't complain about her health. She complained of something else.

She was always suffocated and terrorized by her schedule, by her father's name, by the idea of a bachelor's degree and a Ph.D., by decency, by diligence!

It wasn't surprising that the constantly suppressed libido of Iulia Hasdeu ended up a complex trauma with fatal consequences. When it comes to inferior beings, their subconscious resolves that issue in a completely different manner. The preservation instinct transforms, from a social point of view in ways to externalize through banquets or parties. The instinct of aggressiveness, which is a primary instinct, if becomes suppressed it can turn into envy, scorn, mockery, etc. Sexual instinct, always compressed by clothing, social order, and sanctions, borrows other external forms, other symbols that even though they have the same root as

---

[17] Vol. *Chevalerie* 131

sexuality, they become conventionally allowed: close dancing, wearing revealing clothes during balls, wording, and hints, etc.

When it comes to superior and cerebral beings, eroticism finds refuge in spiritual instincts, in artistic or literary creations. While instincts are always egocentric for both categories, at the moment they become expressed by symbols they become social.

Therefore, a suppressed wish becomes a poem when that person has talent, or it becomes a novel or a theater play in which intrigues and passion, which are usually objective, become subjective when the author lends it to the character they created.

That's why the poet's dream, dreams we'll reveal later, the dreams she confessed to as well as the ones she never confessed to, create pages, princesses, romantic knights in shining armor, and sacrifice. But all those characters love with Iulia's heart and kiss with her maiden lips.

In Hasdeu's time, science had not yet researched these psychiatric issues. Freud's line was not known yet. "The poet acts like a child at play: they create an imaginary world which they take seriously, a world they are greatly attached to even though it's completely different from reality." The main characters are, as Freud said, "partial egos," part of the author's ego. The world imagined by a child or by a poet is but a projection of their wishes, animated proportionate to the emotional talent.

That's what happened to the persistent eroticism that Iulia Hasdeu turned into spiritual creations.

This sacrifice might have been attributed to the great amount of talent as well as to its quality. Literature received her works as a gift, but her life stripped her of those gifts.

While Hasdeu was working hard on *Magnum Etymoloficum*, his daughter was giving everything to graduate high school and pass her final exams, despite the heavy teenage dreams on her shoulders and her inspirations. She could barely see, but she was studying, barely breathing, hiding in her books until five in the morning. She slept little, ate on the run, didn't play the piano anymore, she didn't relax anymore…

A serene face with blue eyes was still appearing from time to time among the pages of her books like a fog floating from oblivion. Was he even real? She didn't know if he was in England, if he had just moved to another apartment, if he had graduated, if he would visit Paris, or if he was under her window while she was focused on something else. Sometimes she would find herself saying: "Albert James, Albert James?" She often repeated her pseudonym used for the poems she was going to write in that year, published in *Bourgeons d'Avril*, which was Camille Armand, sometimes Armand Camille. Her father stated her chosen pseudonym was the first one mentioned. One of Byron's books in the Archives' library, *Childe Harold*, which Iulia Hasdeu read in 1885, was marked with her usual signature, but next to it the name Armand Camille is visible, Camille probably being a nickname. Iulia Hasdeu was not confident in her work and that was the name she wanted to write under when reaching the highest peaks of artistic conscience. A pseudonym!

The 22nd of May 1885 came with a blow to the heart of France, which produced an echo in Lilica's heart: the passing of Victor Hugo. Two days before the unfortunate event, Lilica found out his end was near and wrote a eulogy to the great master.

No, you will not die, Hugo! You frightened
Death. With her head bowed in compliment
She will back away from your sacred bed
And with respect, she'll delay the moment.

Before your brilliant and unequaled mind
Like the morning star shining on night's sky
Oh, grandfather, if I can call you that,
Death had to bow her head in respect...[18]

Poets are prophets; it's always been like that, but Iulia Hasdeu was the exception. She found out about the passing of her spiritual grandfather, she was shaken and cried, and wrote to her father:

"Victor Hugo died today at 1:30 in the afternoon, at the age of eighty-three years and three months.

And this is the terrible news that shook all Paris, all France, all Europe, and the whole world: Victor Hugo is dead.

As for me, I am devastated, I am heartbroken; the front page of the newspaper was framed in mourning, with big black letters saying: 'Victor Hugo has died... a brilliant light was extinguished...' I felt like I was stabbed in the heart. Dear Father, while writing this letter the quill trembles

---

[18] V. Hugo, *Bourgeons* 183.

in my hand, I feel overwhelmed, and I try in vain to cry. Oh, we can't cry when we're in such pain…"

And she continued retelling the sad event, which she first found out about from a market vendor, who was a great admirer of the poet, "…we owe a tear for the ones who made us cry for others."

In the footnote of that letter, Iulia Hasdeu added she had visited Eylau Avenue with her mother and they had signed the guestbook: "Madam and Miss Hasdeu from Romania, for the greatest of poets and citizens." She ended the letter with: "I cannot express the feeling when being so close to the wall behind which he, Victor Hugo, was laying; my heart was racing in my chest, my hands were shaking, and I turned red, red, red…"

By the end of July 1885, Iulia stopped writing, except for the dedication to her friend, Marie from Paris, on the occasion of the birth of her little brother, whom Iulia got to see sleeping and smiling.

Your lovely little brother might have seen
The charming days of yesterday past
He might have come to bring you joy
When he flew out of paradise…

(A une amie… Bourgeons…78)

Besides this short poem, she wrote a true love confession during the time she was studying for her final exams with the same friend, a poem that resembled a reproach called *Je N'ose* (*I Don't Dare*):

I might have a few things to say
But I don't dare, 'cause I'm afraid…
I can already see you laughing,
And in mockery freely displayed.
Your mouth resembles a red rose…
You will just smile in amusement,
And I'm too shy, and I don't dare
To look into your eyes' allurement.

I would like to be your king
And I want you to be my queen,
But even if you hated me
I'd still die for your devotion

I might be foolish, it is true,
But I know how to feel emotion...[19]

These lyrics were only a few of the ones she wrote for her loved ones in November of that year; other poems showed the same thirst for fearless, exigent, but not brought into the open as it was: (*A Celle Que J'aime — To the One I Love*).

You make a martyr of my heart
But no matter how hurt it is
Before my feelings fall apart
It's yours until I die, Marie...

Her inspiration while writing these poems was part of the same state of mind and state of her soul that was responsible for manifesting a normal love — as we mentioned before — which was usual for many other sentimental teenagers.

Besides, Marie, the recipient of these poems, who had honestly loved them, decided to commit an indiscretion despite Iulia's protests and shared them with other people. She shared them with the French language and literature professor, Maurice Albert, and confessed what a great talent Iulia Hasdeu had. The professor was already familiar with her work and was only half surprised. He knew she was a great writer, but he didn't know Iulia was into writing poetry as well. Marie Mavrodin showed him the poems Iulia had written for her. He read them, smiled, and called Iulia to see him.

"Did you write these poems?" he asked with a serious expression.

Lilica blushed, glanced at the sheet of paper, glanced at her teacher, and frowned at her classmate. She answered in a weak voice.

"Yes, Professor. Please forgive me, they're silly, but..."

"Excuse me, Miss Hasdeu, but allow me to decide that."

"Please forgive me. I won't do it again... I only showed them to Marie..."

"Oh yes, you'll write more!" he answered with an amused authority.

"What?"

"Yes, yes you will; but..."

The professor allowed a few moments to pass before answering. Lilica raised her eyebrows at him.

---

[19] (*Bourgeons* 100)

"But?"

"But… after you pass your finals! You, Miss Hasdeu, are very talented! But poetry requires dedication and a lot of work! Believe me!"

"I know, Professor," she confessed.

"Oh! You know! So you've written more?"

"Yes, I mean no…."

"Don't make excuses, miss. I didn't accuse you. I'm only trying to advise you. But this isn't surprising. You're Bogdan Hasdeu's daughter after all."

What followed between the two friends was not far from a catfight, but in the end, they shared warm hugs.

Finally, Lilica was about to take her final exams. They passed successfully, the small disciple passing the first part of the baccalaureate with the grades she was used to.

The student was more ready than any of her other classmates. She passed the analytical exams because the ones focusing on synthesis, science, and philosophy were in the second part. She gave everything to classic languages, such as French. Math came second.

It was the middle of June. Every window was open in the classroom. The warm air brought the scent of freedom, song, and games from the outside, the soul of Paris pulsing with life in every corner.

The Bois de Boulogne was giving away a grand prize for the horse races that was worth a fortune. There were more races in Auteuil. Paris was buzzing. The traffic was heavy with carriages, galloping horses, and shouting drivers. Children were laughing, ladies were giggling at the sight, newspaper boys were announcing the news about the grand prize.

The students heard bits and pieces of the outside world, but their faces didn't resemble any of the pleasantries of the boulevards and streets. Their faces were red from heat and emotion. Iulia's eyes were wider than ever.

During the French examination, she was asked about Molière, about the characteristics of his characters, and the era in which the great comedian had placed his heroes. Lilica was comfortable talking about this.

Not long before these exams, the young poet had started working on her great study that she would get back to in 1887, called *Mon Molière* (*My Molière*), following the template she'd used for *Mon Shakespeare*, *Mon Corneille*, and *Mon Sophocle*. This was probably the most complex of her studies, and it was supposed to be even bigger considering that of all the work of Jean-Baptiste Poquelin (called Molière) she only talked about Celimene's lover, Alceste the misanthrope, from the comedy with the same name. (*Le Misanthrope*).

She analyzed the character Alceste in a critical philosophical way, discussed pessimism and misanthropy from the perspective of Plato, Lucian, Jean-Jacques Rousseau, Shakespeare, Boileau, La Rochefoucauld, François Coppé, Sainte Beuve, Goethe, Schiller, Kotzébue, Labiche, etc., for having literary works on this subject or for their own comments on Molière. They were studied and quoted by Iulia Hasdeu with remarkable analytical skills.

"Molière gave all he had for this comedy about the Misanthrope," said Jules Janin.

"I don't believe that statement," said Iulia Hasdeu, "or, the most I believe of it is half. An individual, whoever they are, is never typical. A genius creates types and doesn't copy them. No doubt, he may observe the ones around him, but he guesses more than he observes. Two centuries would have not been enough for Shakespeare to observe everything he guessed. Alceste is the type of a man; so, he doesn't mirror Molière.

"I started this study to compare Molière's and Shakespeare's types of misanthropes. I will return to this when I finish. While Timon represents the highest level of misanthropy, we can even say, to a supernatural degree, Alceste is so different from him that we could even call him a misanthropic philanthropist. And yes, he is but a misanthropic philanthropist. He is very comical without being ridiculous by doubling his personality in this way. His heart makes him a philanthropist, while his reason makes him a misanthropist…"

There are two conclusions that anyone could reach after reading her study. First, she could have written amazing theater plays because she had been blessed with so much culture and a critical spirit. The second conclusion is that she had gathered so much knowledge during her few teenage years, even though she was busy day and night.

Her victory in the exams was therefore explainable because luck had no part in it. Professor Albert was delighted and congratulated the student for her perfect answer.

In Latin, she was fortunate to have to translate and comment on the work of Cornelius Tacitus. Iulia Hasdeu was very fond of him. She had read *The Annals* for school, and for her pleasure, she read *Agricola, Germania,* and *Dialogus de Oratoribus*. By reading, we also mean writing commentaries on the subject.

She had to translate a fragment of the twelfth book of *The Annals*, and she did it with an accuracy worthy of the good tutors she'd had. The professor stopped her on the part about Nero's speech and asked her how she explained the way in which the brutal Nero had been able to write such a speech. But the student knew it had been written by the wise Seneca, and she started on an extensive dissertation that had to be stopped by the professor. Of course, she had the same result in that exam as in the French exam.

She wouldn't have had any problem no matter the author she would have had to translate because her reading was up to date when it came to Livy, Horace, Virgil, Catullus, Tibullus, and Propertius. The proof is shown by her numerous quotes and mottos at the beginning of her poems.

The first part of the final exams was finished with exceptional results that brought her countless congratulations. Her mother was by her side constantly, laughing with emotion, dabbing her eyes from time to time. She was the one who informed Hasdeu of Iulia's accomplishments.

In the following letter, Hasdeu wrote to his family saying "the dog survives winter but only it knows how it did it" as an allusion to his daughter coming out victorious. But the revengeful nature always takes its toll. The poet was feeling well, she was happy, but her face was pale, her headaches had returned, and sometimes she was getting dizzy. Sometimes she spent her day lying down or strolling through the park, laughing, singing, but her mind didn't know any respite, and her soul was not at peace. The vital fluid in her heart was in turmoil at almost seventeen years old. She loved, as we know she loved. A friend. That was her only testified love. It might have been a part of idyllic poetry that found refuge in her heart and resonated with Marie's heart. She answered this love as anyone would, with warm friendship, and friendly love, but not as passionate as Iulia might have wanted.

I don't know how you can sleep
When the moon shines above us all?
Wake up at once, my lovely friend,
The air's so sweet after nightfall.

I want to tell you, my dear friend
My lovely black-eyed soulmate

The reason why I cry and fret,
The reason I stay up so late.[20]

Her dear friend was probably less romantic than her and sleepier, and she didn't respond to such monogenic callings; the poet wrote the following for that reason:

I know her; she's deceitful,
Her eyelids show emotion
But her heart doesn't feel it.
She swears to be faithful;
But she is like a swallow:
Fickle and disloyal.

The last part of this poem called *Vieille Chanson sur un Nouvel Air* (*An Old Song in a New Melody*) was like a rewording of the melody from "Rigoletto": "La donna e mobile…" The woman is fickle…

Yes, a woman's like a leaf
Collected by a passing breeze
Floating away, carried by the wind
I know it is true, nothing can be done
Despite me not approving of her way
I'll still love her as before anyway.[21]

She always used the same tone when writing about women. They were always fickle according to Iulia Hasdeu's poems and her later comments.

At the same time, when she found herself alone, missing her homeland and her good childhood friends, Florica, Matilda, and Hermina. She wrote an ode to her Dacian origins, *Chanson Dace* (*Dacian Song*). The last line says, "But you, Dacian, keep your head high!" In one of her patriotic fragments called *Six Soeurs* (*Six Sisters*), one that was supposed to have been expanded to a great historical poem, Iulia Hasdeu praised the six Romanian regions crossed by the Danube and the Olt River and cooled by the Carpathian Mountains.

In it, the Olt River tells the Danube about the places of its origins, the lands it flows through, and what the Carpathian Mountains see:

---

[20] Nocturne, Bourgeons 125.

[21] (*Bourgeons…* 48)

Torrents of red blood,
And blue waters flowing through the meadow
Turning shades of purple flowing through the country.

The nostalgia of the same sights from home seen through a lacey fan, the ivory branches, and the paintings were remembered by someone from the family of Hasdeu's good friend, Theodor Speranția, who had seen him and was eager to share impressions of those times.

The poem *L'éventail* (*The Fan*) was written during the "good old days" of gentlemen and ladies in corsets, with a thin waist and with fans covering their features.

She felt like she could smile behind the shady lace,
Her eyes were stealing glimpses of the surrounding place
Protected by its shadow, victorious and haute
She watched the marquis kneeling, nervous but full of hope.

The fan remained forgotten on a red cushioned sea
The lady had left hastily, her carriage discreet.
The next day, someone who's seen in her the bliss
Returned the missing object on her doorstep: the marquis.

And that's the way the fan placed in its rosy case
Was fast asleep again, dreaming in its embrace,
Remembering the bosoms it used to cover up
Regretting the illusion that vanished at wind-up.[22]

A salon, a serenade, a minuet, a harpsichord! These were the setting of that lacy poem, despite the turbulence caused by the delicate and discreet love that Iulia Hasdeu dreamed of. The poem could have been signed by Sully Prudhomme, or François Coppée in their youth.

Around the same time, she wrote the ballad *Le Pauvre Page* (*The Poor Page*), which laments the fate of the poor pages who were used as toys by influential people.

Pages, adored so by the ladies
The ones who would offer their souls,

---

[22] Bourgeons

Do not give in to their temptation
Because they're cruel and deceitful...

The same mirage of a past love is shown in an imitation of Walter Scott's work, *Chanson du Brave Archer* (*The Song of the Brave Archer*)[23] in which Iulia told a story about a young man in old heroic Scotland, which could have been molded by the man with blue eyes.

Son of Scotland, yes, I was born for you,
Despite the dangers you may run into,
I want to unite my destiny to yours,
I want to live and die for our souls,

Look at me, brave archer, I am beautiful:
Strong, with olive skin, dark hair, playful.
If you want my love, I'll be most true
It will be forever for my one and only: you...

I'll put my hand in yours, always and forever
And follow you believing, be by your side wherever.
We'll bind our souls together and for eternity
In death, we'll be together just like in life, full of glee.

Was this fantasy or a testimony? Or both? Who could know? One thing is for sure: she wanted him, and she wanted him in a way that was worthy of her love. The poem *Le Souhait d'une Vilaine* (*The Wish of a Villain*) was a reflection of her characteristic and expressive mind:

If I were the chatelaine
Of some noble manor
That dominated the sight
Of its wide dark region.

I'd wear my hair in braids
Adorned with emeralds,
I'd listen to the ballads
Of the gentle bards.

---

[23] *Chevalerie* 12.

I am destined to be
The wife of a knight

That would be my victory
As won in a fight
The bard would tell the story
Of his brave adventures

My name would bring him glory
If sewn on his flag
Floating in the breeze
On top of a rampart.[24]

During the time when Iulia Hasdeu was writing these poems with perfect French prosody and blooming inspiration, romanticism, especially in France was not at its peak, despite Lamartine, Musset, Gautier, Vigny, Nodier, Deschamps, George Sand, and especially Hugo. They were not born from the poetic work of Iulia Hasdeu as a bud of April.

The ballads of those nights with moonlight, the theme adopted by all romantics, were constantly calling to the fifteen-year-old girl, especially the nocturnes sung by wise Selena when guiding lovers in *Il Fait Nuit* (*It's Nighttime*)

It's dark and everything is sleeping,
Except for the wandering wind
Who wanted to give the rose a kiss
Not wanting it to fall asleep...
Playfully he makes the trees sway

Around the moon dance
Clouds from the heavens,

And its prying light
Won't inconvenience this evening
But it's watching the two lovers
During their walk.
The flowers the wind touches
Fragrance the air around them

---

[24] Chevalerie 45

Everything displays emotion
In the mysterious woods.

There's no noise in the leaves
The sleeping nightingale
Has stopped its chatter
For its friend, sleep.
It's the hour of the loyal lover
Who watches as everything sleeps,
From the doorway of his beloved,
By her side, dead or alive.[25]

That was how Iulia imagined her loyal lover, watching over her sleep and dreams, just as she would do for the one chosen by her heart, the slave of eternal love. All these poems were written in 1885 after passing her final exams, and before she took another trip to the mountains, written with care and accuracy, but they were not created during her hours of respite no matter how inspired she felt at that moment. They were laid on paper after hours of hard work, of persistent thinking. They are creations that would honor any French poet. We say that so we don't overshadow the quality Romanian poetry born from the genius of Eminescu, Alecsandri, and Gr. Alexandrescu.

But she needed rest. A break in the mountains, filled with fresh air and sun, laziness, and fun. Did Iulia Hasdeu find all of this in the place where her parents decided to take her?

Another resort was chosen, one in Zurich, surrounded by elegant villages, on the shores of a lake, embraced by fragrant evergreen forests, one of them being Wartenstein. In the second half of July, Iulia found herself in this small, charming village with Gothic towers, villas, and tall hotels rising towards the sun and the fresh air. The surroundings were new, inviting, and joyful. Lilica was happy and her soul was being called by stars and electrical spheres. She was lively, showing her mother so many places and lines where nature had imprinted its grace and eloquence. They took walks together, but her mind couldn't take a break as her mother wanted.

"Maria told me you are writing poetry again when you're supposed to be resting. Please, dear, leave them aside from now on. You worked enough."

---

[25] *Bourgeons* 168, 1885.

"I'll stop, Mother, but they need to leave me too! Look there, far away; look how the sky calls the earth and the clouds kiss the forests. Their white arms embrace the peak… there is love and kindness in nature. But people won't take it as an example."

"You can't change the world, Lilica. Come on, drink your milk! These people have really good milk. Drink, my dear, drink!"

"Later, Mother; let me talk to my good father who loves and spoils my soul."

But the girl's rest was in truth a toil. It was a battle between abstinence and urges, between the rest prescribed by doctors and the turmoil of her mind. A week passed in this way. However, August said "Enough!" God had listened to the prayers of this poet and shared a bit of his creative spirit. "Come on!" A big locust was flying before her; behind her, a spring was trickling its cool water towards her, and God saw it all. And that's how *Chanson du Faucheur* (*The Song of the Reaping*) was born.

The pale wheat falls reaped
The bees gather and buzz,
Crickets are hiding in the grass
To sing about the summer God gave us.

God gives springs their freshness;
And if he wills in the field
The reaper has shade always
From the swaying amber leaves.

God gives the reaper his health
And harvest to all of his lands;
He gives girls their beauty
And gives us dear friends.

Let's all praise the Lord…

Let's sing His praises morning and evening,
And may He hear our song
A pious fragrance of incense
The hymn of our joy.[26]

---

[26] (*Bourgeons* 1885).

Forgetting for a second about castles with marquises and pages, her affection was turned towards the modest children of the earth; the poet wrote: *Chanson Hongroise* (*Hungarian Song*) about the face and soul of a brave knight (wearing a sword, spurs, and a whip). Thinking "The brunette girl I love is not a countess" but "her feet are bare; her hair is braided."

It was enough for her to imagine the rustic love and a horse rider for her dreams of knightly romance to come back, dreams of loving a "brave knight," a Roland that she was restlessly searching for.

Oh, find me, find me on this earth
Knight without reproach and fear:
Gentle with his lover, invincible in war,
Who never fights except for honor;
A loyal lover bound by an oath,
Oh, he's the one that my heart seeks for.

There was just one hero such as him in the world:
It was Roland…
Roland is dead! And my life is over…

Wartenstein, August 1886[27]

This poem had Roland! Others had Bayard! Another had a joyful bard who travels with his loyal dog, singing serenades under the window of his beloved. Another poem had a betrayed Valentin: "Oh, I know you'll betray me!... But I still believe in you." In another poem, she scolded the unfaithful and fickle knight.

You promised her eternal love
You had to love your lady and for her
Be ready to fight, to win or die;
And you betrayed your word, sir knight…
You must serve your lady, as you serve your God.

Another creation of hers punished the unfaithful knight, making him fall on his knees before the woman he'd caused to suffer.[28]

All these were internal screams from every fiber of the body; they were desperate calls. Her heart was craving an ideal world: "Oh, find me, find me on this

---

[27] *La Fiancée de Roland* — Roland's Fiancée, Chevalerie.

[28] *Souvenir-Bourgeons* 28.

earth, Knight without reproach and fear; Gentle with his lover..." We wonder if she was not waiting for her perfect knight, that Lohengrin brought to her by a fantastic swan, a man who was gentle, brave, and loyal.

The lyrical heart of the poet might have become calmer if only she had more years to live...

The same summer brought her the memory of the death of a poor bull she had seen killed in the arena, an animal that understood it was time to go only after its whole strength left it. The poet wished for a similar death, one that came after a fight, after irreparable defeat...

But it's equal to what despair gives him
A good death is his strongest wish.
So when everything abandoned him,
Despite all his faults, God forgives
The man who knows to die well.

"To die well!" A fifteen-year-old child thought of this when her soul was joyful, when her cheeks were rosy, while listening to the thrilling song of the blackbird. What secret wish persisted in the mind of the girl, even at eight, nine, ten, fifteen years of age?

From time to time, her constant refuge in love for a friend came as salvation, as an overflow of emotions she let free. She would have confused her love in those Swiss woods, on those shady paths where it seemed she could hear the voice and see the beauty of that beloved girl. She would have told her that on her knees... However...

Nothing could touch her heart,
Her heart didn't feel either love or hate[29]

But the end of August took her away from that earthly heaven with fir trees, flowers, butterflies, and sun, but lacking angels, and the train brought her back to Paris with its noise, sorrow, memories, and books.

She had plenty of time until the second part of her final exams. She had to reenter the temple of creation, tune the harp, and give a voice to the cherubims and the seraphims. Her soul was refreshed, reborn, pulsing with life, but melancholic. She raised her head towards the sky like a lily spreading its golden pollen.

---

[29] Feuille verte d'églantier – The Green Rosehip Leaf. Bourgeons d'Avril.

At that time, the poet wrote the parable of Marta and Maria, that Maria who, just like Iulia, "...took the most important part: my soul!"

She wrote the gentle pious poem called *La Vièrge au Manteau* (*The Veiled Maiden*), in which Virgin Mary, embracing the cross on which her son was suffering, covered his cold feet with her cloak...

And Jesus told her: "Thank you, woman!"
She wrapped him in the sacred veil,
He closed his eyes, released his soul.
But Mary could no longer wail.[30]

It was the most profound evocation of a supreme moment! It was a delicate comprehension of the female essence from the consolation of a divine maiden. "Mary could no longer wail..." The mother had given her son the last possible consolation; she covered his cold feet with her veil and her warmth... and at that moment the son gave his last breath. This "Thank you, woman," even though it seems cold in contrast with the tears of his mother, has a deep meaning. He didn't thank his mother at that moment, but the womanly kindness, and the generosity of the feminine soul!

The poet praised the same feminine gentleness in *Pétrarque à Laure*, one of the most massive poetic creations of Iulia Hasdeu, in which the feelings of love and adoration compete with mature thoughts and clever poetic expressions.

Oh, you, who were the pride and love of my life,
Oh, Laura, I've always served you with passion.
The God that has given the rose its perfume
Has given me pure love for your beauty.

And Petrarch confessed that:
Our love is purer than earthly flames
Makes us forget our bodies and unifies our souls
A charming love that is sweet like honey.

Laura for him is: "A masterpiece of God with a flawless body."

Further on, when it comes to the eternal feelings of the heart, the poet said:

The soul is everything; it is God's touch in nature
The soul cannot die. It's the murmuring spring,

---

[30] *Chevalerie* 106.

The forests, the mountains, the universe, one day
All might be shadow and smoke,
But, my love, our souls are immortal,
Making our love eternal!

May the man find beauty in everything;
May he love the buds of June flowers,
The forests, the streams, the blue sky;
Every true and righteous deed of the heart,
He will find God in the end![31]

We believe that Petrarch himself would have approved with all his heart of the poem written by the almost sixteen-year-old girl, for the way she knew how to depict his great undying passion.

The poem *Magdeleine* joins the pure and dogmatic atmosphere of love with the mystical passion that Christ forgave and preached in His godly manner. It has a motto from A. de Musset: "May the earth rest lightly on them! — they loved it."

Forgiveness is my only mission
– Just like my Father told me to –
My soul's at peace with its condition
After the love's fire burned true.[32]

Her poetic spirit, however, caught flights in another field as well, one bordering innocence, the candor of love, the gratitude towards her parents when evoking childhood, and everything that had been dear to her during those ripe years. That's how the poem *L'armes d'enfance* (*The Tears of Childhood*) was born, a creation dedicated to her mother.

Oh, charming days of childhood,
Sweet tears I shed for nothing,

Tenderly wiped by mother's hands…

She wrote a second poem, *Amour Maternel* (*Motherly Love*), in which she expressed her feelings towards the daily love and care of her mother.

---

[31] *Chevalerie* 16, 1885.

[32] *Bourgeons* 52, 1885.

Motherly Love

"A Mother's love how sweet the name
What is a mother's love?"
(J. Montgomery)

When children choose to come to this early plane
They remember their wings, their flight in the light
They always miss heaven, revisit it in dreams
This world is their torment, a drama like no other.
But to comfort their pain, their tears coming in streams
God gave them the best gift, the arms of their sweet mother.[33]

That was the sweetest homage the parents could have received from a child whose heart God had gifted with so many talents! Similar to the love she felt for her parents and other childhood experiences, Iulia Hasdeu cried for her memories of home, cried about her fatal uprooting, despite her great fondness for her second home, which was France. Those were the days in which she wrote *La Roumanie* (*Romania*), *Patrie* (*Country*), *Le Grelot* (*The Bell*) which was dedicated to her good friend Florica, who was a student in Bucharest, *Une Nuit* (*One Night*), *Les Perles* (*The Pearls*), and *Prisonnière Roumanie* (*A Romanian Prisoner*).

In the poem entitled *La Roumanie*, with a motto from the German poet Tiedge, Iulia Hasdeu invoked the muse to sing about her beloved country, where "God's smile made the mountains rise" and the people working at the foot of the mountain were "the path to the East."

Below your feet, you'll see this earth
At sunset, between two royal rivers,
The mountains, with their mysterious woods,
A beautiful corner that might make you quiver.
By looking at it you'll see it's a utopia
Is the land of God so blessed with harmony
– Muse, you will tell him why:
        Because this is Romania!

The nostalgia of her uprooting that caused her such sorrow was poured into this homage, which was more than a poem or a glorification of her country (that had

---

[33] (*Chevalerie* 1886).

started, as Hasdeu stated, during the war in 1877-1878), which was only a small fragment:

Alas! We have no other hope when dying
Only the thought of suffering no more
Oh, country, our land that's crying...

Oh, country! For you, our only treasure,
We fought, and we will fight again with passion,
We hold a strong belief in our hearts with courage
That one day we will be worthy of our lineage,
Worthy of our Latin ancestry, whose fate
Was more about its life than about its death...[34]

Doesn't this show, just like other creations, that poets are the prophets of a nation?

In *Le Grelot* she remembered a trip to the countryside in the mountains and described an evening scene, the nearby lake, the calm, quiet mountains, and the gentle, melancholic sound of a bell coming from somewhere in the forest:

I think about you with all my heart,
About your voice calling me from the shadows,
Guiding my steps when the night was dark.
I think to myself, how would my life be
If I still heard your voice in the shadows...

In *Les Perles* she talked about the longing she felt for her country, which was alive and persistent in her nationalist heart:

Put on the white pearls

I want to follow you, bird
And fly with you in the blue sky!

I want to see the waves of the Danube
And the golden mountain peaks
Shone in the rays sent by God.

---

[34] (A la patrie — Chevalerie 173).

She expressed the same reveries and longing for her country, for the national dances, for the rivers and the springs in the poem called *Prisonnière Roumaine*.

In *Une Nuit* (written in August the following year), Iulia brought up the church from the Archives with its crosses and graves, in the same manner as she did in the poem *Le Cimetière* (dedicated to Florica who was by her side at the Archives, walking among graves, a scene we mentioned before).

After describing her memories in the churchyard, the whipping willows, the cypress trees, cherry trees, acacias, and the time of joyful play between them, the poem said:

It passed just like a fleeting dream
The joy of our long-gone childhood
But maybe at the end of our road
We will return to our old cemetery
Our hearts have been long separated on land
But the bright morning will shine on us
When we've gone like an evanescent dream!

The same warm place of childhood, the same cemetery surrounded by whipping willows in which she wanted to be buried next to her friend, was mentioned by Iulia on a small piece of paper her father was going to find one day among her notebooks:

"Oh, my dear church in Mihai-Vodă, my dear yard, and the small garden that I used to tend and water with so much love in the past! Oh, the cemetery where I happily climbed trees, where I had fun deciphering the names inlaid in the tombstones! Oh, my dogs, my songs, my beautiful black kitten! Oh, the two elderly women who have been part of my departed childhood! Alas! If you saw me now, I don't believe you would recognize me anymore! I no longer understand the language of animals and flowers; I can no longer read the names on the graves; I don't know how to speak with the elderly anymore... Oh, my poor church! I don't even know how to cry anymore."
(April 10th, 1885)

It might have been that "evil of the century," or the migraines, or the chest pains if we looked at the reality. It might have been the sorrow from being away from home, or a matter of the heart. Or maybe all of them combined. Who knows? Certainly, the girl was suffering.

From a psychological point of view, Iulia Hasdeu had two feelings that were opposing each other; school and crowds excited her; when she was alone, she was full of sadness and pessimistic thoughts. That pessimism we know from her secret confessions she had started when she was around eight or ten years old, seemed to be the mystical root of a true tragic premonition. She was carrying the death intuition in her heart, death was following her, smiling at her. She was not afraid of it, but it seemed she was calling it on purpose.

It's incontestable that besides this psychological state she was tormented by a tangible reality: her uprooting, her incipient illness following her measles and her bronchitis, and love, or the thirst for love that was constantly hidden. On top of that, there was another discernible element.

We know that Iulia Hasdeu was inclined toward romanticism before she left her home country, due to the books she was reading, and it was enhanced by the atmosphere in her home. Hasdeu, who was a romantic as well in both poetry and criticism, was horrified by the realism and naturalism that was still developing back then. He didn't speak of Gustave Flaubert, but he completely despised Émile Zola, his successor. It might have been the fact that he was Jewish, or because his literary work was focused on the realities of life, with its beauty, but also with its horrors and crimes.

Already having this predisposition, Iulia Hasdeu was entangled in the French romantic literary current that was still going strong during those times and was the epicenter of every art enthusiast. French romanticism was indeed taking its last breaths, but "the evil of the century" was still an epidemic. At the time when Iulia Hasdeu was gifted with a romantic sense, all the representatives of this genre, with Victor Hugo at their helm, came to enhance it, so realistic literature didn't satisfy her at all. The work she had left for us to explore was nowhere influenced by the Goncourt brothers or Flaubert, even though Flaubert had already made an impact in France starting in 1850, especially with the case of *Madame Bovary*. Zola became equally famous before 1880, especially with his series *Rougon Maquart*, *Une Page d'Amour*, and *Le Rêve*, but Iulia despised them even though most romantic young girls read them with enthusiasm.

There were other objective writers such as Bourget, Barres, even Daudet who received a great amount of fame back then.

Iulia Hasdeu was in her element only when she was reading romantic literature. Unfortunately, nobody was aware of her literary productions. It is believed that her professors, Bréal, Albert, and Leger, tried to deviate from the artistic path of the dreamy poet, who was reading Taine out of obligation, but wasn't influenced by it in the least.

Trapped in the sea of books and notebooks, protected by a medieval knight's armor, Iulia Hasdeu fed her creations with her flesh, like an esoteric pelican. She read to suffer. She used her suffering to write. Besides the English romanticism of Byron, Shelley, and especially Shakespeare with its morbid *Hamlet*, Iulia Hasdeu read less pessimistic romantic literature, such as Racine, Corneille, and especially Molière, which was enough to see her spiritual reaction following it and deduce the healthy influence she might have gotten if she chose to read at least some of the contemporary critics and realists.

In this spiritual situation, next to her lyrical and deceptive poetry she added priceless works written in 1885, which have the same essence.

Among them, there is a dramatic sketch written in prose, which she wanted to expand, later on, called *Alcee et Sapho*, which came as an attempt to create an alternative literary version of the poet Sappho from Lesbos.

To help you see how Iulia Hasdeu created a literary work of great proportions, it is enough to reproduce all the material she had to study and use as sources for her inspiration, which is noted at the end of her sketch:

"Sources: *Erynnae vatis quae extant residua, aetas patria, scripta*; Upsalae 1826 — Richter, Sappho und Errinae; Quedlinburg 1833 — Malzow, *De Erinnae Lesbiae vita: Petropoli* 1836 — Welcker, *De Erinna, dans Creuzer, Melemata e disciplina; antiquitatis Lipsiae* 1817. — Hock, Alcaeus und Sappho, Berolini 1862.

To be compared: Sappho de M-me de Stael, — Sappho de Grillparzer. — Sappho de Lyly (?!?).

She started the sketch in 1885 and completed it in 1887. It was about the well-known rivalry between the poet Sappho and the poet Alceu. Sappho challenged her rival to a lyrical duel to prove to judges and to the nation which one of them was better. The duel took place. Alceu did his best with his lyre and received applause. Beautiful and seductive Sappho approached Alceu, and while her body captivated his eyes and remained silent, she won with her lyrics. But triumph made her a martyr. She loved Alceu and wanted him to win. After a few scenes in which their love was trying to live in vain, she threw her lyre in the sea and followed it.

Among the characters in the drama, Iulia insisted upon one that was Sappho's and the author's passion, her friend Errina, a young student of Sappho who was

Iulia's age. She was falling in love with Alceu as well. The girl was shy, a sentimental poet who was also destined to an untimely death.

One of the few dialogues Iulia talked about, there was a sweet and captivating lyrical perfume. She poured all her gentleness and inspiration into Errina especially.

Errina (to Sappho)

I haven't spread my perfume onto any meadow. Ah! Sister, my lovely sister, that handsome young man! Did Apollo himself appear before me at the temple? I still want to laugh at the expression I must have had. I laugh, I laugh... Oh, I'm laughing like a fool... Play, I'm done now... I'm done. I won't laugh anymore. I'm not laughing, am I? Tell me, tell me, tell me fast sister, my love, my fierce young lioness, my majestic tulip, my green-eyed goddess!

Sappho

You are mad! What young man did you see at the temple of Apollo?

Errina

Gods and Goddesses! He was so handsome! You know, I brought you some primroses... Oh! I found them in the woods near the temple. Here, I have a lot of them. There, more...more... I also found a nest of blackbirds on the lower branches of an elm tree, but I didn't disturb it. The mother was in there. After that, I saw old Chronis looking for herbs for her ill son. I helped her find some, and to thank me she promised to give me a beautiful white veil for the festivity in your honor, my doe...

Would Madame de Stael have fully approved these inspired and finely crafted lines?

In the following parts, there is one where Errina sang to Cupid, a song written under the name of *Anacréontique*, with a note of inspiration from *Anacréon*. Her father reproduced it in Greek in *Bourgeons d'Avril*. Fair-haired Cupid was walking among the roses when he pricked his finger on a spine.

He blows on his finger, he sucks it and squeezes it,
But in vain! He went to the goddess of beauty
And sulking he told her: "I don't love flowers anymore!"
And Venus smiled and replied: "You whisper.
You're beautiful like them, child, and you cause sorrow,
We love you, but you pierce the hearts!"

From mutual confessions, Errina found out who Alceu was for Sappho, and when she told her she was going to die because of him Errina swore to follow her... Both the master and the poet loved in vain... And it was true, she indeed followed her!

Errina was portrayed vibrantly and expressively. Iulia Hasdeu's confession at the end of the sketch was pleasing:

"No, I am not Errina; or, if you want, she is me at sixteen years old, not as I was but as I would have wanted myself to be, as I would have been if I had a Sappho in my life. But I was denied that joy, so let me stay in my childhood dream, let me believe that Errina is neither me nor anyone, that there are no Errinas in the world; she's an illusion, a ghost, an ideal created by my soul that has never existed..."

However, her father defended ancient Errina, who was a real person who passed away at nineteen years old as a maiden poet. He insisted on the bond between the fate and the soul of that maiden and the soul and fate of his daughter, which were almost identical... mentioning again she had foreseen her death.

Next to these lyrical expressions in which Iulia, besides epic legends or historical facts, focused on her feelings and dreams, sketching other poems and plays with epic characters, in which it's noticeable as always how she had studied and how carefully she had compiled her historical sources. She was attracted by two topics at the same time, that might have been influenced by the reading list required for her final exams, one of them being *Popée* (the subject of a drama), that she had extracted from Tacitus. The poet sketched the script of five acts she was planning to expand later on, in which the figure of the brutal Neron was supposed to be the main character next to the female hero named Popeea, his mistress, and Octavia's rival. She was sent into exile by the arsonist emperor of Rome, where she met Strabo, her former lover, and Anicet, the commander of the fleet. The plot and the action were the settings for an imposing drama that could have had a successful composition.

The second work, written in the fall of 1885 but was completed in 1887, was *L'ami de Trajan* (*Trajan's Friend* – the sketch of a lyrical drama). Besides the emperor, the drama features other characters such as Longinus, Trajan's friend, and Pliny the Younger's and Seneca's disciple, Albinus, one of Trajan's loyal officers, Decebal, the noble Dacian king who was a prisoner of the Romans, Dokia, Decebal's daughter, with a wonderful moral character, and Sarmiza, Dokia's nanny, as well as slaves and soldiers. The plot revolves around Sarmisegetuza,

Decebal's refuge after it was conquered by Trajan. How the story evolves was masterfully crafted: Dokia's intrigue and cunning, Longinus' sacrifice of becoming Decebal's prisoner to facilitate the attack, the way Dokia shows her love towards Longinus, the letter Decebal sends to Trajan to ask him to give the attack up without success. After Trajan conquers Sarmisegetuza he turns Decebal into his prisoner, which resulted in Dokia's death after she drinks a vial of poison she found in Longinus' belongings. All these scenes, with the decorum, details, and fluidity, prove the deep knowledge of theater and scenic effects that Iulia had. And we're only talking about a sketch that was drafted in two versions, the second version containing a Dacian hymn published in *Bourgeons d'Avril* on page 114.

Before she concluded her artistic creation from 1885, we have to remember two of Iulia's important mentions, first from that year, and the second without a precise date. First, *Amen,* which the girl wrote on the fifteenth of December as a reflection of her sixteenth birthday celebrated on the fourteenth of November.

"My birthday was on November 14th, 1885 when I turned sixteen years old. When I woke up in the morning on this day, starting the life of a young woman, I picked up Victor Hugo's book *Chants du Crépuscule* (*Songs of Twilight*). Chance made the book open at the page I've read the most, a page that I knew by heart, marked by a dry white daisy. My eyes fell on the following lines:

Put your spirit out of this world,
Put your dreams somewhere other than here;
Your pearl is not found in our waves,
Your path is not found beneath our feet...

I immediately turned these verses into the motto of my life. Nobody knows how many tears I spilled onto this sacred page while swearing to myself to be faithful to this motto I have chosen. Others might say it was too bold of a sixteen-year-old, but many women with wrinkled faces and gray hair don't understand the torments of the heart that I've been through and don't believe they're real! But I'm not worried about that; yes, I will glide

...above the other women:

I have courage and strength. May God not abandon me and protect my white sail from winds that would tear it down. Ah! I was born to love; I know that, but it doesn't matter anymore!

To be conquered without knowing you're in danger is a triumph without glory!

I want to be victorious, and I know I will be! And when I will have passed through every difficulty in life while staying pure, my glory will be even greater. I'll have to conquer the war with myself to have a complete victory."

The second mention, which belongs to Hasdeu, refers to the unknown activity of the girl, the titles he'd found in manuscripts containing thirty-four dramas, eighteen comedies, and twelve novels or studies which would have been written in detail later, sketches that we've mentioned before. When it comes to the dramas and the comedies, Iulia even mentioned the French stages she would have wanted them to be played on.

Chapter X

A Deceitful Zephyr

The beginning of 1886 found Iulia Hasdeu in full poetic bloom, but also very busy getting ready for the second part of her final exams. Would it be difficult to guess which one of those activities she preferred? Even though she didn't write as much as in the previous year, she still had an impressive collection of creations. But more than in the year past, her poems reflected the increasing torment of her caged feelings, pouring tears and laments from the poet's heart. It seems that Eros was cruelly plotting against her and some of the events of that year confirmed this theory.

Besides the poem *Vers le Passé* written in January 1886, which was a persistent echo of her callings, her other poems breathed the air of castles, seasons, and flags carrying the names of lovers through meadows. Her own words testified to the poetical nature of these dreams of chivalry:

> This heroic life is filled with perils
> That come to haunt my childish dreams;
> It tastes bitter and I often regret
> To be born in these sophisticated times,
> Where we need honor and idyllic love
> Without which only fools can be poets...

The defining word of her dreams, childish, which was not used in a derogatory way, reflected how tired Iulia was of this persistence of her heart. We could say she was tired of this heroic life which she always dreamed of and wished for, but which she couldn't find anywhere.

On the day of Epiphany, Iulia and her mother joined the Romanian Catholic service in the small and poor church of St. Jean de Beauvais, which from the street looked more like a small customs office. In those days the church was led by one of the future hierarchs of the Romanian Church, one of Hasdeu's friends, a priest with a remarkable intellect who was destined to become the Metropolitan of

Moldova under the name Partenie. Mother Iulia, unlike her daughter, preferred to pray in Orthodox churches, but she often joined the Sunday service, taking time to speak to the gentle priest.

At the helm of the Romanians gathered for that particular service was Vasile Alecsandri, standing proudly in a black trench coat, his forehead wide, his gaze full of respect and dignity. Mother Iulia greeted him, the poet replied, and Lilica sent the bard a smile full of admiration. The two women were surrounded by many acquaintances and a few friends that Iulia was candidly looking for. Maria Mavrodin was standing further away from her but moved next to her to exchange a few words.

On the opposite side where men were gathered, Lilica's eyes spotted a face; they widened, turned back towards the iconostasis, then slowly turned towards him again. It was the English, Irish, or Scottish poet, she still didn't know which one of the three he was, the student, the neighbor on the second floor. "Is it really him?" she asked herself. Who else? His thick hair was combed back, his face couldn't be anyone else's, his wide collar. His blue eyes were reflecting the stained glass and seemed even brighter and more expressive. Those were his eyes, the eyes encompassing the Nordic Sea, and those eyes were watching her insistently. A discreet greeting obliged her to return it.

"Who did you greet, Lilica?" whispered her mother.

"Me? Oh, yes! I believe it was Councilor Petrescu…," said Lilica.

"Do you know him?"

"Yes, from the passport service office… You know…"

And the religious ceremony followed its course, and every Christian in the room was feeling it body and soul. All except Lilica…

"Why is he in a Romanian church? Is it really him? Did he find out I was here and come to see me? Maybe he isn't even an Englishman. It would be funny if he was French. Or a Russian! But he doesn't have a Russian accent! Then why does he speak and write English so well? Why didn't I ask him? That's ridiculous. How come I speak and write French so well then? And where was he until now? What if it isn't him?"

While her mind was tormenting her with all those questions, their eyes kept meeting. The young man's eyes were joyful, but Lilica's eyes were grave and frightened. The voice from the altar was coming down from infinite piety, with white doves, almost imperceptible. The choir blended harmoniously with the people's hope. They were singing something. But what? Lilica was not able to distinguish it. Was it just one song or more? There was only one song resounding in her heart, a song she kept pushing away but that kept coming back. She tried to understand the song in the church: "All of you baptized into Christ accepted Christ into your body! Hallelujah!" The choir was singing with pianissimo modulations that were rising and resounding through the church. Did she accept Christ into her body? Was she worthy of him? "Oh, God." She was carrying his cross on her delicate shoulders. The cross was heavy, pressing down on her body in punishment! "No!" Someone had told her that only happiness is the same in everyone's soul, but sorrow is always different! Who was telling the truth then? Who? And why would God punish her? Was she in love? "Oh, God of love! Is this path in your world a punishment? And what is love?" Her gaze rested on the right of the altar door. The man dressed in a mantle was standing there, the mantle that the ungodly threw money at, the man with grave eyes full of forgiveness, understanding, and kindness, himself the symbol of love. He was the son of the Virgin, the divine son… Lilica bowed her head and crossed herself as a symbol of her own sorrow.

The service ended. After the customs that followed, Alecsandri took a few steps to the side and waited for Mrs. Hasdeu. They met and discussed it casually. After greeting him, Lilica politely replied to the questions of the Romanian Minister, while glancing toward the people that had started to leave the church. Marie walked away after gently squeezing Lilica's hand.

Lilica and her mother returned home. Mother Iulia seemed content and still full of the feeling of the religious service; Lilica was lively but restless.

The table in the girl's bedroom displayed a beautiful vase of fragrant roses. Lilica rushed inside and buried her face in the soft pets.

"Mother! Such beautiful roses!"

"They're beautiful indeed, but I wonder who brought them. Maybe Jeanne or Marie? But Marie was at church with us!"

"Of course, Mother! It must have been Jeanne Créhange!"

A moment later there was a knock at the door. It was the administrator.

"Good day, ladies! Well, what do you think? My roses are delicious, aren't they?"

"Your roses?" asked the mother.

"Forgive me for daring, Mrs. Hasdeu. I know that today you celebrate the Lord's baptism, so I brought you the flowers for this holy day."

"Thank you, you're so kind!" said the mother, sneaking a silver coin in the old woman's hands.

"For nothing!" said the administrator. Before she went out the door she whispered in Lilica's ear. "The young man is downstairs. He's waiting for you. Just a minute. Go quick!"

Lilica's mind lost focus. Oh, if Marie was there with her, she would go downstairs with her as soon as possible! But alone? Why didn't Marie join them? Why didn't she tell this secret to anyone?

Her torment increased. "No! No!" She mustn't go downstairs. She couldn't. What lie could she come up with for her mother? It was as if lies lived somewhere in the wilderness of Tiber or in the American jungle. It felt as if they were not near, spinning like air, like smoke around her head, some transparent, some opaque… One of them was right on Lilica's table. Well, half a lie anyway, which was her letter to Matilda Constantinescu in Bucharest.

"Oh, look Mother! I forgot to give the letter to the administrator. I'll run downstairs and give it to her. I'll be back in a second…"

Her hurried steps took her past the door, through a hallway, slowing down the stairs, first thumping and then softening, resembling the steps of a cat. Ten more steps. Eight more. Three more. She could see the door. Should she go in? She waited a moment. Her fingers wrapped around the doorknob, one finger raised, but…

She knocked. The door opened, revealing the administrator.

"Madame, I forgot to ask you… here, please be kind and…"

"Take it to the mailbox! Perfect! But… excuse me, miss… there's a gentleman who wants to…"

The young man took one step, took Lilica's hand in his, and gave it a gentle, respectful squeeze.

"Forgive me, miss. I came back for two or three days, and I wanted to see you. After this, I'll continue my journey to India.…"

"You came to our church, but…" said Lilica barely talking over the thumping of her heart. "India?"

"Exactly. I wanted to see if your health was improving."

"I'm doing well, thank you."

"How about your migraines? I can't get rid of mine either. Did those pills help you at all?"

"Oh yes! They helped me so much back then."

"Can I give you another box? I made them especially for you, that's why I asked you to come down, so I could give them to you personally before departing."

"Oh, you're too kind. Thank you. I'll take one today."

"I want to congratulate you on your results in the final exams."

"How did you know?"

"One of your classmates told me."

Her mother's voice that always followed the girl's moments, steps, and absence suddenly pierced the air.

"Lilica! Lilica!"

"Oh! My mother's calling me. Goodbye!"

"I also wanted to let you know that my poor father passed away, and the day after that, Gypsy followed, his poor pug…"

"Oh, my condolences… but I have to go… Goodbye."

And Lilica ran up the stairs.

"What took you so long? It was just a letter," said her mother.

"Well, you see… the administrator was not, I mean she was, but she was just then coming down from...the third," said Lilica, turning her eyes from the scolding gaze to the roses that seemed to smile at her and give her comfort.

Who was that classmate the young man was talking about? Who cared about her feelings?

And that's how February passed, without one single warm day, without news, without flowers. The roses had bowed their heads and scattered their petals one by one, just like happy memories, turning black, shrinking, losing their fragrance, until they became foul, and the delicate petals became shadows despite tears and care. But she didn't throw them away. She threw them in the fireplace and watched them until they turned to ash.

Only one of them was left in the crystal vase on the table. Iulia was watching it dying there, isolated, taken away from its world, uprooted just like her from the land of its birth:

In the crystal vase with fresh water
Or on the coffee table next to the fire,

A poor rose is withering
Regretting the blue sky above it.

I am like you, oh withered flower
Uprooted from my native land
Longing for my beloved country
Just like you in your crystal vase.[35]

There was also a previous version of this poem:
Time flies
And it steals from us
Our memories:
Joy and sorrow,
Everything fades away
Without ever returning.

Lilica has troubled days and sleepless nights. Was she waiting for someone? Was she waiting for something? She kept asking her soul, just as always, but its echoes were vague, almost imperceptible when it came to her questions. Even the pages she was reading, but not quite understanding gave her no answer. What accord? What escape from Bach? She was nervous, angry, seemingly chosen to be a distraction or generate attention. She couldn't give herself a definite answer. Nothing! Nobody! Nowhere! What would Roland or Bayard do for her sorrow? Would they abandon her with a box of headache medicine? Was Mr. James the shadow of love? And he was departing to India…

Did love warm impulses in such a way? And again, she remembered that *Amen* of the past December: "Oh! I was born to love, but why does it matter?"

"Your path doesn't run under our feet!..."

Why did he come back? To give her the pills, of course! Her migraines were nothing compared to the pain in her heart which caused an infinite river of tears.

Do not try to stop me from crying
As long as I am blessed with tears.
I overcome my pain by crying;
And hope for something from my tears!

---

[35] La Rose au Vase — Chevalerie 124

You know not that I've cried so often
But you can see a ray of hope
Which is the same as it is for flowers
A small refreshing drop of dew.

You don't know tears relieve
Any despairing heart?
It is the last joy
Most often sung by pain.[36]

A few days later she wrote another poem with the same rhythm, like testimony and a lament against her fate:

Alas! Everyone betrays me in this world
When all you try to do is love.
When there's no one to share it with you
What can you blame for it?

What did I do to this world
For it to inflict upon me
Such cruel torture?...[37]

Around the same time, she wrote a sonnet dedicated to her own heart, of course:

It wants to cry when pain is bitter,
But its voice is always muffled.

It is the first to hide the pain
Bleeding under a joyful mask;
Nature made it firm yet bashful.

Therefore, poor heart must always lie!

A majestic lie! How many words in this human universe would have changed their fate, for good or worse without its intervention?

Her mother often found her with her forehead resting on the window, or with her fork unmoving on the plate.

---

[36] Ne me Défends pas de Pleurer — Bourgeons 122

[37] Découragement — Bourgeons 137

"What's the matter with you, Lilica?"

"Nothing, Mother!"

"Is something bothering you? Are you ill?"

"How could I be ill when you're so good to me, Mother?"

"What are you always thinking of so intensely?"

"What? Nothing! I just miss home; I miss my father and my friends! But it will pass. Here, I can laugh, and I can sing!"

She ran to the piano, tried to play a *doina*, a Romanian song of lament representing the cries of the old. Her soul bled profusely under her mask of happiness.

Reading André Chéner she heard an echo in the lyrics of his poem called *Les Maux qu'on Dissimule en Ont Plus d'Amertune* (The Concealed Evil Is More Bitter), which was the inspiration for her poem in which she talked about her false happiness. "Pourquoi Je Suis Gaie" (Why Am I Happy) had a motto from the lyrics of the poet mentioned above, and might have been addressed to her mysterious friend:

If you ask me why I'm happy
Even though my poor heart hurts
You just cut a little deeper
When you doubt I'm torn apart.
When you see me joyful, chatting

You believe I have no woes.

Well, you are wrong because this sorrow
It is not a light or trifling whim
Digging at a naive heart;
Alas! But no, my pain is grave,
And I might hide it behind laughter
So go! You do not understand!

What do you want? I just want joy.
Oh, horrible mask hiding the tears!

One must know pain to feel compassion,
Will understand the sinful shame
And will be blessed with innocence.

Those times came with muffled, tormented screams in the heart of the sensible child who was going to an inner tragedy, playing with ghosts and evil spirits in her mind:

Oh, poor sheet of paper on which I pour
All that is good inside my mind,
You know not the pains that ail me
And I don't dare confide in you.

You see me as the world sees me,
A serene face, a mocking gaze,
But you don't know the pain I feel
Which slowly tears my heart to pieces.

You can complain, my loyal sheet of paper
You are the only witness to my pain,
Because there's no more cruel torment
Then smiling while holding back your tears.[38]

As a profound reaction of the heart that had gone through too much, without friends and love, the poet turned her eyes to God, the supreme refuge of hope.

My hope resides with you, Father, you're the only one I believe in…

Oh, my heart yearns for you, my only hope![39]

While praying to this hidden God that never shows his face to his devotees, even though they love him unseen as he is, she asked him to release her from the prison of questions without answers, and bless her with childish innocence, because children don't ask God questions, and that is the reason why he protects them.

Oh God! Allow me to believe in you
With my eyes closed, in service to your will:
To see you in your glory in the sky,
To always have the innocence of children![40]

---

[38] A Ce Papier — Chevalerie 135

[39] Invocation — Chevalerie 166

[40] *Credo — Chevalerie* 145- March 1886

As a result of her trying to find refuge in the innocence of childhood which brought her closer to God, Iulia Hasdeu turned her attention towards children and lullabies, fairy tales, fantasy:

Nani, nani, sleep my love,
Mommy's darling treasure

Sleep without knowing heartache
Knowing only pleasures...

While she was watching the little children playing in Luxembourg Park, she observed their hard work:

Their faces are flushed and kissed by the wind –
Alas! A kiss of betrayal that often kills –
The joy of innocence!
Their game is just the labor of childhood!

She remembered the stories of childhood and fully understood the sweet lies they told:

I go back to my poor stories
Innocent, gentle comforts.[41]

On another page she said:

It is the poetry for children
That opens up a theater in the sky

How to believe in one true love|
When after fighting for it so
It crashes like a wingless bird?
And how can we believe in honor?
How could honor be a reward
In a time when money is God?[42]

Sometimes while isolating herself in this other world away from artifices, the poet turned her attention towards delight, comfort, nature, where she was going to pull in one of her estranged friends. She dedicated a poem to Laura Laurian, whom

---

[41] Encore les Contes Bleus — Bourgeons

[42] idem.

she accused in a letter of spending too much time in an evil circle. She walked a path through a ravine, a cluster of linden trees and acacias brightened by sun rays, surrounded by thorns and nettle, but in a surreal atmosphere given by the soft sunset:

Right now it doesn't matter what path we wake
We will just walk together holding each other's hand![43]

The poet had some words to say about a young, cold English girl whose personality didn't match her youth and beauty:

She's just a beautiful young girl,
Shining like the sun to please us;
It would take lightning to make her eyes shine,
To make her heart vibrate from under its veil
Just like a bird singing from a bush.

If you don't have fire in your heart
Alas! What good is it to have beauty?[44]

One day she asked a little bird what the meaning of life was. The little bird seemed to answer her that all it needs to care for are her nest and her mate, and a little bit about happiness:

My joy is in singing for nature,
To love, to sun, to flowers, and woods,
But I don't ever think of the future…

Jealous of the birds' life that revolved around flowers, sun, woods, and love she ended the poem with an innocent wish, one of those often found in poetry written by teenagers, even those with a great amount of talent: "Becoming a bird is all I wish for!"[45]

One time she turned her thoughts to the daughter of Juno, Hébé, the goddess of youth, begging her to gift her heart with immortality:

Share the contents of your divine amphora,
And share the spring of life and love;

---

[43] *Bourgeons*, 129, May 1886

[44] *La Beauté — Bourgeons* 145, February 1886

[45] L'oiseau — *Bourgeons*

Color the dawn in the color of roses
And shine your rays to give us the dawn

The heroic scenes of the century showed love, bravery, and songs, fascinating her and causing her from time to time to separate her bitterness from false love while turning what she perceived as a punishment into redemption. She saw the one inciting to love with flowers and songs under the windows:

The bard has managed to enchant
The blonde chatelain.
The lady has told him before
She craved passionate love.

The bard was cruel even so
He didn't want to give
Whatever she feverishly needed
Whatever her heart craved.

While the lady stabbed her heart because of the cold-hearted bard, he sat there drinking a last sip of wine before the fallen woman. But God didn't forgive such cruelty and the bard was forced to wander the world with the image of his dead lover always imprinted in his mind.

And for the rest of eternity
Her heartbroken ghost
Will punish his disloyalty
By enhancing his guilt...[46]

If her obsession with chivalry was enhanced in the time of war, times of peace gave way to lovers, making women give their hearts and their lives for the man of their choosing, and also prompting Iulia to write the ballad of Aymer:

He wears his brazen heart like armor.
He likes to drink for those departed.
And still, a maiden stole his heart
Making him dream and be less guarded.
He'd die in a melee for honor,
And when his heavy lids would close

---

[46] Le Minnesinger et la Châtelaine — Chevalerie 56

Just as the heavens did for Roland
They'd take his soul to Paradise.[47]

But even though she was inclined towards her usual refuge in romantic love, the poet kept going back to true friendship, when two souls miss each other and shed tears for each other, the way she at one point had done with a few friends.

You are the one to understand my heart and suffering,
And often shared your tears in consolation.
It appeased me to sit together crying...

Sweet childhood mirages, adorable chimeras,
That lied to us about a happy future,
One that wouldn't change, one without dismay,
When we would love each other, long time past our decay![48]

Iulia dedicated another poem to the same friend who was going through a sentimental disappointment, a poem entitled *Encore à Elle*.[49]

You, whom I long accused of callousness
Whose icy heart I wept over so often,
But who became my friend by instinct,
I now know you've also known love and pain!

That "who became my friend by instinct" was a phrase showing love towards her friend and might have been a way through which she acknowledged that suppressed and deviated love she had honored before. The word "also" came as a confirmation that Iulia also had felt the pain of love.

The same friend was the recipient of the poem *À une Jeune Fille* (*To a Young Girl*). "For your heart has suffered and your eyes have wept."[50]

The bizarre poem entitled *A Quoi Pensiez-vous?* (What Are You Thinking About?)[51] was dedicated to her as well.

---

[47] Chevalerie 63

[48] Séparation — Chevalerie 175

[49] *Chevalerie* 149

[50] Bourgeons 177

[51] Chevalerie 61

In May, before dedicating her whole time to studying for the final exams, Iulia Hasdeu sketched another love story called *Thomassine Spinola*. Ludwig XII, the main character, was passing through Geneva where he was received ceremoniously by everyone, including young and beautiful Thomassine Spinola who asked him to consider her as "the lady of his thoughts," as she loved him just like Laura loved Petrarch. However, the king chose to take her with him as his mistress. Disappointed by the fact that her love was not understood, Thomassine committed suicide to avoid dishonor.

Again, while sketching the plot and the characters, Iulia Hasdeu showed her rich literary culture and the true historical sources she used every time. We must mention one of the works written by the sixteen-year-old girl on the pure love she was dreaming of. One of the young poet's written reflections was about the pure love she craved:

"Platonic love is the love a woman feels for her God, no matter if she's married or not; however, she doesn't suffer if her God becomes a man."

This can be seen as a paraphrasing of another of her reflections on complex love, almost evangelical as Apostle Paul had called it. She was talking about complete abandonment without justification:

"If you love someone, you don't think of the reasons why you love them; you will love everything that others despise about them."[52]

As an introduction to the drama, she wrote a poem dedicated to Genova in a different rhythm and rhyme than she was used to, a poem in which we can see the same setting as Eminescu's poem *Veneția* (*Venice*), published almost two years prior in *Convorbiri Literare*.

Under the starry sky
Proud
Like a queen
Where the infinite sea
Melts away in its shores.

The whispering waves
Softly knock in its docks

---

[52] *Cugetări*, quoted by Gion.

Singing a hushed song
In the calm eventide.

An inspiring hymn,
Pious melody,
A vivid high note
To the sky from the Dome.

Meanwhile, the girl's knowledge was increasing by the day, and it happened that one day a conflict broke out between her and her father. Somehow, he was defeated and admitted his guilt.

Busy with the difficult job of continuing to write *Magnum Ethymologicum* after the first volume was published around that time, giving every second of his time to his sources, parallels, deductions, and linguistic transformations, the scholar didn't have time for literature, while Lilica's knowledge of literature was increasing exponentially.

In a letter dated the second day of Easter in 1889, Hasdeu wrote to his dear family, telling them various details about their home, spending, especially about the amount of money they needed for the trip they were going to take to Romania to satisfy Lilica's yearning for home, as well as details about the inheritance left by his uncle Bleslas in Vienna who had left them the ranch in Hotin and some smaller items.

Through this same letter, he informed them of Pană Constantinescu's daughter (who was a director at Cantemir), Matilda and Lilica's friend, and couldn't help but add that "she had turned as ugly as she can be." On this occasion, he told Lilica that their friends, Zaharescu family, might visit them in Paris in June with Florica, quoting a line from Lilica's friend to her friend saying *"Mon mari/ Comme il est petit!"* (My husband/ He is so small!).

Hasdeu told her: "Forgive me, but *mari* is written *maryx* according to the new grammar rules since chez is written *cheux*; that terrible *cheux, cheux, cheux,* that I can even see in my nightmares... Everything is well at home, I send thousands of kisses to both of you, and I'm eager to see you in our dear home. Your loving husband and father, Bogdan!"

The irony was a flaw of this "loving husband and father," or in Lilica's words, "hobby." Some philosophers state that this type of irony, which is far from proof of superior intellect, is a specific trait of fickle, even primitive spirits. So, Max Nordau, the one we borrowed the idea from, who was a famous explorer, stated the natives of Central Africa were rolling on the ground laughing every time they saw him writing, and the superior man was "genuine through the condition of his intellectual work" because humor is not the same thing as jesting. According to his ideas, humor was sourced from coincidence, from disproportion, from contrasts that touch each other and produce laughter as a manifestation of pure intellect. Humor is the balance between reality and fantasy, between imperfection and perfection. Satire relies on trivial methods, sourcing from contempt, sometimes from malice. The irony is close to that, being born out of imagination, from forcing reality to blend in with fantasy. The humorist doesn't cause pain, but the ironic man feels pleasure when using his skill.

Hasdeu's spirit was always burning, and his sarcasm was always alive, thriving from daily irony, and we know this great man juggled with his words sometimes successfully, sometimes being defeated as we would shortly show. The philologist tried his irony with his daughter in that letter, and she sent him the following reply.

"Oh, Father, I received your lovely letter last night! The first time I read it I didn't know if I should laugh or be angry, but I ended up with tears from laughter.

My God, it was so silly of me, but anyone else would have misunderstood. The first time I sent Florica a letter, I told her about my final exams, and I wanted to let her know that I didn't change, that I am still a child in heart and spirit. She replied to my letter with a long epistle in which she tried to convince me she is now an extraordinary young lady, knowledgeable and rational. With all my faith in her, I fell into her trap. I believed in her as one believes in a prophet, thinking that such an extraordinary young lady as her, a student in the sixth year of high school at Matei Basarab would have read Molière, an author read by twelve-year-olds at Sévigné. Now, in *Les Femmes Savantes* (*The Learned Ladies*), Act II, Scene VI, Martine says:

My Lord! I didn't stay silent like you,
And I speak straight like they speak in our house.

These lines have become proverbs and ten-year-olds know them as well as *Our Father* and *The Creed*. *Cheux* is part of a dialect spoken in Picardy, and the song says:

Do you know how to plant cabbage?
In the same manner we do? (*A la mode de cheux nous?*)

If I remember correctly, I told Florica I kiss Madam Zaharescu's hand like that. It was a more pleasant way of wording it, and Martine's words are so well-known even by those who don't know the dialect of Picardy that I honestly couldn't have imagined that people wouldn't understand what I meant. Besides, I'll say it again: I was a fool. I was naive enough not to realize that people in Bucharest don't know the common sayings in France…"

After receiving the letter from his daughter, Hasdeu pulled Molière's book off the shelf, opened it to that specific play, and found out that it was true, and Lilica had described the grammar lesson Bélise had given Martine. The only difference was that his edition had the words *Ma Foi* which were replaced by *Mon Dieu* after the old edition in 1734.

Any excuse would have been in vain. Facing such a formidable adversary, persistent irony became dangerous, especially when compared to his direct and cruel arrow, the child answered with delicate irony. She was amazed at Florica's ignorance, and the whole issue ricocheted upon the magister who had adopted Florica's opinion.

The old man gave up completely. He couldn't joke with a student who was so well informed on the work of famous writers, so he replied to her letter in the following words:

"My mistake! My mistake, dear Lilica. Your friend Florica didn't tell me anything of this terrible *cheux*; the fault is mine and only mine, especially because I don't know Molière's work from heart, even though I've always admired him. But I'm somehow glad I made a mistake because it made you send me this exceptional letter that proves once again that you're great at having a debate and poor people who'll dare to criticize you in the future. You will manage to turn their spirits inside out, just as I used to do!"

He ended the letter after telling her more about his success with *Răzvan și Vidra*, and about some money-related issues he was having with the Jewish bankers.

But this small duel that made the young girl victorious against her opponents would become the subject of laughter during the summer that was approaching when Lilica would visit Bucharest.

A logical conclusion to that occasion when Iulia's literary work, her culture, and especially the sorrows of her soul were still unknown, she noted something on a piece of paper among her manuscripts, a note her father would find later on: "Who would reveal you before their eyes? Death! 1886."

In June, while she was studying philosophy, psychology, and metaphysics, Iulia's soul was flying through the ethereal space. She saw herself pass through hypothetical or mystical transcendence, through everything related to the meaning of life and its origin, always haunted by Cupid's smile, the being who creates wide worlds and destroys them in seconds. That was when Iulia Hasdeu wrote a poem about the love she was always running from, feeling undefended before it, a love she completely despised. That candor, that critics entirely attributed to her brilliant mind, might have been purity, a cleanness hiding in her tormented soul, which caused that perpetual search for refuge in innocence:

I never loved! Love is not fit for my age
I laugh at its persistent blushing face

… … … … …

I am told that Love will punish me one day

But until then:

You, who always praise Love to me
Why steal sweet innocence from me?
Leave me this fleeting moment to enjoy
My age says, woman, my heart says childhood joy!

… … … …

Let me flee from all women's sins
To be beautiful without knowing beauty exists
Without knowing of the charm I was born with
And not know the desire it brings with it
To live with satisfaction and with glee
To let my heart keep its naivety!

  This poem took a weight off the girl's shoulders by allowing her to confess her feelings and liberate herself from "the presence of sadness that repulses and hurts me," after which she was free to focus on her studies.

  The second part of her final exams took place in July 1886 at the Sorbonne, which Iulia Hasdeu passed by presenting written works and oral presentations on rhetoric and philosophy. Before her exams, she'd read everything suggested by the curriculum, from Greek classics (Demosthenes, Socrates, Plato, Aristotle) to Bossuet, Descartes, Boutroux, etc. Ionescu-Gion stated the exam was brilliant, informed, and complete. She received her diploma on the twelfth of November of the same year.

As we mentioned before, two main reasons contributed to Iulia's trip to Romania in the summer of 1886. First, the child's health seemed fine, second, she was greatly missing her country and her friends.

At the end of July, the mother and daughter took the train to Bucharest and spent the whole month of August with Hasdeu and with her friends whom she found changed, some married, some wanting to get married, normal changes brought by her five years of absence. They took trips to the mountains and to the seaside, which were great opportunities for Iulia to rest and heal her body and soul that had been so challenged by illness and melancholy.

Before leaving, Iulia dreamed of enjoying walks with one of her most treasured friends, and activities that she had greatly missed and waited for:

We'll walk along a narrow path
On golden carpets of dry leaves
Wind will be blowing walnut trees
And blow our hair with its sweet breath.
……………….

I like to dream of August twilight
Of evanescent happy times.
Alas! Searching for it is a sweet plight,
When it fades away without leaving any signs.

Against our happiness, against our love
Something always obstructs this image
'Cause all we can enjoy is just one day
Before death shatters our dreams with its black glove.

Even if Iulia was just dreaming of this time, August saw her in the company of her childhood friend, that "silly ugly girl" named Florica, who was already married, but whose delicate, friendly, and devoted soul was intertwining with Iulia's. Following this meeting, she wrote a poem in which she compared her friend's presence to a ship approaching blessed land:

My friend, I only feel this sweet intoxication
When I feel you so close to my heart
When I hold your hand I feel elation
When you look at me I don't want us apart!

One day of the same pleasant month of August, Iulia embarked on a boat ride on Cişmigiu Lake by herself and was once again astonished by the everlasting splendor of nature, with all its flowers, birds, and waves, but at the same time, the questions from Lamartine's *Le Lac* returned to torment her mind with the mysteries of life:

The sun was smiling in the glowing sky,
My boat was lightly gliding on the tide
When suddenly a cloud of grief raised high
Above my agonizing heart that cried.

... ...

I just wanted to cry in peace my sorrow
... ...

You held me and my bleeding heart, dear lake
Carrying me on your bright emerald waves...
... ...

You seldom notice the human misfortune
Impassive and cold as it is in your nature
Quietly flowing in the wind's direction,
Oblivious to our many afflictions.

Before a tombstone, we mourn our dead
That lay under our feet before their time
From here I see you beautiful and bright
And hear the ground laughing at my poor life.

I wonder if men could rule the Universe.

What is our meaning on this earth?
Our pride won't move this serene world.
It witnesses our birth and our death
We live and die, and the earth remains cold...[53]

When she returned to Paris, the girl didn't show any of the shadows of her loneliness. She was as joyous as any girl returning from a ball. Before her father

---

[53] Rêverie — Bourgeons 148

she acted measured, before her mother she was loving, and before her friends, she molded to their souls. Being part of society was making her feel happy. Everyone knew her mind was filled with literary plans, but nobody knew how much she was planning. Despite his superior intuition, Hasdeu didn't suspect anything, and he couldn't see the heaviness pressing on her heart. If anyone ever asked why she was looking out the window, or why she was not getting enough sleep, she would throw a joke with a smile on her lips.

From the first day Hasdeu together with Ionescu-Gion, Theodor Spenanță, Pană Constantinescu, Matilda, Florica, Maria, and Ermina greeted Iulia and her mother in the train station, the balcony with roses, the courtyard of the archives, and the surrounding park resounded with her cheerful laughter, the laughter of a child enjoying every happiness in the world...

Fated isolation! She spent her time with her father discussing philosophy, literature, including Molière and his dreaded *cheux*, reliving the brilliant moments of her final exams, memories that earned her many kisses from her father's bushy mustache. They debated Leopardi, Carducci, Oberman, Goethe, and Schopenhauer. The recent graduate riposted against the optimism of the scholar from Bessarabia, as well as against his sarcasm related to oblivion and Nirvana, however, she never revealed the bitter feelings in her soul, a soul that would soon be covered by the veil of death. She didn't even show a hint of her thoughts, many of them hidden at the bottom of her suitcase or in her apartment on the Rue de Condé. There was a fatal wall like a gravestone between them, blocking the optimistic influence her mature father could have cast on the dying girl.

One of the dinners in their home hosted many intimate friends of the family: Theodor Speranța, Constantinescu, Zamfir Arbore, Ionescu-Gion, and Condurachi, the one who was replacing Frățilă as the secretary for *Columna lui Traian* newspaper after the latter's departure. They took their seats and patiently waited for Iulia, who was running late. Her mother looked everywhere but couldn't find her. Where was Lilica? She must have hidden somewhere. However, five minutes later she joyfully walked into the dining room and apologized for the delay.

"Please forgive me, ladies and gentlemen, as I had my full attention on a murder."

"What? What?" asked her mother.

"I sketched a drama with six characters, and I mixed them up quite terribly. I killed two of them. Now I have four left.... And I don't know what to do with them."

"You know what?" said Speranță. "Kill them all, because the dinner is getting cold!"

The meal continued in a friendly and opulent atmosphere, with scents from the nearby park, no clouds, and no negative interference from anyone.

The guests toasted shots of brandy to the happy parents and their daughter, praising her and showing her all the admiration for the way she looked.

"You look like a twenty-year-old lady!" said Constantinescu.

"Why not twenty-one?" asked Hasdeu.

"One year of life is one extra achievement, dear Father," prophesied Lilica.

"That only counts when you're old," said Speranță, "but at our age…"

"Well, truth be told," said Arbore, who was still young, "I fully agree with Miss Lilica. She's like a Șiras rose, she's ageless."

"You mean I'm exotic, Mr. Arbore?" asked Lilica.

"No. I mean you've reached a beautiful maturity," corrected Arbore.

"She resembles her father," said Hasdeu.

"Here maybe," said Mrs. Constantinescu, pointing to her cheek, "she resembles her mother."

After dinner some guests gathered on the balcony to serve some coffee, others gathered in the garden. Lilica walked ahead, and Ionescu-Gion took the opportunity to run after her.

"There's a full moon tonight," he said.

"I can't see it yet," said Lilica.

"It's behind the bell tower. You'll see it in a moment, and you should sing it a song in Romanian," said Gion.

"My heart only sings in Romanian, Mr. Gion. It's just my voice that got accustomed to the French language. I do it on purpose, I'll only write in Romanian later on; if I'll be alive, we'll see," said Lilica.

"How can you say, 'If I'll be alive' when you're a sixteen-year-old girl?"

"Almost seventeen."

"Either way, you're young, beautiful, and so admired."

"Admired by whom?"

"By us all…"

Lilica walked towards the balcony, somehow annoyed by the professor's courtship.

But the night was claiming its domain, and the conversations and jokes ended once the guests started trickling out. Lilica opened herself up to her hidden world. The yard and the church were veiled in darkness, but shortly after that, the darkness was banished.

The moon showed its face to Lilica, helping her get immersed in the fantasy surrounding her.

It's nighttime! The birds are quiet in the trees
The moon is shining its white light on us
In our courtyard, in our park, in our cities.
Dark silhouettes of high majestic walls
Rise high under the stars as the night falls.
This night is more enchanting than the day.

***

The church, with its great brown arched gate
With its dome shining in the moonlight,
With its great Byzantine cross in sight.
Willows are swaying over the silent graves
And the laments of owls raise towards the stars
Somber predictions of our disparaging fates.

***

Oh! Who could make this night ideal for me,
Make this moon shine brighter than a precious gem,
Make this gentle breeze last and keep flowing free?
Oh how sweet seems this short reverie
Fueled by my love for my dear country.
Then why is the distance a quiet melody?[54]

During another evening, within the walls protecting so many sleeping souls, some sleeping their eternal slumber, others sleeping their life away, Iulia Hasdeu remembered the lines of *Le Saule*, a poem that had brought so many moments of

---

[54] Une Nuit- Bourgeons 124

melancholy. Her lyrics trickled on the papers like whispers from the depths of her heart.

The weeping willow bowed like a shy maiden,
Its branches swaying in the autumn wind
Caressing the forgotten slabs and crosses
That lay upon forgotten who had sinned.

Their murmurs are just muffled songs of pain
So sad and distant, echoes of the soul,
They are the whispers of the dying men
Taking their last breath, losing all control.

The dead could hear the willow's song and
They felt reborn by its caressing song
So grateful by the willow's dark protection
One fleeting glint of hope, love, and no wrong.

....

Oh! How much I love your sweet melancholy
Oh, Wind!
Keep singing your sweet song, sweet melody,
Help me remember those lying here under my feet.[55]

September came with the clinking of bells. The whipping willows seemed to bow their heads in prayer, calling for their fate.

At the end of the month, Iulia packed her suitcases, visited her friends one last night to take her farewells, and paid a visit to Dr. Calinderu, who found no sign of illness. Shortly after that, the two women were waving their handkerchiefs from the train and wiping their tears.

The train took them far away, flying away like her memories, took them to a place where the smell of roses still seemed to linger. In the drawer of her nightstand a small box was waiting for her: "for headache..."

Jeanne Créhange and Elli Scott greeted them with kisses and news. Paris was the same as always. No matter what events challenged it, Paris stood proudly before everything. It absorbed a little bit of everything, but its peak was always high like

---

[55] Le Saule — Bourgeons 103

a jewel. It presented both its faces to whoever visited it, either Dante's Inferno or a Christian Paradise. The metropolis was luxurious and full of color. Details were lost here, but everything of great proportion resounded in chaos. A few echoes from the past betrayed excitement from long ago. Other than that, it was only opulence!

Jeanne informed Lilica of the news that had an impact. The girl heard everything, swayed, and rediscovered the old Paris! "The good old days!"

The place where we believe in love and honor
Where we gave our souls to our land
Where we would gladly die for our ladies!

A place where in our days we now praise sin
And we replaced whatever we once treasured
How could we even find the love within?

Iulia could visualize the times of Roland again! The times of Bayard and Don Quixote that Paris was no longer worthy of.

As a distant cry of the holy lands she had just left, Iulia Hasdeu sketched another drama before starting university, "A plan for a drama or an opera in three acts," named *Les Heiduques* (*The Outlaws*). The plot takes place in a village in Moldavia surrounded by woods and orchards, with an old church. A Jewish innkeeper tries to seduce Marioara, the lover of an outlaw called Michael the Black, after the girl broke her engagement to Vlad the Shepherd. Vlad persecutes Samuel the innkeeper because he's Jewish, so he agrees to help the girl and the outlaw meet in secret. Michael is afraid of Vlad, but he's especially afraid of his love for Marioara. Starting with these main characters, the author sketched the plot in multiple episodes. If Iulia had the time to finish it, it could have become an exceptional representation of the times in which outlaws were heroes, symbols of the struggle against corruption.

When it came to her inspiration and her literary accomplishments, Iulia Hasdeu was very busy just like any other young author. She didn't wait and didn't let time take the reins. Her ideas, her imagination from which she was living her intellectual life knew no respite, were lively and spontaneous. Once she had an idea, she had to write it down. She rarely had an inspiration that she left for later. Of course, works such as *The Outlaws*, *Thomassine Spinola*, or *Sappho* took more time to be elaborated, because Iulia needed to research facts and opinions. However, most times Iulia wrote very fast. She stated as much on an envelope received from

Konstanzer Hof with the occasion of a trip to Constanța (probably from the previous year), that her father was going to find among her manuscripts:

"Camille Armand (a pseudonym she likes to hide behind) always wrote effortlessly. Her pen ran and ran on paper. Her inspiration was rich and ardent. Thank God, she wrote whenever she had inspiration because her soul was brimming with it. Her pen seemed to burn the words on paper…"

"So," her father added, "she was making a psychological study of herself for her own pleasure; and if death would have spared her, nobody would have seen these intimate monologues."

"In November 1886," said Ionescu-Gion, "Iulia Hasdeu was a university student, happier than ever, in full health and in her thirst for knowledge she chose to join the Faculty of Letters at the Sorbonne in Paris."

On the second of November, Iulia turned seventeen years old. Even though she "looked twenty-one-years-old," tall enough, maybe too short (her father was quite short as well) she had a full body and chubby cheeks. Two days before starting classes, the poet had a strange dream. She told her mother about it the following day, and Hasdeu stated she also put it in writing around the same time.

That dream became a mystical symbol for Hasdeu especially after the passing of his daughter, like a confession from the afterlife. But it was a bizarre prophecy even for the seventeen-year-old girl…

The poem Iulia wrote following this dream had seventeen stanzas dedicated to Professor Maurice Albert (with a motto from Petrarch) and had the following content: There was a blue-eyed woman with angel wings walking towards the girl and pointing to the hazy horizon, bidding Iulia to follow her. She felt trust, so she obeyed, and the angel steadied her whenever she would trip on the path full of slippery stones and ravines. Suddenly, the woman pointed toward an icy mountain peak showing from behind the clouds. The cold wind was freezing their breath. For some reason, Iulia let go of her guide's hand and she lost her consciousness. When she regained it, she took one great step and saw herself on the snow-capped peak, with the abyss at her feet and the sky above her head… All around her there were eagles, hawks, and vultures that terrified her; the stone cliffs, walls of ice, and fog that started to descend warned of a terrifying night. There was no sound, no whisper. "I'm alone and the world lost track of me." She was the only human in the dark chaos. Shivering, she embraced a pine tree and started crying. She prayed and waited to die. Suddenly, the sky brightened with a strange light. There, close to paradise, she saw the angel who had guided her on the mountain. Her prayer and fear had been heard, and the girl was saved. And there she was rising to the sky, with a ceremonious hymn welcoming her to heaven.

The new life she discovered at university temporarily suspended her poetic activity. Iulia found new philosophy and history books, carefully organized them on her desk, and consulted them after every class, not only to understand the new knowledge she was acquiring but also to verify the information from the source.

As a pleasant diversion for her soul, the artist found solace in the fine arts and music. From time to time, she sat at her piano and composed her own melodies to go with her poems, such as *Invocation a Hébé in Mi Major*, or *L'air du Papillon*, a sweet melody for children in la major, as well as *Sursum*, or *Requiem*, a melody that was going to be harmonized by G. Ștefănescu and today can be found in her mausoleum.

After puberty, her voice had become louder and more defined. Her warm mezzo-soprano voice, almost contralto, contrasted with her physique, which could have fooled anyone into believing she was a lyric soprano. After hearing Lawers in Lohengrin she had acquired great respect for him and asked him to tutor her weekly, lessons that flowed easily after her studies at the Conservatory.

Meanwhile, thanks to her friends in Paris, she met a beloved French painter, Maillart, the one who gifted her that wonderful portrait of herself found in the Romanian Academy, also reproduced in this volume. The painter also gave her lessons in watercolor and gouache.

Iulia's mother closely watched her every step, except her classes at university, and wanted to observe the painter and the musician by entering their circle of friends, visiting with their families, and later taking full control of the classes.

Diogène-Ulysee Napoléon Maillart was almost fifty years old at that time (47-48) and he was well-known for his historical-mythological paintings, having received awards from the great French Salon, and he was also a knight of the Legion of Honor. Therefore, he was a trustworthy man who shouldn't be the cause of the mother's jealousy. So, what was the woman thinking? She probably wanted to be better safe than sorry. When it came to Lawers, who was younger than the other artist, she saw him as fraud.

Among her new colleagues at the Sorbonne was young Broșteanu, a snob that Iulia couldn't stand and had no kind words for, especially since the Oltenia native walked like a peacock before the serious and intelligent girl.

The Sorbonne was a sanctuary for Iulia. Some of the classes she was attended were philosophy, Lenient's class taught by Gustave Larroumet (a master of the conference) and Paul Janet's class taught by Gabriel Séailles. Other professors whose classes she enjoyed were Louis Leger, Jules Martha (Latin literature), Paul Girard (Greek literature), Ludovic Carrau (director of studies), and Leger (comparative French literature).

Most of them were aware of Bogdan Petriceicu Hasdeu's fame and cast their full attention on his remarkable daughter. Besides, Michel Bréal, who had become the general inspector of superior education, had his eyes on Iulia Hasdeu and often joined her classes. Carrau noticed the student during longer debates, and Leger was a true friend and protector of the family.

One day, her friend Elli Scott visited her. She was happy to discuss the current events of Paris, especially since she didn't know the city well, except for Condé Street, Odéon Square, and Racine Street that connected St. Michael Boulevard to the Sorbonne, so about 300 meters.

Her mother assisted at the meeting as usual. Elli waited for a moment of privacy, and when the mother finally went to bring a few glasses with water, she whispered to Lilica.

"I have to tell you something. I'm about to get married."

"Oh! To whom?"

"I can't tell you, yet, because it's a work in progress… but you'll be the first to know all the details."

"I congratulate you from the bottom of my heart, Elli. What does he do for a living?"

"You're questioning me, dear Lily! Well, I can tell you that much. He's an architect."

"Architect?" said Iulia, her eyes wide.

"You're surprised. Why? You don't think I would prefer an officer? But 'for lack of thrushes, one eats blackbirds.' Architects are not a bad deal either, especially if they truly love us."

"Yes, of course, Elli! And… listen," whispered Lilica. "Tell me… do you love each other?"

"Oh, yes Lily, we are madly in love with each other! If you only knew! He adores me… We met last evening, and he told me he'll come in a few days to ask for my hand in marriage. Oh, Lily, if only you knew, my dear Lily… Last evening — but please keep this to yourself only — we shared a kiss! Oh, if only you knew! Listen, have you ever kissed a boy?"

"What a silly question, Elli!"

"Forgive me, I know you. Of course! But I'm so happy that I would like every girl to know how it is to be kissed by the one they love. Oh, he's so passionate! I can still feel his mustache on my eyes, on my cheeks, on my… mouth. Apologies; he kissed me on the mouth… what was I supposed to do? I let him… Oh! What a feeling! I was trembling like a leaf and had shivers down my spine! That scoundrel! He grabbed me in his arms, he squeezed me, and…"

"Enough, Elli!" said Iulia, standing up.

"Are you upset, Julie? Forgive me…"

"I'm not upset," said Lilica, biting her bottom lip, "but I can hear my mother returning…"

And her mother walked in holding a tray with jam and cold water. Elli drank a bit, and Iulia emptied her glass, smiled, touched her mother's arm, and said: "Elli is a very sweet girl, right, Mother?"

"Do you even have to ask, Lilica?"

After Elli's departure, Lilica returned to her desk and opened a book, but her eyes ran far following the steps going down the stairs, sounding further and further away, disappearing to a place where shivers go from the lips down the spine, in the strong arms that fell limp… Was that what love felt like? Was it the way Elli wanted it? Who would want another type of love? Was there another type of love? Oh, of course… one that was pure, chaste, ideal, without embraces, without lips… Love that dematerialized… One that forgot about the body, that threshold of death, and that only cared about the soul. That was her love, the one that was based on sacrifice! That was her side of the world.

Love was silence, peace, depersonalization, especially an insatiable thirst one suffered for in secret. What was the chalice from which one could drink love?... Only one: "suffering in silence" as Sully Prudhomme said.

Le meilleur moment des amours
N'est pas quand on a dit: je t'aime,
Il est dans le silence même
A demi rompu tous les jours.

Heure unique ou la bouche close
Par sa pudeur seule et dit tant;
Ou le coeur s'ouvre en éclatant
Tout bas, comme un bouton de rose;

How did this wizard of whispers know what was inside her heart?

But the student had close friends that knew how to creep into her heart and be a constant presence in her life, without her even knowing it was happening. Plato had taught her what true friendship was… and, just like Crito, Socrates' friend, all three were her friends just like Harmides and Lisimah. The idealism enhanced by moral essence, Plato's noesis, was boosted by an invigorating serum that surpassed chaotic sentimentalism. Zenon, Epictetus, and especially Marcus Aurelius became great friends of hers, as well as Tacitus, Herodotus, and Strabo who comforted her in the hours when music and painting did not succeed in doing so.

Chapter XI

Decay

Christmas and New Year's Day of 1887 found Iulia caught between obsession and preoccupation, between uneasiness and tranquility.

If her poems from the two previous years focused on pulling the weeds out from among the flowers, her new knowledge made her pluck out the daisies, roses, and wildflowers as well…

Starting in 1887, her seconds were running out faster than ever.

"The year 1887," said Angelo de Gubernatis (loc. cit.), "must have brought a lot of sadness to the young girl's heart. Her poetry suffered from it; it became pessimistic and every line had a tinge of despair to it. She used to dream, but even this seemed to have vanished. Painful premonitions were the only things she was paying attention to, ignoring the voices of nature she had once listened to. Laughter bothered her, so she found comfort in solitude, in museums, already tired of dying."

What Hasdeu's friend stated about "this heavenly flower who grew on earth" was completely true, with one exception about the "tinges of despair," as those had started years prior. That last year was the time when something happened in Iulia's life, something that can be read in the last lines of Sully Prudhomme's poem, *La Vase Brise* (*The Broken Vase*).

The world sees just the hard, curved surface
Of a vase, a lady's fan once grazed,
That slowly drips and bleeds with sadness.
Do not touch the broken vase.

It was a conclusion that announced moral agony.

At the start of the university year, Elli Scott was by Iulia's side. "What's new in your life, Julie dear?"

"Nothing besides studying Greek for my class. I want Girard to be pleased with my progress. How about you?"

"Everything is going well. I actually postponed it."

"What?" asked Iulia, confused.

"What do you mean 'what'? My studies!"

"Oh!"

"What did you think? You know I'm engaged."

"I congratulate you and wish you luck!"

"Thank you, dear friend; but you know… I can't read anything anymore."

"Anything?" asked Iulia, smiling.

"Believe me."

"You can't read things in people's eyes either?"

"Oh, that…! That passed… Now… we're a bit further along…"

"??!!"

"I mean… we love each other! Oh, Julie! When you know love, you will understand that books don't do it justice… Love overwhelms you, distracts you… intoxicates you… believe me, dear Iulia… Nothing is sweeter than love in this world…"

No other period of intensive study was fuller of thirst to obtain knowledge and to obtain the necessary material, but during that year Iulia Hasdeu looked for answers to her soul's questions, calling for them hopelessly, exceeding the limit of her powers.

As soon as she finished her daily classes at the university she ran home and sat at her small desk with drawers and concepts, with sketches and notes. That's the spot where dinner found her almost every evening, and that's the spot her mother left her every night before bed. Sleep avoided Iulia, but she didn't feel the need to sleep. She always went to bed after midnight, the image of the pages still imprinted in her eyes. She woke up every morning around four or five, and the silence of dawn found her mind fresh, just as if she had slept for eight hours. Was the medicine helping her and giving her energy, or was it the impulse calling for her from the depths of her mind? Or maybe it was the darkness in which the blue eyes were hiding… However, neither Mignon, nor its puppy, Marin, who walked around her feet whining and wagging their tails, nor the cat, nor her mother's caresses had any effect on her chaotic thoughts… Lilica was creating, reading, asking questions. She talked to scholars, to the apostles, to God just like an equal, daring and curious. Her soul was tirelessly fretting before resting for eternity, asking for its right to find answers. What was that love God was using as a distraction, while people were suffering because of it? Was Elli's love true love? Was that the only form of true love?

Sometimes she felt tired, especially when her eyes started hurting and when her cough returned. She wanted to rest, but nobody could give her the rest she needed, as that would mean her heart had stopped beating. A type of long rest, generous, and lethargic! Where were the heroes of so many novels? How did they survive so many disappointments? Did they ever come out victorious?

The one true love of young Chimène,
Her father and her duty
Consumed her life, consumed her beauty
In the home, all began.

***

Night and day the young maiden
Trapped in her solitary tower
Sings sadly from her lonely cradle
About her fate and lack of power.[56]

What was her good friend, the muse, doing at that late hour of the night when the poet was calling to her so feverishly? Did she abandon her as well? Where was she? Who was she embracing in those moments? There she was! Iulia could feel her gliding toward her with her white wings.

...Oh, muse of my dreams
Why do you come to me with your eyes full of tears?
And from your black veil, you bring in the late hours
Why are you gifting me only with withered flowers?
... ...
Alas! I feel like an old woman with a most heavy heart
... ...
Tired, and pale, and fickle is how I see my youth
Slipping away from me, and I can't hold it back
I'll let it go. I'm tired, and that's the bitter truth.
I'm starting to forget, my life, my dreams, my youth...

---

[56] *Chimène.* February 13th, 1887 – *Chevalerie*

....
Please take your inspiration and your sweet songs to others
....
For me, everything's silent, empty, and without colors!

***

Don't come to me at night with your charming songs
Just leave me in my sleep, in my dreams without clouds.
I just want to enjoy the lethargy I'm feeling
I want to drown my sorrows and numb myself by dreaming.[57]

Even the muse greeted her with tears, with withered flowers, and not even she could bring Iulia's lost childhood back, so she had to ask God himself, she had to summon Him as she had done so many times before, and maybe ask Him to elucidate the enigma and explain the demon of destruction.

What is this sentiment of infinite lament
That tugs at my poor soul when everything seems great?
....
I poured my heart in learning and studying all I can
To understand what only God knew when it all began.

Spring was approaching and God touched the earth's heart with his finger.

Oh, God! I feel the life rekindling into me
....
And yet, this immense joy somehow oppresses me
So overwhelmed I am, that joy escaped my grip;
The zephyr with its fragrances and with its soft caresses
Disturbed my peace and my ever so sweet sleep.

***

And once my heart awoke, my pain came rushing back
The tears are flowing freely, from the spring that's my heart.[58]

---

[57] *Lassitude*, February 15th, 1887 — *Chevalerie*

[58] *Tristesse*, February 20th, 1887 — *Chevalerie*

Those cries for help with tears of blood that dripped from her life's energy and emptied it steadily appeared to sometimes be a comfort for her, a feeling of martyrdom for an idea, or the heavenly love like the image of the Virgin of Orléans. She wanted to write about the life of this saint, a woman who had been defiled even after death:

"This name so noble, so pure, so beautiful, so holy, the holiest of them all after Christ's name…" with an invocation from St. Thérèse: "I'm dying because I won't die!" Iulia Hasdeu started her fragment of *Jeanne d'Arc*:

I mourn my life and youth, but these complaints
Are not towards my king, nor my dear saints.

Meanwhile, her mind imagined Marguerite d'Ecosse, the figure of a martyr girl whose life Iulia made up epically, trying to emphasize the delicate femininity of life:

In truth I'm ill, my soul is pained
My heart is burning in my chest
But woes are pointless to me now
Life doesn't matter, I'm over it somehow.

Everything around me causes me disgust
I'll empty my heart all of feelings if I must.
I wish to die despite still having life in me;
To rest and to feel not in the eternal sleep.[59]

And that's how the muse with teary eyes and soft wings would visit her over and over again, trying to dispute the scientific studies that seemed to reject her as well. As soon as she had to start working on projects, the student chose to temporarily abandon poetry and asked the muse to kindly give her a break.

In March of that year, Iulia had to complete an assignment for her philosophy class, a project that Professor Larroumet greatly appreciated, even though he had a few corrections to offer.

She wrote to her father about it, but her letter contained some half-truths as well:

"…March started with a clear and sunny sky, with the fragrance of violets and hyacinths, that extraordinary flower that sparked the imagination of Greeks, who said it was produced by Apollo's tears mixed with the blood of

---

[59] *Chevalerie* — February 1887

young Hyacinthe. It's one of my favorite flowers, and sometimes, when I stroll with my mother through Luxembourg Park, I buy bouquets of violets and hyacinths from a beggar who always offers them to me from his ice-cold hands.

There's not much new happening in our life; it is as dull and regular as the ticking of a clock. The day before yesterday, Mr. Larroument gave us the results for our assignments, and out of thirty students, only six were above average, me being a part of that small group. The young poet André Bellesort, a former student of the Henri IV school, scored 13 out of 20 points, while I was in second place with 11 out of 20 points. Mr. Larroument said the only mistake I made was writing in a scientific style, and that is the fault of Philosophy. It's been over a year and a half since writing my literary works. I hope that my writing style will go back to what it used to be as time passes."

The last sentences, as well as her general attitude for everything that was outside her heart, were half-truths.

When it came to plans for the future, Iulia had in mind to destroy everything that didn't suit her, keeping only what was valid and essential, her superior inspiration (that's why she was dating her works), and only publishing her mature literary works. Iulia was deep in the academic mindset when writing that letter to her father and she stated she didn't write any more literary works. A poetic mindset would have made her confess to some intuitions or prophecies, making her appear more cautious.

In that letter, after telling him more details about her classes and her professors, she told him about Broșteanu "who's a rare type of idiot," whom she portrayed in a way that reflected many of the students in Paris, a snob and ready for everything but learning. Among others, the student that Broșteanu didn't know at all, told her father how she caught him plagiarizing his works. He kept bragging about a speech he'd given at the death of one of his former professors, Caloianu, a speech that presumably had been reproduced in newspapers and appreciated by a big audience. Iulia was very intrigued about how such a mediocre boy could write a well-received speech, so she asked him to show it to her. And Broșteanu did. She was amazed and appalled at the same time when she saw the speech was indeed amazing, however, there was one problem: the beginning was Bossuet's funerary peroration at the death of Henrieta de Anglereta, and the ending was a fragment from Pascal. There was nothing about Caloianu in the text.

Iulia asked her father to pay a visit to the office of *Amicul Poporului* newspaper, which in 1887 was in Craiova, the newspaper that had published that speech:

"... Is this how we're supposed to live in Romania? Only reading novels by Gyp and Georges Ohnet?... What a beautiful and modern civilization... A beautiful civilization indeed!"

This is just a delicate fragment she wrote in a way to be respectful towards Hasdeu, but we feel that we must present the true way she felt about Broșteanu, that "rare type of idiot, even though he's from Romania!"

In another letter dated April 4th sent to Hasdeu on the occasion of Easter, Iulia shared past events from Paris with him, some trivial, others very important, but she took that opportunity to tell him about her wish to visit Romania over the summer and see the wonderful cathedral in Curtea de Argeș. Her father had recently sent her a new album about this cathedral, a building "which will forever be linked to the sad memory of three women, three mothers, one being the legendary wife of Master Manole, and the other two no less real and significant. Despina and Elizabeth..."

Among other news, she told her father about her constant migraines, and about a few trips to le Bois de Boulogne, where she'd seen "the pretty painted socialites, women of the half-people who can barely be distinguished from real ones." She exclaimed: "Those are what most consider to be beautiful people! Well, not me! Their beauty won't last two years. I prefer our beautiful sun-kissed peasant women, with chubby red-cheeked infants at their breasts. Those are what I consider to be beautiful!"

It was a bitter profession of austerity for that barren world, as well as a moving homage to the Romanian peasant! All good, however, the girl didn't confess one thing to her father who was so far away: the state of her physical and mental health. No word to her always worried father on these problems, which were dearest to his heart. Even though work was crippling him, he ardently missed his precious child.

That's why she avoided burdening him with the true reality and allow him to only know the comforting feel of her academic success and her apparent glowing health that Lilica's cheeks were showing at that time. Obviously, that was the child's wish; she became isolated within herself for eternity.

Iulia Hasdeu's soul was in constant agony:

I wish I was asleep deep underneath the ground
In the eternal silence, eternal mystery
Just lying in my coffin inside my quiet tomb

Protected from my sorrows and from old misery,
Finally sleeping soundly!

***

I understand I'm young, and I love life no doubt
But death feels so enticing, the only real way out
To rest in the embrace of the eternal slumber.
… … … … … … … …
I love Death's gentle whisper calling me from beyond.
The pain in my chest's burning and Death will soon respond.
No one on earth can hear me, no one can hear my wails
Nobody can feel pity, only my friend, sweet Death.
… … … … … … … …
A child and a butterfly seem so alike just now
We mourn together in our hearts, were connected somehow
My heart is pained and sometimes it can feel truly broken
So I cry for Death to save me now from all the pain unspoken.
But God said no….

***

One girl can hope that someone will reach a helping hand
And will tend to her wounds and won't misunderstand.
Nobody really knew what pain hid in her soul
She chose not to confide; she chose to hide it all;
She shared only smiles, laughter, and gentle charm,
Dying like Polyxenia, without causing alarm.[60]

This poem is maybe more than a supreme testimony. It's a testament!

She didn't want anyone to intrude in her bitter isolation from the world, that world that only made her suffer, so the charming young woman wanted to die without anyone knowing her tears and her pain because "modesty commands it!"

Was her heart yearning for death just because of a slight intuition fed by her recurring poor health? Or was it because of the ever-growing melancholy? It might

---

[60] Jours d'Angoisse. April 1886 — Chevalerie

have been the reverse of suppression. Her excessive candor and modesty could be explained by that thirst for perfect love.

Hasdeu was working tirelessly on the second volume of his great dictionary which he was planning to release soon. Completely unaware of the bitter fretting in his child's heart, the great scholar and father was veiled by the sad fatality, not being able to help his dear daughter who was alone!

What was her mother doing? She didn't want to ask too much of her. She could see things only on the surface. Her motherly devotion that was present day by day, her generosity, and the humanitarian nature that was shared with everyone were just as useless to Lilica.

In the letters Iulia sent to her father she tried to only talk of trivial things from Paris or Bucharest. She asked about a dog, about a black cat, about old Anica or her daughter, about the flowers, etc.

Hasdeu wrote his thoughts on that maternal generosity at the end of February 1887, as an urge to focus everything he had on his daughter:

"Generosity is indeed a great trait, but the beginning of generosity comes from one's own family; only when you have the means to keep your family comfortable can you think about helping others. That's what Jesus Christ said, and nobody was more generous than him; he said that in a time when nations didn't have embassies everywhere, because those — not Mrs. Hasdeu — are the ones in charge of helping victims in foreign lands if those victims indeed deserve to be helped. No man could say I don't do my duty to my family, maybe even overdo my duty; however, when it comes to strangers, even if I wanted to help them, I can't, I don't have the means.

Too bad my wife doesn't read the Gospel; I have it memorized; that is the only tool to teach people what true generosity is! 'Don't give dogs what belongs to your sons.'

I will sacrifice everything for my family, and I'll never refuse them the right to see a doctor, get a ride somewhere, follow the tonic diet of Dr. Damaskino, or anything else; but I have the right to not work for strangers. Their relatives should work for them, and the Embassy should help them in foreign countries. If the embassy doesn't have money to spare, how do they expect the Hasdeu family to have money?

I'm just sitting here suffering because I know my Lilica is ill; I cannot describe how much I suffer…"

In the beginning, this letter says "On the sixteenth of February, I turned fifty-one years old...," there are two main ideas we can understand from it: first, his real age is written in Hasdeu's hand, so he was born in 1838, not in 1836 as some have stated. The second idea is a contradiction. In the lines written by him in 1889 to Angelo de Gubernatis in a letter meant to praise Iulia and her work, Hasdeu said: "...she was healthy and in very good shape until last year..." Meaning until 1888! He painfully stated that starting with 1887 he suffered greatly because of Lilica's illness.

Ionescu-Gion was also confused about the poet, writing about it in a new issue of *Revista Nouă* saying that "At the end of 1886, beginning of 1887, she was as ready as ever to fight," but a few lines below say that "She had started to vomit blood. This happened at the beginning of 1887."

The truth is, the illness had not begun at the beginning of 1887, but long before that, right after getting bronchitis two years prior. The tonics and teas had just delayed the hemoptysis, but the girl knew she was ill because of the sudden fits of cough. The seed of the disease had been planted during the time she had the measles, and only her good shape had slowed its progress. "Why should I care?" said the girl heroically, making everyone believe that was the start of the illness.

Lilica was not indifferent to it. It's possible that at the time Ionescu-Gion wrote the article, he was not familiar with the whole poetic activity of the girl, because all her confessions were dated. If at the time when her first symptoms appeared people still believed they were harmless, when her suffering was doubled by her sentimental disappointments, and by her regular migraines, how could anyone think about anything else but fatality? She wasn't blind, but she had blinded everyone around her.

The hidden poison Elli Scott had fed her was enough to increase the speed of her internal decay because the direct sensations and her own opinions had crushed her heart. The contrast with her friend's happiness, with her excitement, and confessions was decisive. This was a truth talked about by the great Dante in one of his poems: "There is no greater sorrow than to recall in misery the time when we were happy."

The contrasts coming from outside were also evident between her deep sorrow (which was unknown to others), and people's happiness.

It seemed Iulia Hasdeu was fighting life and fighting death at the same time. She was working on various university projects for which she was reading day and night, gathering the necessary materials for that work she was planning on expanding soon, inspired by Larroument. It was the *Logic of Hypothesis*, a daring study, controversial but subtle, which was a true statement of her intellectual capacity. She purchased various books, such as *Le Fondement de la Morale* (Schopenhauer), and *Logique de Port Royal* (Ch. Jourdain) which was a commentary on A. Arnould's and Nicole's work. Iulia sat for hours in the library of the Faculty of Letters, enriching her mind with everything written on logic, jumping from one hypothesis to another. Copernicus, Kepler, Huygens, Newton, Hume, Leibnitz, Cuvier, Bacon, Plato, Aristotle, Socrates, Thomas Reid, Descartes, Schopenhauer, etc., all came to gift her with the fruit of their minds, despite her crushed body and soul, despite her using every last bit of her energy to leave behind a tribute of her life.

In that study, Iulia combated the Scottish school system when it came to "human understanding" represented by Thomas Reid who claimed around eleven contingent truths through which he wanted to show that everything is tangible, that human understanding carries the questions and the answers in the form of rationality, that nothing is metaphysical, that Descartes' skepticism was unfounded, and he stated that men have complete freedom to think and express their will. Iulia sided with Maine de Biran, Edgar Quinet, and other opponents of the Scottish school who claimed the elements of hypothesis are always imposed by logical and verified understanding, and that hypothesis is indispensable to the phenomena that are not part of experience and induction.

While giving a speech on her study and commenting on the great philosophers, Iulia explained their opinions by using her critical thinking, concluding the logic hypothesis was valid in every case and equal in validity to an experimental demonstration.

Of course, during these weeks of soaring ambition, Iulia wrote the symbolic poem *Le Cavalier Nocturne* (*The Nocturnal Knight*), a description of herself, of her transcendent soul, touched by the mirage of the eternal "beyond" that accompanied her all over, watched her like she was prey. At someone's advice to stay away from the "soft melody" around which "the dead from the realm of Tartarus" were dancing she replied:

I keep on my path
Despite rain, despite snow
I'll follow my destiny
Nothing stops me now.

***

I do not fear death,
My direction is sacred.
I'm the one Fate has chosen
My genius is my weapon.

Higher! Higher always
Higher! That's my plan.
Love is my undoing
I'll avoid it as much as I can.

***

You'd like to know my name
My name and my whole past
Ambition calls me, though,
And I'll do as I'm asked.[61]

That spring, when the bitter taste of jealousy she was feeling for her friend was still tormenting her, she wrote a rant against lies and duplicity called *La Femme (The Woman)* with a motto from Tibullus: "*Ah, crudele genus, nec fidum femina nomen!*"

Oh, you, heart of a woman, always an enigma
A blend of divine fire, sin, artifice, and stigma,
All-gifted mystic creature, that cannot be explained
With empty heart or cold, loved, desired, or chained!
Your smile can be evil, you're treacherous at heart
You have so many flaws, your face is cold and hard:
Your words, your look, your figure
You hate whatever lives
You believe all your lies!
Your character all proves.
Poor women, you live for that
And have knots in your souls!

This digging into the depths of the woman's nature was not accidental or new for her. It's not quite clear how she studied this by socializing with various women.

---

[61] March 13th, 1887, *Chevalerie*

Her genius intuition on causes and manifestations was supplied by the literary works she'd read with extraordinary attention.

One of her comments on women says:

"There are some women with an exquisite smile; even if they're ugly their smiles still brighten their faces and give them beauty.

And there are other types of women, even beautiful ones, but who have a hideous, repulsive, even disgusting smile. They pout their lips, narrow their noses, and make their cheeks sink in, showing how jealous, intriguing, nasty, and insufferable they are. We know each woman has her smile, but if they don't plan the way they smile in advance it becomes just a convention…"[62]

How many of Iulia's acquaintances and friends could have seen themselves described by those lines? In another of her writings the poet said:

"A woman has many qualities in her heart, but they're mixed in with many flaws that paralyze the qualities; she thrives from being impressed but she forgets easily; she is capricious and inconsistent; she is kind and generous but she is jealous, hence her craving for intrigues; she is frank and genuine but weak and cowardly because of hypocrisy, perfidy, and lies. Finally, her qualities and flaws are part of the body's chemistry, they come in combinations, but she's always at risk to have her qualities changed to vices."[63]

There is a certain amount of objectivism in the way she was thinking, but she was still crippled by the bitterness of true and loyal friendship, despite being disappointed. As an escape from that artificial, ugly, perfidious world in which children were not children anymore after losing their honesty and candor, Iulia called on Azurina, the muse of stories to take her to her bright world:

Oh fairy, let us go and forget our misery
In the land of chimeras, and follow our destiny
Let us run to the holy and unknown lands…

Her oil paints were almost forgotten. She drew two-three strokes a day, but the brushes refused to listen to her. Harsh lights covered the canvas, but the colors looked right only in her heart. The piano received her smiling with its white keys, but her hands were gliding on them inconsistently... Every melody sounded sad, in

---

[62] Ionescu-Gion: Iulia Hasdeu

[63] I.G. loc. cit.

a solemnity reminding one of an organ. She only liked the first part of Beethoven's *Mondschein Sonata* because of its slow and dark feel. *The Funeral March* of the *Third Symphony*, the masterpiece of the deaf genius spoke to her more clearly than ever! But of course, since it was dedicated to another unhappy genius the girl so admired: Napoleon I.

One evening while playing another funeral march belonging to Chopin, a melody that sounded like a blessing to those nearing their end, a harmonious and melodic line that seemed to come from heaven seemed to make death sound... sublime. Iulia's mother tried to appreciate it:

"Lilica, that sounds like a melody played for someone who passed away; can you stop playing that for a while? It's making me cry... wail..."

"You're right, Mother. This funerary march was composed to make people cry. Chopin was an unhappy genius just like so many others destined to die young..."

"Leave him, dear. Play something more suited for your age, so I can enjoy it as well."

"For my age? Hmm... Okay, for your enjoyment I'll play a Transylvanian song..."

So Iulia played a traditional song from Banat, a lively melody that seemed to have been composed by an intoxicated musician.

"Well, Lilica, that's what I call a good song! It suits you, my dear!"

It suited Lilica as it suited a Gypsy playing Chopin from a cimbalom...

Easter passed, and so did spring with all its flowers, like ephemeral tears. Roses didn't bloom and her vase was empty like a coffin waiting for its occupant...

After the first-year exams, for which she had studied intensely, Iulia got ready to travel to Bucharest. Hasdeu gave up on taking her to Switzerland after he saw no improvement in her health, even though Drs. Damaschinoș and Percheron had told him to try again. The girl was excited to see her country, especially since she had received an invitation from Bishop Ghenadie to spend a portion of her vacation at Curtea de Argeș.

The train ride seemed long and dark to Lilica like it had never seemed before. It was overbearing, hot, and boring.

She finally arrived in Bucharest and was happy to see the park surrounding the Archives, the bell tower, the gate under it, the weeping willows swaying over forgotten graves, the cypress trees, and finally, Agrippa and his Agrippina, her grandmother, Mrs. Svârlescu, Florica, and Matilda. There were flowers everywhere around the church and on the graves.

During the first part of August, she stayed at the Archives, visited her friends, strolled through Cișmigiu, enjoyed carriage rides, and took a trip to Sibiu with her family. Meanwhile, Drs. Măldărescu and Calinderu gave her repeated checkups, but aside from some weakness common with students, they couldn't find anything wrong with her lungs, even though the girl was still struggling with coughing fits. However, she was the only one who knew the cruel reality. In her mind, she smiled bitterly before the diagnosis. Sometimes, she would hide under trees and think about the refuge from "the other side."

Where was the man with blue eyes? The poet might have abandoned his Scottish shepherdesses and might have started singing in some salons in Calcutta, or London. Nobody knew.

In the poem *La Muse et le Poete* (*The Muse and the Poet*), dedicated to S. Prudhomme, a poem she had written at that time, she praised the divine poets who used to be "Gods on earth":

They were seated at tables, by emperors and kings
In Greece, they were requested to sing in tournaments.
....
In Rome, if a poor slave would prove he was a bard
Then he would earn his freedom, and honor, and a guard.
....
Today every beginner claims to write poetry
....
But poets are most useless, ignored, going hungry.
....
Believing they can write, but they're not really poets.

After a long lesson given to young poets by this veteran, Iulia joked about mad scientists who believed poets were mad and genius men were demented, but the reality was not quite so.

In July, sitting under a cypress tree close to the tombstones inlaid with love declarations, Iulia Hasdeu wrote the symbolic legend called *Le Chevalier et la Mort* (*The Knight and Death*). Eude, disguised as a knight and riding a horse resembling the one of Bayard, was the incarnation of Iulia's own dream. The knight was riding at night through the thick fog after fighting heroically, and he was exhausted. Suddenly his horse stopped in the dark and told his master a specter was waiting ahead. Eude unsheathed his sword ready to fight but a voice told him "Do you wish to fight Death?" The knight stated his identity and asked who the specter was. "Son of this earth, I am death." "O, Death, have you come for me?" asked the knight. "So be it! But I want to fight. I know you'll defeat me, but I wish to die fighting." Death accepted the challenge and said:

So far, for love you only had disdain
… … … … …
You didn't know, dear healer,
That love opens the skies?
… … … … …
You will get to regret your past
You will regret in your last hour
Not having your lady in your arms;
Your knightly pride is your undoing
'Cause God might have blessed you
… … … … ….
…but suddenly under the pale moon
The figure of a woman appeared before his eyes
Her beauty was angelic, warm like the afternoon;
…. His tears were hot, however, and he fell to his knees
He spoke to his beloved, his words sad shaky pleas:
"Your celestial beauty was only made for me
And if I was to lose it, nothing else matters, dear."
She turned around and left, his eyes losing her shape
The Lord of death returned and wrapped him in his cape.
"Oh, Death, I'm ready! Come take my soul away
Living without love is too much of a weight."
And Death then snatched its prey.

In this legend, Knight Eude had a truly heroic name inspired by Count Eudes who became the king of France in the 1st Century, during the times of the Carolingians, which fascinated her. Iulia borrowed the name for her legend, and even though she was inspired by true love she didn't want to obey the "true love's kiss" after running away from it her whole life.

A few days later, Iulia and her parents left for Curtea de Argeș and they spent a week there, in the care of Bishop Ghenadie Petrescu. After Hasdeu made sure his family had everything they needed he noticed Iulia was feeling well but her cough was persistent. That time he had allowed her to take books, even though she needed all the rest she could get. The family was visited by peasants dressed in flowery traditional clothes, with sun-kissed cheeks; they could hear flutes playing from across the hill, and the silver bells of the monastery were clinking with angelic tunes. After two or three days of enjoying the mystical monastery built by Master Manole, they were surprised by a few friends from Bucharest who came to visit them for a few hours, among which was Ionescu-Gion.

"The one writing these lines," said Ionescu-Gion in this eulogy "saw her in Curtea de Argeş in July 1887.

"She was glowing, beautiful, happy, with a slim waist, with shiny eyes, playful, friendly, amusing, with no trace of coyness, wanting to take part in every conversation that focused on ideals and art. She matched her father in humor and irony, she knew everything about the topics being discussed, but she was breathing life in and thriving on the power of her mind, her most splendid quality."

It's not hard to imagine what Gion was feeling for the girl from that description. There's little left unsaid. He must have had a true sympathy for her that was not yet defined by love, a sincere admiration for the witty student, even respect for the magister's daughter. It's possible Hasdeu saw him as a serious match for his daughter, a few close friends of the old man even confirmed this idea. But Iulia was loyal to her legendary dreams, and we don't know if she could have been happy with the attentions of Professor Gion, a man she often joked about, a man twelve years her senior. There was no similarity between them, which was obvious.

After a week of resting among geraniums and carnations, the buzzing of bees, and the songs of the monks, Lilica returned to Bucharest at the end of August. In the first days of September, she joined her father on a trip to Iaşi, a city that surprised and amazed her, surpassing Bucharest in her eyes.

When she returned from Iaşi she sent a letter to Gabrielle, her friend from Paris, giving her details about her summer vacation. She said nothing of her sorrow, nothing of the signs Death kept sending her trying to show her the mirage of the "other side," nothing of her supreme dreams. The only thing she talked about was the fun she'd had.

One of those evenings was the moment when Hasdeu finally found out about her poetry. While resting on the porch, Iulia finally confessed to the many works she had scattered through her notebooks. At his insistence, Iulia read a few of her poems to him. He listened with tears in his eyes, with the expression he always had when his spiritual soul was flattered, and tightly hugged the young poet.

"Bravo, dear Lilica! Why didn't you tell me earlier? Do you have any idea how talented you are? Bravo! Please read some more!"

"That's enough for now! I have to revise them."

"But you must publish them, my girl. Let me have them..."

"No! Not yet! Later, after I revise them. I'm too young anyway. I can still wait!"

But, as Hasdeu stated in *Burgeons d'avril*, seeing how opposed his daughter was to that idea, he stole four of her poems: *Les Contes Bleus*, *Larmes d'Enfance*, *Dédain*, and *Le Souhait d'une Vilaine*, after which he gave them to Clavel (the director of *Etoile Roumanie* newspaper) who published them accompanied by notes of amazement. She was surprised by his actions and sent him a letter:

> "If there's anything that I'd want to forget more than the regret I felt seeing my humble creations published, is the way you interpreted them. I believe that by now you've realized I detest artificiality and posing and that I love honesty and truth above everything else, which are two qualities I hardly even see in children today. Therefore, I want to remain a child at heart despite everyone trying to force me to grow up. I hope you understood the polite message I'm trying to give you. Thank you..."

I.H. Buc. September 9th, 1887

We know she created works that are far from childish, especially philosophical and deceiving ones, most of which were written in the fall of that year. They were painful as slicing blades, especially the morbid ones written in the following year.

The end of September found Iulia traveling back to France, a tragic country she couldn't abandon.

After getting situated in her apartment on Rue des St. Pères No. 76, she proceeded to rediscover Paris with its cosmopolitan life, which was disgusting for a soul that was always searching for the "beautiful heroism of times past." The devotion to great causes, which became like a unique god,[64] made Iulia Hasdeu feel disgusted with Paris, a feeling described in *Paris Dantan* (*The Old Paris*), in which she glorified the beautiful society of the times passed, with marquises, honorable men, poor students "that fed on beans, sang, and slept on straw beds," with knights, and cathedrals full of devotees.

Iulia's eternal nostalgia was a mirage that affected Eminescu as well as other poets or writers whose dreams and loves could only be found in a veiled world of

---

[64] Il est Passé, sonnet — *Chevalerie* 164

perspectives that had been buried by the centuries. Those were poetic worlds that came back to the surface in her time as well, proving that beauty still existed, and social doctrines were still somehow linked to human morals. But how would the world change?...

After spending an evening celebrating the engagement of one of her friends, Iulia wrote *La Chimere* (*The Chimera*), blaming those who believed they were happy for believing in the chimera of love.

If a pair truly love each other
And always live happy times
In Germinal like in Brumar,
It is because they trust no other
Than the Chimera's cult bizarre.

Notes accompany the poem. She states that she wrote them during the engagement celebration, when the lovers "looked so happy, and I truly found love, as I have not experienced it, I said to myself: They are truly happy! They're crazy, but they're happy."

We know Iulia was mocking the love she had not tasted by looking at the literary works created by that honest but tormented soul, so we can understand how she felt about writing those lines. The rest can be seen in the medical studies on the states of mind of patients suffering from tuberculosis. At that time, Iulia Hasdeu was already displaying a few of the traits of that specific psychology, being sarcastic when others assumed she was in great health, being disgusted with life and the world, sometimes being outright rude to others. It was the dark line death was drawing over the last part of one's life. She was getting ready for the "afterlife," trying to adapt to eternal darkness...

Nature starts looking like a catacomb in her eyes. In November, shortly after turning eighteen years old, she wrote the bitter poem *La Feuille* (*The Leaf*) with a motto from Heine:

Vois, les arbres ont pris des formes de squelettes.

So many leaves...
Pale, dry, fallen leaves, trampled under our feet
.....
Poor fallen leaf! Oh, you mirror our fate
Our sad destiny, and our disgrace:
We are born but don't know what we're meant to be

What are we? Where do we go? It's secret… a mystery
What will we become when we leave this plane?
That we'll never know. That is death's domain.

.....

Oh, dear God! Dear erudite and scholars,
Do you all understand that heaven's full of color?
The millions of planets, galaxies, and stars
Float around us unchanging with their eternal charms;
And our Earth is tiny, minuscule grain of sand

.....

Body, mind, spirit, intelligence, all that
What do you think tells you? Your science is a lie.
Dear scientists, your answers are hurting our minds
We cannot understand it, you can imagine why.
Is man a soul and body, or a machine, you say?
Because we love and cry, why would you search as to why.[65]

It was pain and a cry of panic! Why did she feel so empty? Sometimes the poet was showing anger towards the love she had never known, but she could explain the meaning of her life. Was man a machine? Or a spirit? Why would it matter since men can love and cry?

The taste of the last autumn of her life, while comparing spring with the season of dry leaves, Iulia Hasdeu felt the right to find autumn charming because "in fall, one feels the need to be loved."[66] Even though she always felt the need to be loved, at that time she felt it more than ever, through all the fibers of her decaying body, she was calling for it but love belonged to those who treasured it and didn't mock it, trying to bury it! That's why she was rushing to leave this world that didn't appreciate her enough; she would have rather been in the white Eden with the angels. In one of her written reflections that was cited by Angelo de Gubernatis, Iulia stated how she felt about that sentiment of dying, for that would have been the only happiness she was destined to feel: "Life is a river, and we all must swim across it; the first ones to arrive are the heretics."

---

[65] Bourgeons 179

[66] *Printemps et Automne* — Bourgeons 92

Despite her sorrow, in 1887, Iulia gave her second speech at the Sorbonne, and that one was about Herodotus (*The Second Book*). To prepare for that speech she used all the available material she had from classical and modern historians.

She presented the noble and independent historian as one who had glorified Helade whom he'd described in the first book, as well as a man with a great knowledge of Egypt that he had visited around 459 B.C., after which he described it in the second volume. Iulia showed how Herodotus was impressed by everything in the country of Osiris, by the teachings and the secrets known only by the Egyptian priests who refused to share their knowledge on Egyptian gods by word of mouth. The student's commentary was even more interesting when it explored the way in which Herodotus wrote about Psamtik, the pharaoh, who, wanting to learn if Egypt was the oldest country in the world, took two newborns to raise them away from society and see what their first words would be. The first word was *becos* = bread in Phoenician, which helped him to conclude that Phoenicia was the oldest nation in the world.

Iulia explained, chapter by chapter, how Herodotus described Egypt, the wonderful River Nile, and its course, and how the Greek historian attributed that phenomenon to the Sun; she then continued with their bizarre habits, with the cow cult (Isis was a woman with cow horns just as Io was for the Greeks), with their customs, their writing from right to left, just like the Jews, and with simple but important commentaries.

Iulia's study was presented with her well-known excitement, and it was received with admiration by her professors and her fellow students who took time to congratulate and praise her. Her voice was a bit weaker and interrupted by the coughing fits, which only enhanced the echoes of the praises. A few things were known about the suffering of the Romanian genius; people knew her worries, but nobody knew what a price she had to pay to complete that study.

By the time she arrived home, she was exhausted. Her mother wasn't in the room. Iulia threw herself on the bed, fixing her eyes on the ceiling, clenching her jaw. She just wanted to hold on. But her chin started trembling, her eyes started burning, and she just burst out crying with hiccups, with spasms that shook her body and the bed... She wanted to wipe her eyes with her handkerchief, but she remembered that on her way home she'd had a coughing fit, and the handkerchief was still wet with blood. Suddenly she heard her mother's footsteps. She controlled her crying, turned around to face the wall, and pretended to be asleep so her mother wouldn't see her face. She tiptoed to the bed, bent over her daughter, saw her eyes were closed, and decided to let her sleep, knowing what a day she'd had.

But her eyes rested on the handkerchief that Lilica forgot on the bed. A deaf scream stopped in her throat and made Lilica jump. Their eyes met... and the girl jumped into her mother's arms, in a saving embrace...

"Again?" asked her mother quietly, biting her lips.

"Again, Mother... On my way home earlier, I started coughing hard. This is it for me, Mother. You'll see..."

"Why would you ever say such a thing, Lilica? This is a result of your past illness... It will pass. I'm taking you to Percheron tomorrow. You'll see, my dear, you'll get better... You're young and strong. How was your speech?

"It was perfect, Mother! Girard congratulated me... What's the point? I'm ill! Very ill! My dreams..."

"Oh forget about the dreams," said her mother, trying to swat an imaginary shadow with her hand, remembering her old dreams. The dream she'd had when she was pregnant with Lilica, which had been returning to her memory more and more often. "It was just a dream! Only hags believe in such a thing, and they're crazy!"

Soon it was Christmas 1887. Her mother did everything in her power to distract her daughter from those thoughts, from studies, especially since Iulia attended extra classes in her free time at Hautes Études School, especially the lectures of Professor Jules Soury, the director of Paris National Library and the creator of the psychology course.

Iulia's mother organized small family gatherings, inviting Iulia's new friends and university colleagues, among which were M. Lantz and Lucia, the daughter of the great August Treboniu Laurian and Iulia's old friend, and they also paid visits to the Leger, Carrau, Maillart, and Lantz families, as well as to Lawers, the music professor. On the first day of 1888, they paid a visit to Vasile Alecsandri and his wife, Iulia taking the opportunity to talk about her poems; they also paid visits to Bengescu and his wife, and their old friends Albert and Gasthon Paris, Hasdeu's good scholar friend.

Meanwhile, Iulia made a new decision. After confessing to her father to having many poems hidden, and after having her work published behind her back and acclaimed, she had realized the true value of her work. Despite being angry at her father and Clavel for publishing the four poems, she decided to start publishing all of them, in turn, under the guidance of Maurice Albert, who proofread them, and who planned to write a preface for them. What had changed the mind of the poet, who four- or five-months prior had told her father she was too young and "had plenty of time." Of course, there were two factors: first was the public acknowledgment of her talent, and the second was the constant whisper in her ear telling her she was running out of time...

Chapter XII

The Eternal Rift

After Christmas, Iulia received the first issue of *Revista Nouă* magazine, a monthly literary publication initiated by Delavrancea, with the collaboration of A Vlahuță, V. Bilciurescu, D.D. Racoviță, Ionescu Gion, I. Bianu, and Th. Speranția. Those young writers and poets asked Hasdeu to direct the magazine, an offer that he accepted, and so, the first issue was released on the fifteenth of December 1887. As a preface, Hasdeu stated what made him want to help those young men:

> "These youngsters taught about everything in so much detail, that I feel like biting my fingers in frustration for not doing the same when I started my career because I might have avoided so many temptations, difficulties, and regrets that I only overcame after hiding myself behind the image of an old scholar with a cool mind and a warm heart.
>
> I was a socialist once, somehow similar to Don Quixote...
>
> I was a realist as well, one resembling Zola, maybe even the ones before Zola, dreaming that perfect men could stay away from plagues — similar to Pasteur's theory — by plucking away the waste of broken society...
>
> I tried Gongorism as well, believing that pompous words could cover the emptiness of thought without essence...
>
> And... and... what else could I say?"

These were the collaborators of the first issue: first, there was Minuzio who used a pseudonym and Iulia didn't know who he was, even though he wrote a serious article about Gheorghe Asachi; then, there was Delavrancea, who took that opportunity to publish the famous *Hagi Tudose*; Vlahuță published the poem *Iertare* (*Forgiveness*); Ionescu-Gion contributed with an article about the Phanariots; V. Bilciurescu published the poem *Plâns de Clopot* (*The Cry of a Bell*) influenced by Eminescu's style; P. Ispirescu contributed the story *Sarea în Bucate* (*The Salt in Your Food*); D.D. Racoviță presented a long dramatic chronicle and various illustrations attributed to I. Georgescu, the creator of Gh. Asachi's statue in Iași.

Iulia Hasdeu read the magazine, and following her father's request for a review, she wrote eight ideas to him. The article on Asachi was great and very interesting, Delavrancea's story had amused her, and she said "it was one of the best ones he'd written." When it came to Gion's article about the Phanariots she said that "it made up for the time I lost reading the article about Răzvan that should have never been published. Racoviță impressed me with his theatrical chronicle. He has great ideas." Finally, she compared Vlahuță with Alecsandri, saying:

> "I can't share your admiration for Vlahuță, even though I only know him from his poems. It's not the lack of talent, as he probably has plenty of that, but I regret seeing him take such a deadly stop when it comes to literary progress. The old France had 1,500 years to produce men such as Zola or Goncourt, and it's still going strong. Stating an old country is past its time to produce great names is a poor excuse (to say it in Zola's style). Really, our poor fragile literature is too young to be drained. We can pity it since the country is barely out of infancy after its revival from a long and painful martyrdom, but why choose young poets who can't write about anything but the erotic dreams filling their heads or about demure women? Vlahuță superior to Alecsandri? That's sacrilege! Alecsandri is the poet of our soldiers and our peasants. He wrote of the exploits and sad history of our ancestors. He celebrated our soldiers who fought and died for independence. Alecsandri is the sentry of Romania, who holds our flag high even during a storm. He always believed that love was the noblest and highest feeling, and he only ever wrote about great, pure, and beautiful things.
>
> I'm not saying he can't write better than he did, and I truly hope he won't be the last of his kind in history; I'm not saying his recent works are not inferior to what he's written so far, we tend to make excuses for the old lion for what he's accomplished in his youth and we shouldn't compare every writer to him.
>
> Oh, praise the days we still have the Alecsandri of our soldiers, the one who wrote *Lăcrimioare* (*Lilies of the Valley*) and *Fontaine de Blandsuzie*. If I was a king, I would praise him with cannon fire as if he was a prince..."

Iulia Hasdeu portrayed a declining Vlahuță after publishing *Lertare* in *Revista Nouă*. The poem talked of a lively girl with a "lazy walk", with her "curvy body," with a "slow majestic sway like the waves of the sea," with a bright face as "a newly risen star," dancing with a young man, seeming to glide. But at home, with her mind full of fresh memories, sees an old hunchbacked man walking towards her bed. "Oh, the irony!" exclaimed Vlahuță who knew that forgiveness was a virtue: "your sweet sins will undoubtedly be forgiven by the men and by the saints," concluded Vlahuță.

It is enough to forgive
Everything men blamed me for
– As my Father has taught me –
Everything that we once loved.

It was inspired by the Savior of the world. Instead of Bayard or Roland, she ended up writing about Vlahuță, a poor old man described in *Certain age*, a cited poem, that gentleman with white hair was not a simple coincidence of situations and people. Was it a variation of mediums?

It was understandable why Iulia was upset with Hasdeu for his appreciation towards Vlahuță and defended that "old lion" in the person of Alecsandri. She admitted to not having read much of Vlahuță's literary work, but she grew up with Alecsandri's poems from the time she was a small child, which was the reason he was so close to Iulia's heart. The future would speak plenty of Vlahuță's decadent attitude...

She sent a letter on the 8th of January 1888 that was greatly influenced by her dramatic state of mind caused by the terrible illness. Her disposition was a sort of silent cry, a bitterness...

"Last Saturday night, I had to visit Maillart and take a few days off. I've been seriously ill for the past few days. Yes, I'm sick. You didn't believe it, did you? My chest is congested and it hurts; my back hurts badly as well. I suffer from a dry cough that tears me apart and suffocates me from time to time. I don't go out, I stopped singing, I take tonics, I cover my back and chest with iodine. I wake up at six AM instead of four AM like I'm used to, but I don't feel any better. The weather here is terrible. It's cold and humid, the temperature staying between five and eight degrees now. With all this humidity there's no chance for my health to improve. It's painful to admit that..."

Her alarmed father replied to her letter and asked her to take care of herself, to stop forcing herself to study, and be consistent with the medication she had been prescribed... He especially asked her to think about returning to Romania...

Neither the French doctors nor Lilica agreed with that advice, and they insisted on another trip to Montreaux in Switzerland, Territet, or Glion. Iulia's soul was crushed more than her body. What would happen to her ideals? How could she obtain her bachelor's degree and her Ph.D.? She had already chosen a study subject for it with her father's help: "The unwritten philosophy and literature of the Romanian nature, theology, metaphysics, logic, psychology, and ethics." She had already gathered her study materials, a lot of it mostly obtained by Hasdeu. How? Was her life already over? Were the hallucinations, dreams, and ethereal whispers telling the truth? How? In the spring of her eighteenth year, when all her classmates and friends were overflowing with youth and enjoyed life as much as they could, laughing, singing, and loving, Iulia had to give everything up. Did she feel hate towards life or was she just afraid of death? Oh no!...

I love my life, I don't fear death,
For Death is the great source of light
And not a deep, eternal sleep
That steals our colors from our eyes.

Iulia saw herself carrying the last branch of her life to the afterlife, through that river of light, finding some comfort that her soul would revive in a new body, maybe one more compatible to its essence.

The mortal body under the ground
Is still fulfilling its earthly duty.
It feeds the soil, fertilizes the mound,
So another child could enjoy the earth's beauty.[67]

Whoever saw the castle in Câmpina could see at the entrance the way those mysterious lyrics had materialized in the hands of the old mage who believed Iulia was just one of the many reincarnations of a soul that had been Elizabeth Tudor and Charlotte Cordey. Trapped in the vortex of mystery that showed their outlines from beyond this world, Iulia allowed herself to be pulled once again in the world of stories, that had fed her childhood with their gentle and fragrant charm. They were a refuge, a moment of respite from her many hours of worry and sorrow.

Shortly before that, during the previous year, Ispirescu, the great storyteller had died. Iulia treasured him, and she remembered one of his most beautiful stories: *Youth Without Aging and Life Without Death*. The memory of that story was

---

[67] *La Mort*, Paris, March 1888- *Bourgeons*

brought up by a study on Irish and Scottish traditions, where Iulia discovered a similar story to the Romanian one written by Ispirescu, with the same Prince Charming in search of the kingdom of infinite youth and immortality. Iulia ended up translating that story into French, proving the similarity. The study was called *A Celtic Tale from Romania.* Iulia didn't want to prove Celtic influences in Romanian fairytales, knowing that stories have the same influences all over the world, and the only varying factors are the characters and the names.

But the story in question had a secret meaning to her, in a time when her youth seemed to evaporate without age being involved.

On the tenth of March, Iulia, feeling hopeless, wrote a shorter letter to Hasdeu:

"Dear Father.

Please don't be alarmed when receiving my letters. From now on they will be short....

I suffered a relapse of my bronchitis in the past few days and I'm feeling worse than ever, forced to stay in my room for at least another week. The weather here is terrible; after a few days of rain, Paris saw a snowfall like never before. The doctor that visits me every two days (to check my lungs) told me that I could be cured by the Mediterranean air alone, but he was hoping the weather here would improve so I could get better, but it doesn't look like that's going to happen. Despite all of this I'm working as much as I can, but for the last two days, I've been bedridden. That's all I can tell you right now if you're even interested. My only wish is for Agrippa and Sultan to stay here with me, despite them not being our blood family...

Your loving daughter, Julie."

The final lines of the letters deeply wounded the father's heart, which was already full of bitterness and anger. That "if you're even interested" was the worst of it. There was no worse insult for old Hasdeu than that poisoned arrow from his beloved daughter, at a time when he was already terrified about her future. The phrase "despite them not being our blood family" was referring to the two dogs Lilica was begging to keep. And Hasdeu replied to her:

"My dear family,

I received Lilica's letter yesterday. She's satirical despite being ill: 'Agrippa and Sultan...despite them not being our blood family.' That means they're great listeners, but I am one as well. The other day I sent Anica with Sultan and Agrippa with Mandy, so she would take a photo of them together; the old woman and Agrippa were patient, but Sultan was impossible to handle, therefore the photo had to be postponed. I assure you all three are healthy and cared for.

You saw Măldărescu's diagnosis. Calenderu told me the same thing, that Miss Lilica will be completely back to normal within two months if she will avoid catching a cold, will eat well, will drink good wine, and won't exhaust herself. Therefore, this topic is out of the way. There's no way she could get her bachelor's this year if she stands by her own description of herself as a 'respectful and obedient daughter.'"

She said Dr. Percheron suggested the Mediterranean. Where exactly? And when? You know summer in Nizza is unbearable. Genova? Where?...

Iulia didn't know any better. She'll "be completely back to normal within two months"? Hmmm... For the time being, she was stuck at home. She was suffering, suffering, suffering for herself, for her dreams, for her parents. Doctors' recommendations were pointless. All they recommended was rest, and that was not helping in the least. Koch's bacteria was not a common bug that could be killed with simple medicine. It hid in a place where nothing could touch it. It was especially hard at work and persistent. The coughing of blood confirmed it.

Iulia's mother sent a telegram to Hasdeu while dabbing her constantly tearful eyes. "She has gotten worse in the past two days!"

Hasdeu received the terrible news, cried, and wrote down the feeling in his screaming soul:

"The telegram I just received saying 'She has gotten worse in the past two days!' worries me terribly. I got out of bed and prayed to God, a deity I have always believed in and who has never disappointed me. I cried, I cried, and I'm still crying. Then I thought about the 'past two days.' That means she started getting worse on Friday, and that was the day she was supposed to receive my letter. I wonder if it didn't upset her and caused her health to decline. I don't know what to believe.

The second calling of my heart was to leave for Paris immediately. But maybe there's no need for it. I'm sure my wife would have informed me at once if I was needed and I would have arrived there with lightning speed.

Lilica already knows enough, maybe too much. I believe you should return to Romania, maybe even somewhere in the countryside where the air is pure, where she doesn't need to work or worry. It would help her. A diploma means nothing. I have none.

My thoughts are scattered. Please send a telegram daily while she's sick, so I stay informed. Should I come there? Should you return? Oh, Lilica, Lilica..."

Those lines were painful to write for a man such as Hasdeu. He cried and prayed! He wrote and screamed! "Oh, Lilica, Lilica..."

His cries summarized everything that was ever hidden in this soul, everything that he had asked his child to do, all the threats!

From "You're Hasdeu's daughter!" to "Oh, Lilica, Lilica..." was a long way. He was only thinking about her Ph.D., but at that time pain made him reject knowledge, hard work, and diplomas. He didn't have a diploma. He had one from Petersburg, another from the Linguistics Society in Paris, he was a member of the Academy of Belgrade, Sofia, and Constantinople, not to mention all the ones from his native country. Nothing. They were all worth nothing! Death opens everyone's eyes so easily. It unifies the specter of the afterlife with the horizons of human vanity. *Vanitas vanitatum! Omnia vana!* (*Vanity of vanities! All is vanity!*)

Seeing the alarm and torment in her father, Lilica tried to convince him she was exaggerating, that things were not that serious, that she had stopped spitting blood. He told him a few friends were taking care of her, as well as her mother, Professor Leger and his wife. She said she regretted not being able to attend her bachelor's exams, but she would study from the bed she was forced to lie in. She was not thinking of giving her studies up. She didn't care for the diplomas... "but once the battle begins, I won't be the one to run away from the fight; and I like my work. I wouldn't give it up for the world."

"For the world." Just like the knights imagined by her who would never back away, even if they were facing Death. And Iulia Hasdeu kept her word.

Hasdeu's heart was breaking to pieces while writing this heroic epistle, but he didn't give up as well. He gathered all syllogisms his logic gifted him in a small reply:

"Nothing is more philosophical and truer than the following statement: Each man, each being loves itself, which is where the instinct for conservation comes from. The only woman I've ever truly loved is my wife. So, when it comes to Lilica, I love myself, I love my wife, which means my love automatically concentrates on her. Is it surprising that the state she's in burns me?

There is a fourth type of love. I deeply love the Romanian nation and the future of Romania. Despite not speaking Romanian well, I sacrificed everything to become Romanian. Well, I believe Lilica will bring pure glory to Romania; how would this glory get bronchitis?...

Nobody in Paris could obtain their bachelor's degree in two years. Therefore, she must fully heal and postpone her bachelor's work until next year. This is what I want her to do from the authority of a father, especially a father like myself..."

Lilica read the dogmatic truth, trembled at his logic, hesitated for a moment, but the revival of her delicate youth kept her steady.

During that stubborn and final fight that exhausted her she heard the echo of true love, the one she had never experienced, the one others had savored especially during the spring that seemingly brought by two blue eyes. She remembered seeing a couple in a church she'd visited at one point, who were there for prayer or to thank God for something:

These young and happy lovers
Have sworn a thousand oaths
To be loyal and honest
.....
...at the monastery's gates.

.....
He would warm up his wings,
For him to pass, sad and old
Most hailed of the gods
Whose youth is eternal!...[68]

Whose sad old past? Everyone's! But especially hers, the one Cupid (the merriest among Gods) didn't allow to taste from the chalice of nectar and ambrosia!...

At that time, she wrote the poem, her second to last (besides some prose sketches) in which she seemed to prepare her luggage for a very long journey. It was the most painful poem, full of the mystical fluid from the "beyond."

It was a synthesis of her most private beliefs, which the smile of that fairy from her dream two years prior had opened to her like a new religion, the only religion of all the inhabited worlds.

---

[68] *Sous les arceaux* — Paris 1888, après *Avril Bourgeons*

Solitude

"Spiritus astra petit"

Come on, my soul, fly in the distance
Towards the sky, towards my dreams,
Towards a space with no human conscience
Where a soul is free from earthly needs.
Let us fly, my soul, fly away
Let's lose track of time and the world.

.....
Let's try and discover the great infinite
Let's see the abyss of which speaks no word.

***

Oh, my dear soul, noble, pure spirit
Let go of the body and surpass your limit!
.....
Once we're up there, free with no guidance
We'll enjoy the solitude and the deep silence.
.....
And we will smile and sigh
At everything, we left behind.

***

Alas! This indescribable torment
Of knowing that you are immortal
Of wanting to spread your wings wide
And towards heaven to ascent.
But suffering still keeps you grounded
Rebelling against your intent.

***

You must be patient because one day
You'll be free from tears and lament.
.....

Oh, my dear soul, let's hope for good
Because God knows when is our hour;
Eternity will wait for us
And patience is our only power.
Oh, how I put my only hope
Into God's hands…

Paris, April 16th, 1888

Following those two poems, which were the last ones she wrote, the muses strayed away from the girl's bed. It was the peak of her romantic talent and real pain, the only realism she accepted until her death.

Since her health was declining, day after day, despite all sorts of medical tricks and medication, Percheron and Damaschinos decided to take her to be examined by Landouzy, a famous lung doctor in those days.

They all gave her the same cruel diagnosis and in opposition to Lilica's stubborn idea of working on her bachelor's degree, they ordered her to be taken to Switzerland, in Territet, a resort she had visited before.

Mother Iulia wrote to Hasdeu to inform him of the diagnosis and asked him to come to Paris at once. Hasdeu was receiving information from other people living in Paris as well, including from Lazăr Șăineanu who was studying in Paris, and who found out the cruel reality from Percheron. Șăineanu had visited Iulia and her mother a few times, and they welcomed him in their home, despite the fact that Lilica despised him for being a Jew, as she admitted to in writing, as well as for him lacking good manners and intelligence. When it came to literature, the young poet had completely different ideas than the philologist in the making. The diagnosis communicated by Percheron was forwarded to Hasdeu from Șăineanu as well.

The old father left his household in God's hand because Mrs. Svârlescu had left and embarked on a lonely train ride to Paris. He wondered how Lilica's health was. He wondered if she was still alive and if he would get to see her delicate being, her gentle eyes, her genius…

He got off the train in Paris and his knees almost gave out. Nobody was waiting for him on the platform. Who would? He knew everyone was at home, but he didn't know what to expect. Contrary to the train, the carriage flew like a dragon. It was going too fast. Was that a sign? Or was it just his imagination? The clock was ticking. The carriage was going at a normal pace, but for him, it felt like it was flying.

Something in his mind was telling him to reach his destination so fast, and when he noticed the familiar streets, he knew their home was close. Maybe his Lilica... God!!!

"Thank you, sir!"

How? Did he thank the driver? That man probably felt as if he was paid double. The old man didn't have any reaction. He started up the stairs. Silence... He arrived in front of the apartment door. Silence! Maybe he was on the wrong floor. No! The name card confirmed it: "Mrs. and Ms. Hasdeu!" The old man leaned his ear against the door. There was no sound... no sign to burn into his soul. He knocked and heard footsteps. His wife opened the door and they embraced in silence. He felt tears flowing on his shoulder.

"She's asleep," whispered his wife.

"How is she?" asked Hasdeu, holding his breath.

"How do you think? Bad. We have to take her to Montreaux or Territet as soon as possible."

"We will. We'll leave tomorrow or the day after tomorrow."

The next day, Hasdeu paid a visit to Percheron. The doctor didn't hide the truth. Iulia had tuberculosis in both her lungs. They were full of holes and bleeding. It was terrible. The child had not followed the treatment as she'd been instructed. Instead of resting, she was overworked. Instead of breathing fresh air in the park, she preferred to be in her room using a gas lamp and staying up all night. She slept little, and read too much...

The family was ready to leave three days later. In his memory of her at Curtea de Argeș, she had chubby rosy cheeks, but now they were gaunt and pale. Her eyes seemed bigger. Her lips were thin and chapped, her smile forced and sad.

The carriage ride was slower than ever. In the train station, the father turned his body into a shield, so nobody could touch his daughter, who could barely stand up. Their travel documents were in order, and the train was ready to depart. And then they were flying. The sights were the same seen through dirty windows, but the white gifts of spring looked like shrouds.

They spent a week in Territet in the "Hotel des Alpes" on the shore of Lake Geneva, resting on the terrace warmed by May's sun. Blue horizons were melting in the lacey mountain peaks that seemed to smile at her. Somewhere, far away, she could still see two pale blue reflexes that were hiding in the shadows…

Traveling exhausted her and she couldn't feel any improvement in her energy like before. Dr. Carrard advised them to move to a resort closer to the mountains, in Glion. They moved into a beautiful villa, "with a terrace, fragranced garden, lilacs, and pine trees, with a beautiful view of the lake and the mountains", as Iulia described to Mrs. Leger in a letter she barely could write.

That was the last letter she ever wrote.

Hasdeu left his family there and with pain in his heart, he returned to Bucharest. In Glion, Iulia continued her sun therapy, kept taking medicine, and even though she was still in bad shape she was feeling a bit better. At first, she took small walks with her mother, and then she was confident enough to go for walks on her own. There was a glimmer of hope in her mother's eyes.

"…there's a less pleasant part of my treatment," she told Mrs. Leger in her last letter, "the cure with arsenic. Taking it is not unpleasant, but the side effects are terrible. Now imagine I'm not allowed to eat anything spicy, anything with vinegar for at least twelve months. I'm also not allowed to eat fruits (strawberries, cherries, apples included…), vegetables, or ice cream. The hotel is serving everything I'm not allowed to eat, and without being modest I can tell you that I need to be quite brave to sit with my mother while she eats a little bit of everything… while I have to resist the temptation! I admit that I'm quite a glutton, so it's really hard to not eat all these things. I 'must be happy with myself' as the Marquis is with the Misanthrope, isn't that right madam?…"

After finishing the treatment, and probably the money as well, Iulia and her mother returned to Paris. She decided to start studying again, but only from her desk at home. Percheron didn't allow her to go to university, write studies, or take exams. However, forcing herself even a little bit was enough for her to start coughing blood again. She didn't have any other option than return to Romania, as they didn't have enough money to spend their time in mountain resorts.

Summer was approaching, so they started their trip to Bucharest. Lilica was upset. She had forgotten how to smile. The secret voice that had been tormenting her entire youth was now silent.

She knew what was going to happen. It was their last trip to Romania, and she was never going to see Paris again. Paris! Her Paris will forever be the tomb of her youth and her memories.

Once in Bucharest, Măldărescu and Calinderu visited her for checkups and recommendations. The yard of the Archives was in full bloom and the trees had fruits, but it seemed silent and barren. Iulia's friends sneaked in, asked about her, and left. Only Florica decided to walk into Lilica's room and smile at her every two days, always assuring her that she looked well. Florica told her about various news from the social life of Bucharest, about her own family, brought her lilies of the valley, daffodils, and roses. Ionescu-Gion was paying regular visits to her crushed father.

The girl's body was giving up. Her cough was getting worse, and it was destroying her lungs.

Doctors kept imposing vacations in mountain resorts, but where? Sinaia? Predeal? No! She needed a mild mountain climate, maybe Agapia…

"We have to travel again?" whined the sick girl.

"Yes, dear Lilica, we have to go to the mountains. You need fresh evergreen air… and Agapia Monastery is wonderful."

"Do you think there's anything left to be done, Father?"

"Do I think? I'm sure of it! The doctors are assuring us as well. It must work!"

"It's useless! But I will go to please you two, dear Father. Only to please you. My life is over. I climbed too far on its peak."

The climb was hard and painful. Now she had to pay the price.

"No, Lilica, you're not right here. The pain and suffering are making you see everything in a negative light. You forget you're young and you carry three generations of this strong family. It's a fleeting accident."

"It's fatal, Father! I'm not afraid of dying, but I don't hate my life either, enough to believe in one more than the other. Whichever will want me can have me. Maybe I'll get to live more 'on the other side' …We'll see! We'll all experience that and we'll discuss it there. Do you believe in this?"

"It's a subject for another time. When you'll be old… you'll get the right to unify these two lives. Death is just a bridge. But now we must speak of flowers, of cherry trees… Do you know they're almost ready to be picked?

"They're red like the cheeks of our peasant women. The only beautiful women!"

"It's true, Lilica, the only ones…"

"And healthy…"

They got ready to travel again, which took a toll on everyone, but especially on Lilica. Mother Iulia gathered everything necessary for their trip, and Hasdeu got the money. It didn't matter if he had enough or not, but Mircuș, the Jew, was a true patriot. He didn't abandon the great Hasdeu in his hour of need, especially since he was the one who was supposed to become a minister.

The train and their friends were all on the platform. After a train ride that was not too long, they arrived in Pașcani and were received with great festivities by the joyful peasants. Blonde women, flowered chemises, waving flags, clinking bells greeted their sister as she was Creangă's Ozana. They passed through Humulești, near Târgu Neamț, the village of the national storyteller who only had one flaw: he was part of the Junimea movement. After a few more hours, they finally saw the towers of Agapia Monastery and the wide valley it was overseeing.

The nuns were fast and friendly. The abbess greeted them from the terrace full of flowers. Iulia breathed in the fresh and fragranced mountain air and listened to the deep silence.

God's kingdom in these places was generous. From time to time, the bells accompanied the sounds of the woods.

But the trip was too much for the sick girl. She was exhausted and her lungs didn't have any more strength to take in the fresh air. Her chest was burning, crying rivers of blood...

Hasdeu had to return to Bucharest to continue his work and he was waiting for news; good news, but there was none. He took that time to read everything he could find about the afflictions of the lungs, especially the ones written by Landouzy, in every medical magazine. He added his own acquired knowledge to the one given by the doctors taking care of his daughter.

Lilica was coughing blood almost every day. Nothing could stop it. On top of that, she was lacking much at the monastery, especially the things that a dying child needed.

Hasdeu had to return to the monastery. Traveling during summer took longer. August wrapped the mountain peaks in a golden veil, but Hasdeu found them somber and found his Lilica with her cheeks gaunt.

He took her back to Bucharest. There she again had to ride in a carriage with tears in her eyes, the ride on the train, to reach the bed at the Archives. The bed... September knocked at the gate with bony fingers and was invited in. It stole the leaves off the trees and gave its offering to the earth...

The parents took turns watching over their daughter who was cradled in a nest of agony, which furiously attacked the delicate, almost dried-up body. Her eyes seemed to be getting bigger and bigger and lost their shine. Melted dreams and mysteries shadowed them.

From time to time her faithful friends stepped in quietly, trying to greet her with a smile, and walked out choking on tears. Iulia used her last powers to smile at them sweetly, calm and serene. She knew what was coming.

"Don't be upset, dear Father! Not you! Especially you! You understand the laws of the Universe and the thoughts God sends us."

"I'm not upset, dear Lilica. I'm just bored waiting for your health to improve because it will improve... but..."

"Who is alone in the world? Only Death. Every turnaround, every attempt to escape takes us towards it. We pay with our lives no matter if we want to or not. Oh, I don't prefer the material side of life. It doesn't need respect. Look what's left of me... I'm hideous... However..."

"Oh, Lilica... how can you talk like that, Daddy's beauty?"

"See Father? I know what the spirit is, I understand it better and better every day. But I disrespected the matter that contains it, which is tributary to it. We all make mistakes and ask too much... way too much... Unilaterality is the great flaw of every system! Spencer solved this problem by himself. His dualism..."

But she was interrupted by a bloody explosion that she couldn't contain.

A few moments later, after her chest found its peace again, Iulia gave her father a worried look, worried about the way her father was feeling at that moment, and continued:

"Please take care of my mother. She needs a lot of moral support. You have other ways to escape your pain, which will console you, but she doesn't have any. She only has her Lilica and she doesn't understand the path I'm about to take soon... yes, yes, Papa... She's not very well either... Oh, Papa, don't neglect the matter."

"But Lilica, I didn't neglect anything."

"I know, Father, I know... I won't complain of anything to you... even though you might have paid a little more attention to my intellect and very little to my soul... No! No, don't be upset! It was my fault as well. I hid the way I was feeling, here, where Death is nesting. I didn't show the world or you, the way I truly am... or the way I truly was..."

"But my child, I know you quite well...Every person is like this; nobody tells people everything about themselves... but I understood you... as much as the distance allowed me to..."

"Oh, the distance..." said Iulia, covering her eyes with her palms... "The distance is so cruel! I wish I never knew it... I know, you have no blame in it, Papa. I'm the only one to blame... only me... and my death wish..."

And Hasdeu pretended to look for something to hide his burning eyes from his daughter.

While in the jaws of death, the girl found refuge in Ispirescu's stories. When she couldn't read anymore, she asked her mother to read them to her, and during the times her hands listened to her commands, she translated them one by one into French. She translated paragraphs, phrases, words... But everything was in pieces, cut apart by spasms. When she was alone, she cried... Oh, if only she would have known a small part of the love she'd always dreamed of. How could Death take someone who didn't even know what love was yet? "It's the worst crime!"

In the middle of September, the girl's face seemed to brighten up. Did God take pity on her? Nothing is impossible for the Creator. It might have been a miracle! Hasdeu wanted to believe in a miracle.

Believe and love, that's all
That God expects of us.[69]

And Hasdeu had faith, he prayed every evening and every moment that was not filled with his scientific or literary preoccupations, which he continued to work on, especially on *Revista Nouă*, which was a magazine with regular issues. Besides these activities that he reduced willingly, the father watched over his daughter day and night, together with his wife.

The brightness of her face disappeared as soon as it appeared. Her cheeks turned the color of wax again.

One evening she got a sudden fit of bloody coughing. Hasdeu wasn't home, so her mother sent for Dr. Calinderu, who was unfortunately out hunting. Towards the evening, Calinderu showed up in hunting clothes but without a prize, and drunk like any respectable doctor. Hasdeu was just getting home and when he saw him looking like he did at that altar of pain, was close to kicking him out of the house, especially since he was an amateur even when he was sober. The pained scholar

---

[69] B.P. Hasdeu — *Așteptând* (Waiting)

found Calinderu to have a fault as well in the death of his beloved daughter. The poem *Așteptând* had a part about him:

> *When you will wish to die, just visit any doctor!*
> *Their job is to bring death, that's all they are good for*
> *They love ending a life; to heal they do not bother*
> *They slice and chop a body, to cause pain they adore:*
> *You will not feel the torture! These butchers have no law*
> *They execute the faultless, kill them without remorse,*
> *Among the common people, they are kings with no flaw:*
> *They're fearless and unmoving, no armies back them up!*
> *When searching for a killer, try a doctor's hacksaw.*

In this stanza, Hasdeu describes the doctor that visited the delicate dying girl, as it was described by an eyewitness... He was a brutal and emotionless hunter.

With or without his care, Iulia's days were numbered. There was nothing to be done.

Her mother went out on the balcony adorned with roses, bit her fist, and let out a muffled cry directed to the churches, the heavens, to the friends that were mute with grief.

Hasdeu couldn't sleep. He sat transfixed near his daughter, or at his desk working, only raising his eyes from his manuscripts to stare blankly at the nothingness. He heard something, maybe a weak voice. Did Lilica say something?

"What a great work... *Istoria Critică*... *Răsvan*... but *Duduca Mămuca*, oh no!"

"Did you say something, my girl? Or did I imagine it?"

The girl's face attempted a nod, and she gave him a sweet warm smile which faded away slowly and sadly... like an enigma.

The old man's mind shattered. What was that? An account? The supreme account!... That small, ethereal life like a lily petal, that intelligent head resting on a pillow... There! Did she speak or did he imagine it? It wasn't an opinion, not an opinion, maybe a belief... Holding his head between burning hands, Hasdeu went over it again and again... The dark muse was creating a story in his mind: *Povestea Crinului* (*The Story of the Lily*), about two crazy parents who wanted to turn their daughter into a boy.

And while the story was taking shape in his mind, the old man was keeping his eyes on his daughter's face, counting her uneven breaths, trying to remember them all by integrating them into his own breathing, living next to the one that was slowly departing...

It was the twenty-nineth of September. The wind blew among the towers, graves, poles, branches, crying through the weeping willows. Iulia's breathing slowed. The phantom of death approached her and stole each breath, one by one... The last!

The clock stopped at 1:30. Iulia leaned into the phantom's arms and passed "to the other side," accompanied by "the solemn hymn of the angels who were celebrating her arrival."

Chapter XIII

Excelsior

(Bellu Mausoleum…March 14th, 1939)

But there she was! Iulia Hasdeu is among us. The earth perfectly preserved her body even after death. No maggot had desecrated the lily.

The magic window of the mausoleum was used by Hasdeu to visit his embalmed daughter daily. He sat at her desk for hours, surrounded by her things, conversing in a language that only he could understand, because Iulia only ever spoke to him. At that time, she could be seen just as she was fifty years earlier. She rested in her white sarcophagus covered with a crystal top, dressed in white, her face white like paper. Her serene forehead and her chestnut curls were frozen in time, keeping the last caresses of her parent's hands, her small straight nose, a final smile on her lips. But her eyes had nothing of this world. They seemed to repeat the same words she'd told her father during their mystical encounters:

"I am happy; I love you; we will see each other again: this should be enough to keep you going…"

Her spirit was escaping from time to time from the eternal excelsior, during the times the angels purified her path she needed to take to get to her father, and she traveled to the mausoleum to visit her earthly body that had been tormented by so much suffering and give it a cold embrace.

Anyone who could forget about their physical bodies could feel it; anyone could hear the martyr's blessing to those who chose to visit her, say a prayer for her soul, and learn the philosophical and moral laws that she had told her father from beyond the grave:

"The religious: Believe! Believe in God! Believe in the immortality of your soul! Believe in the gift of communicating with the ones who passed away!

The moral law: Love and offer help! Love and help your nation! Love and help whoever helps and loves you! Love and help without thinking of anything in return.

The social law: Don't be dishonest! Don't be dishonest to yourself to get respect from others. Don't be dishonest to others to favor yourself. Don't mock hard work, because work is life!

The philosophical law: When you search for the truth you will find it. When you don't want to believe it, you will be blind. When you look for proof, you'll only find denial!"

Her obedient father understood these teachings sent by Iulia and engraved them into the marble of the mausoleum. They remain there like a supreme testament, dictated from the sphere of infinite truth for all those who look for the meaning of life, for hope for their souls, and for fulfillment.

Beyond the veil of eternity, like an angel among her people, Iulia Hasdeu watches over us like a saint!

CENTER FOR Romanian STUDIES

The mission of the Center for Romanian Studies is to promote knowledge of the history, literature, and culture of Romania to an international audience.
For more information contact us at
info@centerforromanianstudies.com

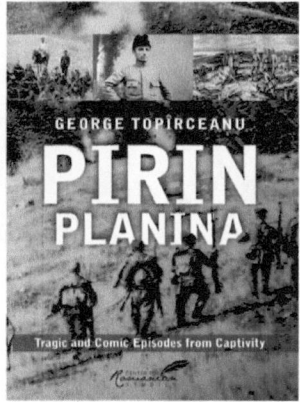
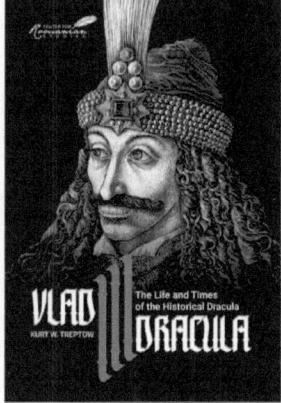

Check out these and other great titles at
CenterforRomanianStudies.com

www.ingramcontent.com/pod-product-compliance
Lightning Source LLC
Chambersburg PA
CBHW060517080526
44586CB00012B/521